REPORTING CHILD ABUSE AND NEGLECT
IN NORTH CAROLINA

JANET MASON
second edition

2003

INSTITUTE OF GOVERNMENT
SCHOOL OF GOVERNMENT
The University of North Carolina at Chapel Hill

Established in 1931, the Institute of Government provides training, advisory, and research services to public officials and others interested in the operation of state and local government in North Carolina. The Institute and the university's Master of Public Administration Program are the core activities of the School of Government at The University of North Carolina at Chapel Hill.

Each year approximately 14,000 public officials and others attend one or more of the 230 classes, seminars, and conferences offered by the Institute. Faculty members annually publish up to fifty books, bulletins, and other reference works related to state and local government. Each day that the General Assembly is in session, the Institute's *Daily Bulletin,* available in print and electronic format, reports on the day's activities for members of the legislature and others who need to follow the course of legislation. An extensive Web site (www.sog.unc.edu) provides access to publications and faculty research, course listings, program and service information, and links to other useful sites related to government.

Operating support for the School of Government's programs and activities comes from many sources, including state appropriations, local government membership dues, private contributions, publication sales, course fees, and service contracts. For more information about the School, the Institute, and the MPA program, visit the Web site or call (919) 966-5381.

Michael R. Smith, DEAN
Patricia A. Langelier, ASSOCIATE DEAN FOR OPERATIONS
Ann Cary Simpson, ASSOCIATE DEAN FOR DEVELOPMENT AND COMMUNICATIONS
Thomas H. Thornburg, ASSOCIATE DEAN FOR PROGRAMS
Ted D. Zoller, ASSOCIATE DEAN FOR BUSINESS AND FINANCE

FACULTY

Gregory S. Allison
Stephen Allred (on leave)
David N. Ammons
A. Fleming Bell, II
Maureen M. Berner
Frayda S. Bluestein
Mark F. Botts
Phillip Boyle
Joan G. Brannon
Mary Maureen Brown
Anita R. Brown-Graham
William A. Campbell
Anne M. Dellinger
James C. Drennan
Richard D. Ducker
Robert L. Farb
Joseph S. Ferrell
Milton S. Heath Jr.
Cheryl Daniels Howell

Joseph E. Hunt
Robert P. Joyce
Diane Juffras
David M. Lawrence
Ben F. Loeb Jr.
Janet Mason
Laurie L. Mesibov
Jill D. Moore
David W. Owens
William C. Rivenbark
John Rubin
John L. Saxon
Jessica Smith
John B. Stephens
A. John Vogt
Aimee Wall
Richard Whisnant
Gordon P. Whitaker

© 2003
Institute of Government, School of Government
The University of North Carolina at Chapel Hill
First edition 1996. Second edition 2003.
⊖ This publication is printed on permanent, acid-free paper
    in compliance with the North Carolina General Statutes.
Printed in the United States of America

07 06 05 04 03   5 4 3 2 1

ISBN 1-56011-455-X

⊛ Printed on recycled paper

Contents

Preface

Since the publication of the first edition of this book in 1996, the General Assembly has made several changes in the laws relating to child abuse, neglect, and dependency. In addition, the enactment of a new Juvenile Code that became effective July 1, 1999, resulted in the reorganization and renumbering of the relevant statutes. The material in this book reflects changes through the 2002 session of the North Carolina General Assembly. Any subsequent changes will be described in summaries of new legislation published by the Institute of Government annually and usually posted on the Institute's Web page at http://www.iog.unc.edu/.

This book should be a useful reference for teachers, counselors, principals, and other school personnel; mental health professionals; nurses, doctors, and other medical personnel; law enforcement officials; reporters; child care providers; and social workers. But the information in this book is important for everyone in North Carolina, regardless of profession, because the child abuse and neglect reporting law applies to everyone.

The book may be useful as a training aid. It focuses on the law, however, and does not attempt to address such topics as medical and psychological indicators of abuse and neglect. Those subjects also should be considered critical components of training in this area.

The purposes of the book are

- to help readers understand when they are required to make reports;
- to explain how to make a report— both when the law requires that a report be made and when, even though a report is not required legally, a person feels that one should be made;
- to describe what happens after someone makes a report;
- to answer some of the questions people ask frequently about the reporting law; and
- to provide broader access to the exact wording of laws relating to child abuse, neglect, and dependency.

Readers should recognize that while the laws relating to child abuse and neglect are important, these are not primarily legal problems. Neither are they problems that can be addressed solely through county social services departments and the juvenile courts. This book is written with the hope that those who read it will be better informed about the reporting law and more aware that the responsibility for protecting children belongs to the whole community.

The Governor's Crime Commission and Prevent Child Abuse North Carolina have provided financial and organizational support for the production and distribution of this book. The Institute of Government appreciates immensely their contributions to helping make this information widely available in the state.

Many Institute of Government faculty and staff members contributed to the production of this book. I especially want to thank Roberta Clark, Nancy Dooly, Lucille Fidler, Katrina Hunt, Daniel Soileau, Angela Williams, and Lisa Wright for their invaluable assistance.

Janet Mason
Gladys Hall Coates Professor
    of Public Law and Government
Institute of Government
School of Government
The University of North Carolina
    at Chapel Hill
2003

Part I

Introduction

1

Purposes of the Reporting Law

A student who regularly skips her physical education class finally tells the guidance counselor that she is embarrassed by the bruises on her legs. When the counselor tries to learn more, the girl just cries and will give no further information.

A young couple voluntarily seeks marriage counseling. The husband, explaining his growing fear and shame, describes a recent incident during which he threw the couple's very young child across a room.

A five-year-old boy goes next door and tells a neighbor that his baby brother won't stop crying, his mother has been gone since yesterday, and he doesn't know what to do.

Responding to a burglary report, police apprehend two males leaving the scene carrying stolen goods. They determine that the two are a father and his twelve-year-old son.

A mother tells emergency room personnel that her child's severe burns occurred when the child pulled a pan of hot water off the stove. The examining physician determines that the child's burns are not consistent with that explanation.

In each of these examples, someone— a school guidance counselor, a marriage counselor, a neighbor, a law enforcement officer, a health professional—has a legal duty to make a report about a child's situation. Most likely, even without a legal duty to do so, these people would take steps to seek help for these children.

Historically, our system of justice has distinguished between legal duties and moral obligations. In the absence of a statute or a special relationship, private citizens are not obligated legally to involve themselves in other people's problems. The North Carolina General Assembly, however, by enacting the laws discussed in this book, has expressed a strong public policy of intervention on behalf of children who are being harmed or are at risk so that they receive the services and protection they need. The law requires anyone who has cause to suspect that a child has been (or is at risk of being) harmed in certain ways to report that child's situation to a county department of social services. (For definitions of key terms specifying the kinds of harm or risk that must be reported, see Chapter 5.)

Although circumstances that trigger a duty to report may involve criminal offenses, North Carolina's mandatory reporting law is not a crime-reporting statute.[1] Rather, it is part of the state's child protective services system, created to respond to children's needs for protection or assistance.[2]

The child protective services system is based on a body of law and procedures that are carried out primarily by county departments of social services and the courts. These laws are in the North Carolina Juvenile Code (the Code), which establishes civil (as opposed to criminal) procedures for responding to children who are abused, neglected, or dependent.[3] The Code requires county social services departments to investigate reported cases of suspected child abuse, neglect, dependency, and death due to maltreatment and to offer services to children and families when those conditions exist. It authorizes social services departments to take steps to protect children in emergencies and to begin juvenile court proceedings when necessary. The Code also defines the court's authority to adjudicate (make legal findings of) abuse, neglect, and dependency and to order appropriate responses to meet the child's needs.

The United States Supreme Court has characterized parents' rights to make decisions about their children as "fundamental" and as requiring heightened protection against government interference.[4] Parents are presumed to act in their children's best interest, and ordinarily there is no reason for the government to intervene in the private realm of a family.[5] The Juvenile Code balances opposing interests, defining the parameters of permissible state intervention into the lives of families and children for purposes of child protection. The Code identifies situations in which the state's interest in protecting children— those citizens who are least able to protect themselves—outweighs the state's interest in deferring to families' privacy and freedom from governmental interference. Because that deference has constitutional dimensions, it is not easily overcome.

Some people claim that the state does too much in the name of protective services, intruding on families' privacy without sufficient cause.[6] On the other hand, when a child is harmed or dies as a result of abuse or neglect, questions arise as to why the protective services system failed to protect the child.[7]

The children in the examples at the beginning of this chapter are entitled to services and protection under North Carolina law. But whether children like them receive services and protection often depends on whether someone knows about the reporting law and actually makes a report to the county department of social services. Everyone has a duty to intervene, to this limited extent, on behalf of children who receive care that is below a minimally acceptable level or whose circumstances put them in harm's way. It is unlawful to ignore this duty.

Notes to Chapter I

1. North Carolina law does not include either a general mandate to report crimes or a specific mandate to report crimes involving child victims. Obviously, despite the absence of a legal mandate, many people do report these and other crimes to law enforcement officials when they know about them. *See* L. Poindexter Watts, "The Duty to Report a Crime," *School Law Bulletin* 17 (Summer 1986): 22–30.

2. The criminal justice system, on the other hand, focuses on apprehending, prosecuting, and punishing people who engage in criminal conduct. Although that system does not focus on the victim, criminal procedures may affect a child victim in these ways: A criminal investigation may involve multiple interviews of the child; the child may be required to testify in the criminal proceeding; the child may feel vindicated or fearful or confused about what happens in the criminal system; and the perpetrator may be removed from the home or otherwise isolated from the victim as a result of the criminal proceeding. A number of criminal offenses involving child victims are outlined in Appendix B.

3. The North Carolina Juvenile Code is Chapter 7B of the North Carolina General Statutes (hereinafter G.S.). The Juvenile Code also establishes procedures for responding to juveniles whose behavior is undisciplined or delinquent, for terminating parental rights, and for the emancipation of minors.

4. *See, e.g.,* Troxel v. Granville, 530 U.S. 57 (2000); Moore v. City of E. Cleveland, 431 U.S. 494 (1977); Prince v. Massachusetts, 321 U.S. 158 (1944); Pierce v. Society of Sisters, 268 U.S. 510 (1925); Meyer v. Nebraska, 262 U.S. 390 (1923).

5. *See, e.g.,* Stanley v. Illinois, 405 U.S. 645 (1972); Reno v. Flores, 507 U.S. 292 (1993).

6. *See, e.g., In re* Stumbo, 143 N.C. App. 375, 547 S.E.2d 451 (2001) (appeal pending in N.C. Sup. Ct.) (involving parents' claim that a department of social services was not justified in conducting an investigation after receiving a report of suspected neglect). See also Richard Rubin, "County Manager Defends DSS Removal of Children," *The Charlotte Observer,* 12 October 2002, p. 6B, and Eric Frazier, "Protective Services Scrutinized," *The Charlotte Observer,* 22 November 2002, p. 1B, regarding public scrutiny of a social services department's handling of a case that involved the removal of ten children from their home.

7. *See, e.g.,* Natasha Ashe, "Lawsuit Filed in Death of 2-Year-Old," *Salisbury Post,* 16 June 1999. Retrieved 8 April 2003 from http://www.salisburypost.com/newscopy/061699lawsuit.htm.

2
History of the Reporting Law

Background

Newspapers, magazines, movies, and talk shows regularly depict how often and in how many ways children are mistreated and even killed by the very people responsible for their care and protection. People strive to understand the causes of child maltreatment, the efficacy of programs aimed at preventing abuse and neglect, and the adequacy of social services and court procedures to deal promptly and effectively with these problems. This has not always been the case.

It was only in the 1950s and 1960s that child abuse and neglect began to be recognized as major medical and social phenomena. In 1962, publicity about a new medical diagnosis—*battered child syndrome*—captured the attention of certain professionals and, to a lesser extent, that of the general public.[1] Reports emerged about the frequent failure within the medical community to diagnose child abuse or to refer cases of abused children to appropriate authorities. This publicity captured lawmakers' attention as well, and state legislatures began to enact child abuse reporting statutes. By 1966, all states except one had enacted laws requiring physicians to report suspected child abuse,[2] or at least

allowing them to do so without fear of liability. Over time, those laws have been expanded both to require more people to make reports and to broaden the kinds of conditions or maltreatment that must be reported.[3]

North Carolina Law

In North Carolina, the law commonly called "the child abuse reporting law" is part of the Juvenile Code. It provides that

> [a]ny person or institution who has cause to suspect that any juvenile is abused, neglected, or dependent, as defined by G.S. 7B-101, or has died as the result of maltreatment, shall report the case of that juvenile to the director of the department of social services in the county where the juvenile resides or is found.[4]

This law evolved from several previous attempts to encourage people to report child abuse and neglect. North Carolina's first reporting law, enacted in 1965, did not mandate reporting.[5] Rather, it served the limited purpose of guaranteeing physicians and certain other professionals immunity from civil or criminal liability for reporting child abuse and neglect. The law required county departments of social services to investigate these voluntary reports. It also created an exception to the physician–patient privilege: when a report resulted in a legal proceeding, the privilege could no longer be used to exclude evidence of abuse or neglect. This first reporting law applied only to the abuse or neglect of children younger than sixteen.

In 1971, a new law replaced the 1965 statute. The 1971 law made some reporting mandatory and created different reporting duties for professionals and for other citizens.[6] It required specified professionals to report if they had *reasonable cause to suspect* that a child was *abused* or *neglected*. It required all other people to report, but only if they had *actual knowledge* that a child was *abused*. The legislature included in the law the following statement of its purpose in requiring people to report child abuse and neglect:

> The General Assembly recognizes the growing problem of child abuse and neglect and that children do not always receive appropriate care and protection from their parents or other caretakers acting in loco parentis. The primary purpose of requiring reports of child abuse and neglect as provided by this Article is to identify any children suspected to be neglected or abused and to assure that protective services will be made available to such children and their families as quickly as possible to the end that such children will be protected, that further abuse or neglect will be prevented, and to preserve the family life of the parties involved where possible by enhancing parental capacity for good child care.[7]

The next version of the reporting law came into effect as part of a new Juvenile Code enacted in 1979.[8] In this law the legislature did not distinguish between professionals and other persons. It required reporting by any person or institution that had cause to suspect that a child was abused or neglected. A 1993 amendment added a requirement that people and institutions make a report when they have cause to suspect that a child is dependent or that a child has died as the result of maltreatment.[9] It also added a requirement that the report include the names and ages of other children in the home if the person making the report knew that information.[10]

Current Law

Since July 1, 1999, the effective date of the current Juvenile Code, the mandatory reporting law has been part of G.S. 7B-301.[11] The reporting requirement itself, however, has not changed since 1993. Every person or institution with cause to suspect that a child is abused, neglected, or dependent, or that a child has died as a result of maltreatment, must report that child's situation to the county department of social services where the child resides or is found. (See Chapter 5 for legal definitions of "abused," "neglected," and "dependent.")

This mandate sounds simple; however, it raises many issues of interpretation, even for those who know about the law and want to comply with it.

Notes to Chapter 2

1. Battered child syndrome was described in C. Henry Kempe, et al., "The Battered-Child Syndrome," *Journal of the American Medical Association* 181 (July 1962): 17.
2. Seth C. Kalichman, *Mandated Reporting of Suspected Child Abuse: Ethics, Law, & Policy,* 2d ed. (Washington, D.C.: American Psychological Association, 1999), 15.

3. Reporting requirements are matters of state law, and statutes differ from state to state. They tend to have elements that are similar, however. Since enactment of the federal Child Abuse Prevention and Treatment Act of 1974 (Pub. L. No. 93-247) states have been required, as a condition of receiving certain federal child welfare funds, to include specified elements in state law definitions of abuse and neglect.

4. G.S. 7B-301.

5. 1965 N.C. Sess. Laws ch. 472.

6. 1971 N.C. Sess. Laws ch. 710. In this law, "professional" included "a physician, surgeon, dentist, osteopath, optometrist, chiropractor, podiatrist, physician-resident, intern, a registered or practical nurse, hospital administrator, Christian Science practitioner, medical examiner, coroner, social worker, law enforcement officer, or a school teacher, principal, school attendance counselor or other professional personnel in a public or private school."

7. 1971 N.C. Sess. Laws ch. 710 § 1.

8. 1979 N.C. Sess. Laws ch. 815 § 1.

9. 1993 N.C. Sess. Laws ch. 516 § 4.

10. *Id.*

11. SL 1998-202, s. 6. G.S. 7B-301 replaced former G.S. 7A-543, which was repealed when the current Juvenile Code, G.S. Chapter 7B, became effective.

Part II
Key Definitions

3

Significance of the Definitions

When a person has cause to suspect abuse, neglect, dependency, or death by maltreatment of a child, that person **must** report the child's situation to the county department of social services.

How do you know when a child is or may be an "abused juvenile," a "neglected juvenile," or a "dependent juvenile"? The Juvenile Code defines these and other key terms.[1] The definitions are important because they determine

- which children's situations must be reported to the county department of social services;
- whether the county social services department has a duty, and the authority, to investigate a case; and
- whether the district court has authority to intervene on the child's behalf.

A court also must apply these definitions when an action is filed to terminate a parent's rights on the basis that the parent has abused or neglected his or her child[2] or in a criminal case involving a charge of contributing to the abuse or neglect of a child.[3]

State administrative rules amplify some of the definitions,[4] and policies issued by the state Division of Social Services in the Department of Health and Human Services provide some guidance for interpreting the definitions.[5] When court orders relating to abuse, neglect, or dependency are appealed, the North Carolina appellate courts may be called on to decide whether trial courts interpreted and applied the definitions correctly in specific circumstances.[6]

The Juvenile Code defines abused, neglected, and dependent juveniles—children whose situations must be reported to social services—fairly broadly. At the same time, the definitions exclude some children whom almost everyone would consider to be abused or neglected. This is because the Code is not attempting to describe all situations in which families and children might benefit from services or in which services should be *offered* to families. Instead, the Code is establishing the scope of the government's authority to intervene in families (or family-like situations) for purposes of protecting children, regardless of whether the family wants assistance. Criminal laws, not the Juvenile Code and its definitions, specify when conduct affecting a child should be treated as a crime.[7]

Notes to Chapter 3

1. The definitions appear in G.S. 7B-101, which is reproduced in full in Appendix A.

2. G.S. 7B-1111(a)(1).

3. G.S. 14-316.1. The elements of this offense are described in Appendix B.

4. Administrative rules relating to child protective services are issued by the state Social Services Commission and appear in subchapter 41I of title 10 of the North Carolina Administrative Code. The Administrative Code is available in some libraries and on the Internet at http://www.oah.state.nc.us/.

5. Policies relating to child protective services appear in Chapter VIII of the division's *Children's Services Manual.* The manual is available for inspection at any county department of social services during regular office hours and can be accessed through the division's Web site. Retrieved 8 April 2003 from http://info.dhhs.state.nc.us/olm/manuals/dss/.

6. Published opinions of the North Carolina Supreme Court and the North Carolina Court of Appeals are available in law school libraries; in county law libraries, in counties that have those; and in many law offices and law firms. Recent opinions can be accessed through the Web site for the state Administrative Office of the Courts. Retrieved 14 April 2003 from http://www.nccourts.org/.

7. As noted above, the criminal offense of contributing to the abuse or neglect of a minor cross-references the Juvenile Code definitions.

4

The People Defined: Juvenile, Parent, Guardian, Custodian, and Caretaker

Which Children Are Covered?

The reporting law applies to all juveniles. For purposes of the reporting law, a "juvenile" is a minor—anyone under the age of eighteen—who is not married, emancipated, or in the armed services.[1] In this book, the term "child" is used interchangeably with "juvenile."

An "emancipated minor" is someone under the age of eighteen who has been released legally from parental control and who has many of the same rights as an adult. In North Carolina a minor may become emancipated in two ways. First, a minor is emancipated automatically if he or she marries. A minor may marry in this state, however, only if

- he or she is at least sixteen and has the written consent of (i) a parent who has full or joint legal custody of the minor or (ii) a person, agency, or institution that has legal custody of the minor or is serving as the minor's guardian; or
- the minor is fourteen or fifteen years of age, the minor and the person he or she plans to marry are the parents of a child, whether born or unborn, and the minor has filed a civil court action and obtained a court order authorizing the marriage.[2]

The second way a minor may become emancipated is by bringing an action in juvenile (district) court for a decree of emancipation.[3] Only sixteen- and seventeen-year-olds may petition for emancipation. A judge may grant an emancipation petition only after (1) the minor's parents are given notice, (2) a court hearing is held at which the judge makes extensive inquiries about the minor's circumstances, and (3) the judge concludes that emancipation is in the minor's best interest. This procedure and marriage are the exclusive means of emancipation in North Carolina.

The reporting law, therefore, covers all unmarried children under the age of eighteen except those in the armed services or with a legal decree of emancipation. The law applies to these juveniles even if they

- live independently away from home,
- are treated by their parents as if they were emancipated,
- declare themselves emancipated without having a court order, or
- have given birth to or fathered children.

Whose Conduct Is Covered?

The Juvenile Code defines abused, neglected, and dependent juveniles in terms of the effect on children of the conduct or caretaking abilities of parents, guardians, custodians, or caretakers.

A "parent," although the Code does not define the term, may be a child's biological or adoptive parent, a person who is legally presumed to be a child's parent, or a person who has been determined by a court to be a child's parent.

A "guardian" is someone appointed by a court to have the care, custody, and control of a child or to arrange an appropriate placement for the child. (A child's parent is considered the child's "natural guardian.") A guardian also has the authority to consent on the child's behalf to medical care and other matters for which a parent's consent ordinarily would be required.[4]

A "custodian" may be either

1. a person or agency that has legal custody of a child—that is, custody pursuant to a court order; or
2. a person who has assumed the status and obligations of a parent, even though that person has not been awarded legal custody by a court.[5]

A "caretaker" is someone (other than a parent, guardian, or custodian) who is responsible for a child's health and welfare in a residential setting.[6] A caretaker might be a stepparent, a foster parent, an adult member of the child's household, or an adult relative who has been entrusted with the child's care. People like house parents or cottage parents who supervise children in residential child care facilities and residential schools also are caretakers. The term specifically includes any employee or volunteer of a division, institution, or school operated by the state Department of Health and Human Services.

Because a person, in order to be a caretaker, must be caring for a child "in a residential setting," the definition does not cover schoolteachers, coaches, club leaders, and others with similar temporary caretaking responsibility for children. If someone suspects that one of these "non-caretakers" has harmed or neglected a child or placed a child at risk, the law does not require that person to make a report to the department of social services. Still, most people can and would take steps to ensure that the child and other children are not exposed to further risk or harm.[7] Appropriate responses might include one or more of the following:

- notifying the child's parents, guardian, or custodian;
- contacting law enforcement authorities; or
- in a work situation, informing the employer or supervisor or, if in a position to do so, taking appropriate personnel action.

If a person does report a problem involving a non-caretaker to a county department of social services, the department will not investigate, since it is not authorized to do so. The law, however, requires the department to relay the information to the district attorney's office and to law enforcement officials if the report describes criminal conduct that results in physical harm to a child.[8]

The legislature has included within the meaning of "caretaker" people who provide care for children in child care facilities, which include day care centers and homes, even though these are not strictly "residential settings."[9] The legal definition of "child care facility," which exists primarily for licensing and regulatory purposes, is complex.[10] It refers to a variety of nonresidential child care arrangements, but contains a number of specific exclusions. Some of the people who are not caretakers, because the places in which they provide care for children are excluded from the definition of child care facility, are those in vacation Bible schools; recreation programs that operate for fewer than four consecutive months; organized clubs such as Boy Scouts, Girl Scouts, 4-H groups, and boys and girls clubs; and drop-in or short-term care provided in health spas, resort hotels, bowling alleys, shopping malls, or churches.

Someone who has primary responsibility for a child's care in a day care center or other child care facility is a caretaker, and so is anyone who has that person's approval to assume responsibility for children who are in the primary provider's care. This might be an employee or a relative the provider asks to watch the children, for example.

Observing or suspecting that a child has been injured or mistreated does not necessarily trigger a duty to make a report to the department of social services. In order for a report to be required, and in order for the social services department to have the authority and responsibility to investigate, there must be cause to suspect that the child's condition can be attributed to the child's *parent, guardian, custodian,* or *caretaker.*

A child who is assaulted by an older juvenile, sexually molested by a stranger, or disciplined in a cruel manner by a teacher, for example, would not come within the reporting requirement—unless, of course,

there was some indication that the child's parent (or guardian, custodian, or caretaker) allowed or contributed to the injury, harm, or risk to the child.

This is not to say that a concerned person has no recourse in these situations. Cases involving people who are not parents, guardians, custodians, or caretakers may be the subject of criminal investigations and prosecutions. They should be reported to law enforcement officials or to other appropriate authorities. These cases do not, however, come within the Juvenile Code provisions aimed at getting protective services to the child and the child's family. Until there is some indication to the contrary, the law assumes that parents (and guardians, custodians, and caretakers) will act responsibly to prevent or respond appropriately to harm that others may cause their children.

Notes to Chapter 4

1. G.S. 7B-101(14). A number of states have changed their definitions of "abused juvenile" or "neglected juvenile" or created special reporting requirements in order to bring drug-exposed newborns under the child protective services umbrella, but no state has included unborn children in the definition of "child" or "juvenile" in a way that permits state intervention on the child's behalf before the child is born. *See* National Clearinghouse on Child Abuse and Neglect Information, "Reporting Laws: Drug Exposed Infants," *Child Abuse and Neglect State Statutes Series Ready Reference 2002* (Washington, D.C.: U.S. Department of Health and Human Services, 2002). Retrieved 8 April 2003 from http://www.calib.com/nccanch/pubs/readref/drugex.cfm.
2. G.S. 51-2 and 51-2.1. *See also* Janet Mason, *North Carolina Marriage Laws & Procedures,* 4th ed. (Chapel Hill, N.C.:

Institute of Government, The University of North Carolina at Chapel Hill, 2002).

3. *See* Article 35 of G.S. Chapter 7B (G.S. 7B-3500 through 7B-3509).

4. In North Carolina a clerk of superior court may appoint a "guardian of the person" (as opposed to a "guardian of the estate") only for a child who has no "natural guardian," i.e., no parent. G.S. 35A-1203(a). The district court, in a juvenile proceeding, may appoint a guardian of the person whenever the court finds the appointment to be in the juvenile's best interest. G.S. 7B-600 (abused, neglected, and dependent juveniles) and G.S. 7B-2001 (undisciplined and delinquent juveniles). For a case in which the court held that an aunt was a child's guardian even though never designated as such by a court order, *see* State v. Jones, 147 N.C. App. 527, 556 S.E.2d 644 (2001), *appeal dismissed, review denied,* 355 N.C. 351, 562 S.E.2d 427 (2002) (custodial interrogation did not violate the juvenile's *Miranda* rights because the aunt was present and the aunt was the juvenile's guardian within the meaning and spirit of G.S. 7B-2101).

5. G.S. 7B-101(8). The second prong of this definition, a person who assumes the status and obligations of a parent, used to appear separately as the definition of a "person in loco parentis," a term the Juvenile Code no longer uses.

6. G.S. 7B-101(3).

7. Some professionals are constrained by confidentiality requirements from reporting these cases if the law does not require them to make a report.

8. G.S. 7B-307(a). The social services director must make immediate oral reports and subsequent written reports to both the district attorney and the appropriate local law enforcement agency.

9. *See* G.S. 7B-101(3).

10. G.S. 110-86(2) and (3).

5

The Conditions Defined: Neglect, Abuse, Dependency, and Maltreatment

This chapter will leave some readers frustrated, because it will not answer some of the questions they hoped it would resolve. When someone points to a child's situation and asks "Is this abuse?" or "Is that neglect?" a *yes* or *no* answer often is not possible. The answer may be "It depends," or simply "No one knows for sure."

People trying to decide whether to make reports should not assume that they alone are uncertain about the applicability of particular terms. The question of whether a given set of facts constitutes "abuse," "neglect," or "dependency" will be asked at several stages in a child protective services case, and it is not unusual for the question to be answered differently at different stages. That is because the degree of certainty required is not the same at every stage[1] and also because at each stage, a different person or entity is called on to interpret and apply the key definitions. In addition to the person deciding whether to make a report, those may include

1. one or more individuals at the department of social services who must determine whether, if the information given in the report is true, the child is abused, neglected, or dependent;

2. other people in the department of social services who conduct an agency review if the report is not accepted for investigation and the person who made the report asks for a review of that decision;

3. a social worker who investigates a report and must determine (with others in the department) whether to substantiate the report;

4. a prosecutor who is asked by the person who made a report to review a social services department's decision not to substantiate abuse, neglect, or dependency;

5. a social services attorney advising the department in regard to whether to file a petition or which condition(s) to allege in a petition;

6. a judge (or the chief judge's designee) deciding whether to grant a nonsecure custody order to remove the child from the home before a full hearing on a petition;

7. the child's guardian ad litem and attorney advocate, and the parents and their attorneys, in deciding how to respond to a petition, including whether to contest it;

8. the district court judge who presides over the adjudication hearing;

9. a three-judge panel of the court of appeals, when a case is appealed; or

10. the North Carolina Supreme Court, when it reviews a decision of the court of appeals.

This chapter attempts to explain what is clear about the meaning of abuse, neglect, dependency, and maltreatment and to acknowledge some important areas of uncertainty.

Neglect

The Juvenile Code defines a "neglected juvenile" as a child who

- does not receive proper care, supervision, or discipline from the child's parent, guardian, custodian, or caretaker; or

- has been abandoned; or

- is not provided necessary medical care; or

- is not provided necessary remedial care; or

- lives in an environment that is injurious to the child's welfare; or

- has been placed for care or adoption in violation of law.[2]

This definition has withstood judicial scrutiny when challenged on the ground that it was unconstitutionally vague.[3] In one case, the court found that the terms used in the definition are given "precise and understandable meaning by the normative standards imposed upon parents by our society."[4] The court said, in effect, that people can use common sense

and generally accepted values to determine what is meant by "proper care," "necessary medical care," or "an injurious environment."

A determination that a child is neglected depends not only on the conduct of a parent, guardian, custodian, or caretaker, but also on the effect that conduct has on the child. The child must either be harmed or be placed at substantial risk of harm in order for neglect to exist.[5] Neglect may take a variety of forms, as described below.

LACK OF PROPER CARE AND SUPERVISION

Neglect may consist of a parent's failure to meet the child's basic needs. It is not necessary, though, for a child to suffer physical harm or be threatened with physical harm in order to be neglected. For example, proper care and supervision include providing a child with a basic education, so willfully failing to enroll a child in school can be neglect.[6] Keeping a child out of needed therapeutic day care also has been found to be neglect.[7]

Leaving a young child unsupervised may be neglect; however, the law does not specify any particular age below which a child cannot legally be left at home alone. Rather, it assumes that parents and others will exercise appropriate discretion based not only on the child's age, but also on the child's maturity and all of the relevant circumstances.[8]

INAPPROPRIATE DISCIPLINE

Neglect may occur through parents' actions as well as their failure to act. Inappropriate discipline that harms a child or creates a substantial risk of harm, but does not cause *serious* physical injury, is neglect.[9] This may be contrary to most people's assumption that inappropriate discipline that causes physical injuries, even if those are relatively minor, is abuse. One court held that a five-year-old child was neglected on the basis that her mother had hit her in the face with a belt, causing bruises, and had scrubbed her so hard during bathing (as discipline for the child's sexual exploration) that the child bled.[10] In cases like that, where the parent's actions clearly constitute inappropriate discipline that is harmful to the child, it is not important for the person making a report to be certain whether the child's condition is one of abuse or of neglect.

Almost any method of disciplining a child—spanking, switching, time out, deprivation of privileges—can be inappropriate and harmful if taken too far. But how far is too far? The North Carolina Court of Appeals has stated the following rule of thumb: "In general, treatment of a child which falls below the normative standards imposed upon parents by our society is considered neglectful."[11] That rule can be difficult to apply. Strongly held beliefs about what constitutes proper discipline can vary greatly among parents, communities, religious groups, and cultures.

ABANDONMENT

The courts have described "abandonment" as a parent's willful refusal to perform a parent's natural and legal obligations to care for and support a child, and also as a parent's willful conduct that shows an intent to forego all the parent's duties and rights in relation to the child.[12] The newborn left in a basket on the steps of a hospital or agency would fit within these definitions, but abandonment also may occur over a period of time. Most appellate court decisions dealing with abandonment arise in the context of proceedings to terminate parental rights, where the issue is whether a parent's abandonment has continued for six months or longer.[13] The case law, therefore, usually involves the issue of whether a parent's conduct over an extended period of time constitutes abandonment, rather than whether initial intervention on the child's behalf was warranted.[14]

Publicity about cases in which parents killed their newborn infants or abandoned them in unsafe places, often after the mother had hidden her pregnancy from family and friends, led a number of states to enact legislation aimed at deterring such acts. In 2001, the North Carolina General Assembly amended the Juvenile Code (1) to allow a parent, within the first seven days of a child's life, to "give" the child to another person without providing any information except the parent's intent not to return for the child; (2) to require certain professionals, and allow any other person, to accept physical custody of the infant in that situation; and (3) to require the person receiving the child to take certain actions, including contacting the department of social services or law enforcement authorities immediately.[15] In that circumstance the parent is absolved of criminal liability for abandonment.[16] A social services department receiving a report of a parent's surrender of a child in this way, however, must begin an investigation immediately and proceed as in any other case of reported abuse or neglect.

LACK OF NECESSARY MEDICAL OR REMEDIAL CARE

"Necessary medical care" and "necessary remedial care" have not been defined precisely. A court had no trouble concluding that a child was neglected when the child's father had both failed to seek treatment for the child's serious burns and refused to allow a social worker to do so.[17] Other deprivations of medical or remedial care may not be as clear-cut, but this form of neglect clearly extends beyond physical harm. The court of appeals affirmed a finding of neglect based on a mother's refusal to allow treatment for her child's severe hearing and speech defects.[18] In that case the court of appeals said, "To deprive a child of the opportunity for normal growth and development is perhaps the greatest neglect a parent can impose upon a child."[19]

A rule issued by the state Social Services Commission specifies that medical neglect includes depriving certain disabled infants of treatment. A disabled infant (under one year of age) with a life-threatening condition or conditions is neglected if

1. the infant is being denied appropriate nutrition, hydration, or medication; or
2. the infant is not receiving the medically indicated treatment that, in the treating physician's reasonable medical judgment, would be most likely to be effective in ameliorating or correcting the life-threatening conditions, unless it is also the physician's reasonable medical judgment that
   a. the infant is chronically ill and irreversibly comatose, or
   b. medical treatment would merely prolong dying, would not ameliorate or correct all of the life-threatening conditions, or

   c. provision of medical treatment would be virtually futile in terms of the infant's survival, and under the circumstances the treatment would be inhumane.[20]

North Carolina is in a minority of states that do not make reference in their reporting laws to parents' religious beliefs as a basis for depriving a child of medical care. Some states include limited exceptions for these cases within the definition of neglect; others have statutes that describe how parents' religious beliefs should be considered in determining whether a child is neglected.[21] In North Carolina, courts consider these issues when parents raise them in individual cases.[22] For a person deciding whether to make a report, however, there is no exception based on a parent's religious beliefs that changes or lessens the duty to report.

INJURIOUS ENVIRONMENT

A child is neglected if the child lives in an environment that is injurious to the child's welfare. As with other forms of neglect, an injurious environment may be one that puts the child at substantial risk of harm as well as one in which the child actually has been harmed.[23] In one case, the court found that a child was substantially at risk because the child's mother had moved frequently and exposed the child to an environment that involved drugs and violence.[24] In other cases, the court has found that a mother's severe problem with alcohol abuse created an injurious environment for her children[25] and that a parent's inability to maintain secure living arrangements is relevant to a determination of whether a child is neglected.[26]

ILLEGAL PLACEMENT

Placing a child illegally for care or adoption is a form of neglect, although one that has rarely been the basis for court action. Several statutes govern the placement of children, however, and cause to suspect that a child's placement violates any of these statutes can form the basis of a duty to report. These include laws that specify licensing requirements for (a) operating, establishing, or providing foster care for children and (b) receiving or placing children in residential care facilities, foster homes, or adoptive homes.[27] A child placed in a foster home by an agency that was not licensed as required by these laws, for example, would be neglected under this part of the definition.

A child also may be neglected if someone who is not legally authorized to place children for adoption places the child for that purpose. Under the state's adoption laws a child may be placed for adoption in North Carolina only by

- a county department of social services;
- another legally authorized agency;
- the child's guardian (but not a guardian appointed in a juvenile proceeding);
- both parents acting jointly; or
- one parent who has both legal and physical custody of the child (unless the parents are married and still living together).[28]

Another group of laws regulates the placement of children for foster care or adoption in another state. Under the Interstate Compact on the Placement of Children,[29] it is unlawful to bring or send a child across state lines for placement without providing the receiving state with certain information, receiving that state's determination that the proposed place-

ment does not appear to be contrary to the child's interests, and complying with other requirements of the compact. These laws do not apply when a child's parent, guardian, or relative is placing the child with a parent, guardian, or specified relative in another state. But a child would be neglected if, for example, a court or agency in another state placed the child with a relative in North Carolina without complying with the compact.

Oddly, North Carolina does not have a statute that criminalizes or specifically prohibits the selling of children. The adoption law, however, makes it a misdemeanor to offer, pay, or accept money (or anything of value) either for the placement of a child for adoption or for a parent's consent to adoption, unless the payment is one specifically authorized by statute.[30]

Abuse

The Juvenile Code considers a juvenile "abused" when the child's parent, guardian, custodian, or caretaker acts in certain specified ways and, as a result, the child is harmed or is at risk of being harmed.[31] Conduct covered by the definition falls into several main categories, discussed below.

CAUSING OR ALLOWING SERIOUS INJURY

A child is abused, for purposes of the reporting law, if the child's parent, guardian, custodian, or caretaker inflicts—or allows someone else to inflict—on the child a serious, nonaccidental physical injury. A child also is abused if one of those persons creates—or allows to be created—a substantial risk of serious, nonaccidental physical injury. No statute defines "serious physical injury." The appellate courts have said that the injury "must be serious but . . . fall short of causing death," and that "[f]urther definition seems neither wise nor desirable."[32] A statute that makes child abuse a crime, G.S. 14-318.4, uses the phrase "serious physical injury" to describe a Class E felony of child abuse. The same statute, describing a more serious offense of Class C felony child abuse, uses the phrase "serious bodily injury," which it defines as

> . . . bodily injury that creates a substantial risk of death, or that causes serious permanent disfigurement, coma, a permanent or protracted condition that causes extreme pain, or permanent or protracted loss or impairment of the function of any bodily member or organ, or that results in prolonged hospitalization.

Serious physical injury does not have to be that severe, but there is no clear minimal threshold for classifying a physical injury as serious. As explained above, however, a child who is put at risk of or receives an injury that cannot be characterized as serious, but that results from inappropriate care, supervision, or discipline, may be neglected.

CRUELTY

A child is abused if the parent, guardian, custodian, or caretaker uses—or allows someone else to use—cruel or grossly inappropriate procedures or devices to modify the child's behavior. Trying to change a child's behavior by using electrical shocks, tying the child to a bedpost, depriving the child of food, or forcing the child to consume inordinate amounts of water are examples of the ways parents and others can abuse children in this manner.

SEXUAL ABUSE

Sexual abuse, for purposes of the reporting law, occurs when a child's parent, guardian, custodian, or caretaker commits, permits, or encourages *the commission of any of the following criminal offenses* by, with, or upon the juvenile:

- first- or second-degree rape (G.S. 14-27.2, G.S. 14-27.3);
- first- or second-degree sexual offense (G.S. 14-27.4, G.S. 14-27.5);
- sexual act by a custodian (G.S. 14-27.7);
- crime against nature (G.S. 14-177);
- incest (G.S. 14-178);[33]
- preparation of obscene photographs, slides, or motion pictures of the juvenile (G.S. 14-190.5);
- employing or permitting the juvenile to assist in a violation of the obscenity laws (G.S. 14-190.6);
- dissemination of obscene material to the juvenile (G.S. 14-190.7, G.S. 14-190.8);
- displaying or disseminating material harmful to the juvenile (G.S. 14-190.14, G.S. 14-190.15);
- first- or second-degree sexual exploitation of the juvenile (G.S. 14-190.16, G.S. 14-190.17);
- promoting the prostitution of the juvenile (G.S. 14-190.18); and
- taking indecent liberties with the juvenile (G.S. 14-202.1), regardless of the age of the parties.

The elements of these offenses and of other criminal offenses involving child victims are set out in Appendix B.

It is important to remember that most of the acts covered by these offenses constitute criminal conduct on the part of the adult, and therefore also constitute abuse for purposes of the reporting law, even if the child apparently participates in them voluntarily. In determining whether a child's situation gives a person cause to suspect that the child is abused, it helps to be familiar with this list, but the person need not master the intricacies of criminal law. If conduct that is harmful to a child does not constitute one of these criminal offenses, the child's situation still may be reportable under another part of the definition of abuse or as neglect.

EMOTIONAL ABUSE

A child is emotionally abused if the parent, guardian, custodian, or caretaker either creates—or allows others to create— serious emotional damage to the child. The statute states that evidence of serious emotional damage includes a child's severe anxiety, depression, withdrawal, or aggressive behavior toward himself or herself or others.

This definition is not always easy to apply, and few cases go into court solely on the basis of emotional abuse. Obviously, serious emotional damage is not always caused by emotional abuse. Children may suffer from depression or anxiety, or be aggressive, for a variety of reasons. Because causation is so hard to prove, many cases of emotional abuse probably are treated as cases of neglect. A parent who creates or allows serious emotional damage to a child probably is not providing the child with proper care, supervision, or discipline, so that the child is a neglected juvenile. In one case involving both neglect and

emotional abuse, the court found that the children had suffered serious emotional damage as a result of the parents' long-standing and acrimonious marital disputes.[34]

CONTRIBUTING TO DELINQUENCY

Finally, a child is considered to be abused, for purposes of the reporting law, if the parent, guardian, custodian, or caretaker encourages the juvenile to commit delinquent acts that involve moral turpitude.[35] Abuse also exists if one of those persons directs or approves of the juvenile's commission of such acts. In North Carolina a "delinquent act" is conduct by a juvenile who is at least six but not yet sixteen that would be a crime if committed by an adult.[36]

Dependency

A juvenile is "dependent," for purposes of the reporting law, if

- the child needs assistance or placement because the child has no parent, guardian, or custodian responsible for the child's care or supervision, or
- the child's parent, guardian, or custodian is not able to provide for the child's care or supervision and lacks an appropriate alternative child care arrangement.[37]

Dependency usually results from a parent's inability to provide for the child rather than from the child's having no parent, guardian, or custodian. The cause of the parent's inability to care for the child is not relevant.[38] A parent's inability might be due to the parent's physical or mental illness, an injury, the parent's arrest, or a natural disaster; and it may be temporary or permanent.

A parent also might be unable to provide for a child because of the child's extraordinary needs. A child's severe illness or disability may create such special needs that a parent's best efforts are not sufficient to provide adequate care for the child.[39]

Even when parents are not able to care for their children, the responsibility for developing an alternative plan of care falls first on the parents themselves. The child is dependent only if the parent who is not able to care for his or her child has no alternate plan or the parent's plan is inappropriate. A child might be dependent, for example, if her single parent had to undergo major surgery and neither the other parent nor relatives nor anyone else was available to care for the child. If the hospitalized parent had arranged for the child to stay temporarily with a responsible neighbor, however, the parent's inability to care for the child would not make the child dependent. If a parent has the ability to make appropriate alternative arrangements but fails to do so, the line between dependency and neglect can blur. If the hospitalized parent left a six-year-old child at home with instructions to take care of herself for a week, the child probably would be neglected rather than dependent.

For the person considering making a report, it does not matter whether "dependent" or "neglected" or "abused" is the more appropriate characterization of the child's condition. If the person has cause to suspect that a child falls within the definition of one or more of these categories, the law requires that person to make a report.

Maltreatment

Any person or institution with cause to suspect that a child has died as the result of maltreatment must report the case of that child to the county department of social services.[40] The Juvenile Code does not define "maltreatment." When a child's death is the result of suspected abuse or neglect, as the Code defines those terms, the law almost certainly requires a report to social services. Maltreatment, though, appears to be a broader term, since the legislature easily could have said "children who die as the result of suspected abuse or neglect." Maltreatment might include, for example, harmful actions by persons other than parents, guardians, custodians, and caretakers.

Interpreting maltreatment as being broader than abuse and neglect is consistent with the General Assembly's creation of a child fatality prevention system, which includes reviews of children's deaths as one means of better understanding the causes of and methods for preventing these deaths.[41] The reviews are conducted by state and local multi-disciplinary teams that have access to records of all deaths of children in North Carolina, from birth to age eighteen. One purpose of the teams' reviews is to identify any deficiencies in the delivery of public services designed to prevent future child abuse, neglect, or death.

A county social services department's immediate response to a report of a child's death due to maltreatment, however, focuses on determining whether other children remain in the home (or institutional setting) and, if they do, determining whether those children require protective services or need to be removed for their protection.[42]

Difficulty in Applying the Definitions

Obviously, terms like "proper care," "proper supervision," "necessary medical care," "substantial risk," and "injurious environment" lend themselves to varying interpretations. Questions framed in terms of whether particular facts are covered by these or other terms often do not yield the unequivocal answers people want. The following are examples of questions that people have asked in trying to understand their duty to report and social services departments' responses to reports, including, in some instances, responses that appear to be inconsistent to someone who reports similar facts to different county social services departments:[43]

1. *If a child is born with fetal alcohol syndrome or tests positive at birth for illegal drugs, is the child abused (or neglected or dependent)?*

A number of states have amended their reporting laws to address these children specifically.[44] North Carolina has not amended its laws, but most, if not all, county social services departments would consider the child's condition, in and of itself, "cause to suspect" that the infant is abused, neglected, or dependent. They would expect the hospital to make a report and would accept the report and conduct an investigation. Some counties, however, might accept the report and conduct an investigation only if there was additional information indicating cause to suspect (1) that the child is not receiving or will

not receive proper care from the child's parent, guardian, custodian, or caretaker, or (2) that the parent is not able to provide proper care and does not have a suitable alternative arrangement. The first group of counties would consider this additional information in deciding whether to substantiate a report, not whether to investigate it.

Policy of the state Division of Social Services—a strong guide for counties even though it does not legally bind them— supports the approach of the majority of counties, described above. It states that "reports of children born prenatally exposed to illegal substances should be accepted for CPS [Child Protective Services] investigative assessment to determine if the home environment will offer minimally sufficient care and supervision."[45] The policy also states, however, that "prenatal drug exposure does not constitute neglect per se."[46]

2. *Is a child neglected if the child comes to school inadequately clothed, dirty, or with untreated head lice?*

If there are no other indications of abuse or neglect, a school is not likely to report these conditions the first time they occur, and social services departments likely would not investigate them if they were reported. If the report indicates that the problem has occurred repeatedly, that it is having a harmful effect on the child, and that the parents are not responding appropriately, most departments would accept this as a report of neglect at some point. When that point is reached will depend to some extent on other information that is available about the child and family. It may be affected as well by policies of the county department of social services. Some departments may take the position that the fact that a child is dirty or has head lice, even repeatedly, is never a sufficient basis for a report.

3. *Is a child neglected if the child is repeatedly tardy or absent from school?*

In two cases the North Carolina Court of Appeals has held that a parent's failure to enroll a child in school was neglect.[47] In one case, the court found that a father's insistence on home schooling his developmentally disabled son was neglect because it deprived the child of the socialization and special education classes that public school could provide and that were critical to the child's development and welfare.[48] In the other case, parents refused to enroll their children in school because the school failed to teach about Indians and Indian heritage and culture, and the parents did not provide a sufficient alternative education. "It is fundamental," the court said, "that a child who receives proper care and supervision in modern times is provided a basic education.[49] Social services departments and the protective services laws, however, are not the appropriate avenues for responding to most school attendance issues. Children who deliberately miss school may be "undisciplined juveniles" and subject to juvenile justice procedures designed to address the child's behavior.[50] A parent who violates the compulsory attendance law by willfully failing to send a child to school can be charged with a misdemeanor.[51]

The initial responsibility for dealing with attendance issues clearly rests with the school principal, who has very specific responsibilities in relation to attendance problems.[52] When a child has accumulated ten unexcused absences, the principal must take steps to determine whether the parent has made good faith efforts to comply with the compulsory attendance law. If the principal determines that the parent has made those efforts, the principal is authorized to refer the matter to a juvenile court counselor on the basis that the juvenile is "undisciplined." If the principal determines that the parent has not made a good faith effort, the principal is required to notify the district attorney.[53]

A parent's failure to make a good faith effort to comply with the compulsory attendance law, or a parent's deliberately keeping a child out of school for inappropriate reasons, also may be neglect or dependency. The younger the child, the more likely it is that parental neglect or incapacity is the cause of a child's school attendance problem. Again, county social services departments' policies may vary in regard to when, if ever, a report based on a parent's failure to send a child to school will be accepted for investigation or substantiated as neglect or dependency.

4. *Does the fact that a minor female is living with her older boyfriend mean that she is abused, neglected, or dependent?*

A minor (someone under age eighteen) who leaves home, with or without parental consent, is not emancipated unless she marries or obtains a court order of emancipation. Her parents remain legally responsible for her care and supervision, and the reporting law continues to apply to her. This remains true even if she becomes pregnant or gives birth to a child.

If the minor is under the age of thirteen and the boyfriend is at least four years older than she is, the boyfriend's having intercourse with her is first-degree rape, even if the relationship is totally voluntary on the girl's part.[54] If the same couple engages in other sexual acts, the male is committing first-degree sexual offense.[55] There is no law requiring that these crimes be reported. A report to social services about the child is required, however, on the basis that the girl is abused, if a parent (or guardian, custodian, or caretaker) is permitting or encouraging the commission of the offense against her. (In some cases the minor might be neglected or dependent, instead of abused, if the parent is not permitting or encouraging the conduct but is not providing or is not able to provide proper care and supervision for the child.)

If the minor is thirteen, fourteen, or fifteen years old and the male is at least four years older than she is, the boyfriend's engaging in intercourse or sexual acts with her is statutory rape or statutory sexual offense.[56] Again, this is true even if the relationship is totally voluntary on the girl's part. There is no law requiring that these crimes be reported; however, a report to social services about the child may be required on the basis that the girl is

- abused, if a parent (or guardian, custodian, or caretaker) is permitting or encouraging the commission of one of those offenses against her;[57]
- neglected, on the basis that her parents are not providing proper care and supervision for her; or

- dependent, if her parents are not able to provide proper care and supervision for her (for example, because she came here from another country without her family).

Any time a report to social services involves allegations of statutory rape or statutory sexual offense (or other crimes), the department must make a report to law enforcement and the district attorney if the report indicates that the juvenile "may have been physically harmed . . . by [a] person other than the juvenile's parent, guardian, custodian, or caretaker."[58] The law does not provide guidance as to what constitutes "physical harm" for purposes of that requirement.

When the girl is sixteen or seventeen years old, there is no crime of statutory rape or statutory sexual offense, regardless of the boyfriend's age. Still, the minor may be neglected or dependent if her parents are not providing or are not able to provide her with proper care and supervision. Occasionally there may be a question as to whether the element of harm or risk of harm is present for purposes of neglect—for example, if the minor is almost eighteen, the relationship is stable, and the couple have a child for whom they are providing good care. That determination might be made more appropriately after an investigation than at the reporting stage.

In cases in which a minor's parents do not condone her living arrangement and have made real but unsuccessful efforts to get her to return home, she might be considered an undisciplined juvenile—a category for which no report is required.[59] In that case, the parents could seek help from the local juvenile justice office[60] or file a civil action in district court asking the court to order the minor to return home and the boyfriend to stop allowing her to stay with him.[61]

Other questions that have similarly imprecise answers include:

- Should the fact that a twelve-year-old girl is pregnant or has a venereal disease always create "cause to suspect" that she is abused or neglected? What if the girl is thirteen? or fifteen? or seventeen? or ten?
- Can a parent's refusal to give a child Ritalin or similar medication ever constitute neglect?[62]
- At what point is a child abused or neglected on the basis that the child witnesses domestic violence or lives in a home where domestic violence occurs regularly?[63]

Sometimes the answers become clear with the addition of other relevant information. Nevertheless, until the General Assembly provides more guidance through legislation or the appellate courts are called on to decide cases involving these issues, they will continue to require (1) very individual assessment in light of the purposes of the reporting law and (2) local collaboration to find the best way to address the needs of families and children.[64]

Notes to Chapter 5

1. For example, a person who has only "cause to suspect" that a child is abused, neglected, or dependent must report. In order to adjudicate a child abused, neglected, or dependent, the district court must make findings based on "clear and convincing evidence."

2. G.S. 7B-101(15). The statute states that, in determining whether a child is neglected, it is relevant whether the child lives in a home where another child has (1) died as a result of suspected abuse or neglect or (2) been subjected to abuse or neglect by an adult who regularly lives in the home.

3. *See, e.g., In re* Moore, 306 N.C. 394, 293 S.E.2d 127 (1982), *appeal dismissed,* 459 U.S. 1139 (1983); *In re* Clark, 303 N.C. 592, 281 S.E.2d 47 (1981); *In re* Allen, 58 N.C. App. 322, 293 S.E.2d 607 (1982); *In re* Huber, 57 N.C. App. 453, 291 S.E.2d 916, *appeal dismissed and cert. denied,* 306 N.C. 557, 294 S.E.2d 223 (1982).

4. *In re* Biggers, 50 N.C. App. 332, 341, 274 S.E.2d 236, 241–42 (1981).

5. *See, e.g., In re* Everette, 133 N.C. App. 84, 514 S.E.2d 523 (1999) (vacating adjudication of neglect because although trial court found that parent did not provide proper care, supervision, or discipline, it did not make any findings that the child was impaired or at substantial risk of impairment as a result); Powers v. Powers, 130 N.C. App. 37, 502 S.E.2d 398 (1998) (evidence showing that mother drove with children in the car while under the influence, that her drinking sometimes rendered her unable to care for the children, and that her problem with alcohol contributed to the children's emotional problems was sufficient to establish neglect).

6. *In re* McMillan, 30 N.C. App. 235, 226 S.E.2d 693 (1976); *In re* Devone, 86 N.C. App. 57, 356 S.E.2d 389 (1987). *See* "Difficulty in Applying the Definitions," below.

7. *In re* Cusson, 43 N.C. App. 333, 258 S.E.2d 858 (1979).

8. Several criminal laws do specify particular ages in relation to the proper supervision of children. For example, G.S. 14-318 makes it a misdemeanor for any person to leave a child under the age of eight "locked or otherwise confined in a dwelling, building or enclosure without leaving some person of the age of discretion in charge of the same, so as to expose the child to danger by fire." Under G.S. 14-316, it is a misdemeanor for a parent (or others in parent-like positions) to permit a child under the age of twelve to possess or use a dangerous firearm, regardless of whether it is loaded, except under the supervision of that adult person.

9. Children are "abused" if disciplined in ways that cause (or create a substantial risk of) serious physical injury or involve the use of cruel or grossly inappropriate procedures or devices. G.S. 7B-101(1).

10. *In re* Thompson, 64 N.C. App. 95, 100, 306 S.E.2d 792, 795 (1983).

11. *In re* Thompson, 64 N.C. App. at 99, 306 S.E.2d at 794.

12. *See* Pratt v. Bishop, 257 N.C. 486, 126 S.E.2d 597 (1962); *In re* Adoption of Searle, 82 N.C. App. 273, 346 S.E.2d 511 (1986).

13. G.S. 7B-1111(a)(7).

14. *See, e.g., In re* Young, 346 N.C. 244, 485 S.E.2d 612 (1997) (insufficient evidence of willfulness to establish abandonment); *In re* Graham, 63 N.C. App. 146, 303 S.E.2d 624, *disc. rev. denied*, 309 N.C. 320, 307 S.E.2d 170 (1983) (lack of involvement with children for more than two years established a pattern of abandonment and neglect).

15. SL 2001-291, amending G.S. 7B-302(a) and G.S. 7B-500, effective July 19, 2001.

16. G.S. 14-318.2(c), G.S. 14-318.4(c), and G.S. 14-322.3.

17. *In re* Hayden, 96 N.C. App. 77, 384 S.E.2d 558 (1989).

18. *In re* Huber, 57 N.C. App. 453, 291 S.E.2d 916, *appeal dismissed and cert. denied*, 306 N.C. 557, 294 S.E.2d 223 (1982).

19. *In re* Huber, 57 N.C. App. at 458, 291 S.E.2d at 919.

20. N.C. Admin. Code tit. 10, subchap. 41I, § .0303(2) (July 1993). The state Social Services Commission adopted this rule in 1985 in response to the federal Child Abuse Amendments of 1984 and federal regulations that require states to include it in their definitions of "neglect" in order to remain eligible for federal child welfare funds. *See* 42 U.S.C.A. §§ 5106a(b)(10) and 5106g(10) (1999); 45 C.F.R. § 1340.15 (2002).

21. *See* National Clearinghouse on Child Abuse and Neglect Information, "Current Trends in Child Maltreatment Reporting Laws," *Child Abuse and Neglect State Statutes Series* (Washington, D.C.: U.S. Department of Health and Human Services, 1999), 12–14.

22. The North Carolina Court of Appeals upheld a trial court's order that children who had been adjudicated neglected and placed in social services' custody be immunized despite the parents' religious objection. The court said, "[O]ur courts do not have a history of routinely ordering the performance of medical procedures on children without parental consent. However, when parents refuse to provide necessary medical care, their inaction can extinguish custody and support a finding of neglect." *In re* Stratton, 153 N.C. App. 428, 433, 571 S.E.2d 234, 237, *appeal dismissed and*

discretionary review denied, 356 N.C. 436, 573 S.E.2d 512 (2002). In *Stratton* the neglect adjudication was not based on the parents' refusal to have the children immunized. G.S. 130A-157 provides an exemption from the immunization requirements based on a parent's bona fide religious beliefs. The issue was whether the parents lost their right to claim that exemption when the children were adjudicated neglected and removed from their custody.

In another case the court of appeals rejected a father's claim that his refusal to permit a mental health evaluation of his children during an abuse investigation was lawful because he objected to the evaluation on religious grounds. The court said, "One may not be compelled by governmental action to do that which is contrary to his religious belief in the absence of a 'compelling state interest in the regulation of a subject within the State's Constitutional power to regulate.' . . . The intent of the statutes requiring the Department of Social Services to screen and investigate complaints of child abuse is the protection of neglected and abused children, . . . which is undeniably a compelling state interest." *In re* Browning, 124 N.C. App. 190, 193–4, 476 S.E.2d 465, 467 (2002).

23. *In re* Safriet, 112 N.C. App. 747, 436 S.E.2d 898 (1993).

24. *In re* Helms, 127 N.C. App. 505, 491 S.E.2d 672 (1997).

25. Powers v. Powers, 130 N.C. App. 37, 502 S.E.2d 398 (1998).

26. *See In re* Evans, 81 N.C. App. 449, 344 S.E.2d 325 (1986); *In re* Adcock, 69 N.C. App. 222, 316 S.E.2d 347 (1984) (moving eight times within a year and a half is evidence of instability relevant to a neglect determination).

27. G.S. Chapter 131D, Article 1A. Unless specifically exempted, a person or agency that violates these requirements is guilty of a misdemeanor.

28. G.S. 48-3-201. Placement of a child by anyone else for adoption is a misdemeanor. G.S. 48-10-101.

29. G.S. 7B-3800 through 7B-3806.

30. G.S. 48-10-102, G.S. 48-10-103.

31. The term "abused juveniles" is defined in G.S. 7B-101(1), which is reproduced in full in Appendix A.

32. State v. Hannah, 149 N.C. App. 713, 718, 563 S.E.2d 1, 4 (2002), *review denied*, 355 N.C.

754, 566 S.E.2d 81 (2002), quoting State v. Ramseur, 338 N.C. 502, 507, 450 S.E.2d 467, 471 (1994).

33. The Juvenile Code also refers here to G.S. 14-179, which was repealed effective December 1, 2002, by SL 2002-119, s. 2. That legislation also rewrote G.S. 14-178 so that it covers all incest offenses.

34. Powers v. Powers, 130 N.C. App. 37, 502 S.E.2d 398 (1998).

35. The North Carolina Supreme Court has referred to "moral turpitude" as involving "an act of inherent baseness in the private, social, or public duties which one owes to his fellowmen or to society, or to his country, her institutions and her government." State v. Mann, 317 N.C. 164, 170, 345 S.E.2d 365, 369 (1986). *See also* Dobson v. Harris, 351 N.C. 353, 341 S.E.2d 728 (1999) (child abuse involves moral turpitude); State v. Collins, 334 N.C. 54, 431 S.E.2d 188 (1993) (burglary involves moral turpitude); Dew v. State *ex rel.* North Carolina Dep't of Motor Vehicles, 127 N.C. App. 309, 488 S.E.2d 836, (1997) (conspiracy to possess with intent to distribute marijuana is crime involving moral turpitude).

36. G.S. 7B-1501(7). In North Carolina, a sixteen- or seventeen-year-old is treated as an adult for purposes of his or her criminal behavior. A sixteen-year-old whose parent encouraged him to steal, therefore, would not be covered by this part of the abuse definition, because a sixteen-year-old does not commit delinquent acts—he or she commits crimes. Still, the sixteen-year-old could be considered neglected, because the parent is failing to provide proper supervision and discipline.

37. G.S. 7B-101(9).

38. In 1997 the General Assembly amended the definition of "dependent juvenile" to delete a requirement that the parent's, guardian's, or custodian's inability to care for the child be "due to physical or mental incapacity." SL 1997-113.

39. Parents of some adolescents probably feel "unable" to provide care and supervision to children who refuse to accept either. While these children are not necessarily excluded from the definition of "dependent juvenile," their needs usually can be addressed more appropriately through systems other than child protective services, such as mental health, juvenile justice and delinquency prevention, or other community resources.

40. G.S. 7B-301.

41. G.S. 7B-1400.

42. G.S. 7B-302(b).

43. See Chapter 11 for related discussion of "screening"—the process by which social services departments decide whether to accept reports for investigation.

44. Some states include these conditions in the definition of "abused juvenile" or "neglected juvenile." Others have special reporting requirements that apply to these children. *See* National Clearinghouse on Child Abuse and Neglect Information, "Reporting Laws: Drug Exposed Infants," *Child Abuse and Neglect State Statutes Series Ready Reference 2002* (Washington, D.C.: U.S. Department of Health and Human Services, 2002). Retrieved 8 April 2003 from http://www.calib.com/nccanch/pubs/readref/drugex.cfm.

45. North Carolina Department of Health and Human Services, "The Impact of Drug and Alcohol Abuse," *Children's Services Manual,* Ch. VIII (Protective Services), § 1440 xi. Retrieved 8 April 2003 from http://info.dhhs.state.nc.us/olm/manuals/dss/csm-60/man/CS1440-10.htm#P163_28739.

46. *Id.*

47. *In re* McMillan, 30 N.C. App. 235, 226 S.E.2d 693 (1976); *In re* Devone, 86 N.C. App. 57, 356 S.E.2d 389 (1987).

48. *In re* Devone, 86 N.C. App. at 60, 356 S.E.2d at 391.

49. *In re* McMillan, 30 N.C. App. at 238, 226 S.E.2d at 695.

50. These procedures are set out in Subchapter II of the Juvenile Code, G.S. 7B-1500 through 7B-2827.

51. G.S. 115C-380. The likelihood of these cases' being prosecuted varies substantially among judicial districts.

52. *See* G.S. 115C-378 and 115C-381.

53. Two bills introduced in the 2003 session of the General Assembly would amend G.S. 115C-378 to require the principal in this circumstance to notify the county director of social services as well as the district attorney. House Bill 203 was introduced on March 4, 2003, and Senate Bill 421 was introduced on March 17, 2003.

54. *See* G.S. 14-27.2.

55. *See* G.S. 14-27.4. Sexual acts include cunnilingus, fellatio, analingus, anal intercourse, or penetration by any object into the genital or anal opening of another person's body for nonmedical purposes. G.S. 14-27.1(4).

56. *See* G.S. 14-27.7A. If the defendant is at

least six years older than the victim the offense is a Class B1 felony. If the defendant is at least four but less than six years older, the offense is a Class C felony.

57. It is not completely clear that "abused juvenile" is the appropriate characterization of the child in this situation. The offenses of statutory rape and sexual offense against thirteen-, fourteen-, and fifteen-year-olds were added to the criminal laws in 1995. The part of the Juvenile Code definition of "abused juvenile" that references a variety of criminal sex offenses has never been amended to include these offenses. Thus, the Code does not explicitly provide that a juvenile is abused if a parent, guardian, custodian, or caretaker permits or encourages the commission of one of these offenses against the child.

58. See G.S. 7B-307(a).

59. A juvenile is "undisciplined" if he or she runs away from home for more than twenty-four hours; is beyond the disciplinary control of his or her parent, guardian, or custodian; or is younger than sixteen and is unlawfully absent from school. G.S. 7B-1501(27).

60. See G.S. Chapter 7B, Article 17 (Screening of Delinquency and Undisciplined Complaints).

61. See G.S. Chapter 7B, Article 34 (Parental Authority over Juveniles).

62. This and other issues relating to medicating children are the subject of growing national attention. See, e.g., the Web site of the Public Broadcasting System, which includes links to the 2001 Frontline documentary, "Medicating Kids: A Report on Parents, Educators, and Doctors Trying to Make Sense of a Mysterious and Controversial Mental Diagnosis: ADHD," and related information. Retrieved 8 April 2003 from http://www.pbs.org/wgbh/pages/frontline/shows/medicating/.

63. This issue also is the subject of growing national concern and of legislative changes in some states. See National Clearinghouse on Child Abuse and Neglect Information, "Domestic Violence: Child Witnesses to Domestic Violence," *Child Abuse and Neglect State Statutes Series* (Washington, D.C.: U.S. Department of Health and Human Services, 2002).

North Carolina does not have specific legislation dealing with domestic violence in relation to child abuse and neglect. In early 2002, however, Chief Justice I. Beverly Lake and Secretary of Health and Human Services Carmen Hooker Odom appointed and began chairing the Child Well-Being and Domestic Violence Task Force, which issued a final report and recommendations in February 2003. Retrieved 7 May 2003 from http://www.doa.state.nc.us/cfw/cfw.htm.

64. Since June 1, 2003, the Division of Social Services in the state Department of Health and Human Services has provided additional guidance in the form of state policy regarding structured intake and screening tools for child protective services cases. North Carolina Division of Social Services, "Structured Intake," *Children's Services Manual*, Ch. VIII (Protective Services), § 1407. Retrieved 1 May 2003 from http://info.dhhs.state.nc.us/olm/manuals/dss/csm-60/man/CS1407.htm#TopOfPage.

Part III

Responsibilities and Rights of Reporters

6
Who Must Report

General Rule

North Carolina's reporting law applies to every person and every institution in the state. It requires "[a]ny person or institution who has cause to suspect that any juvenile is abused, neglected, or dependent, as defined by G.S. 7B-101, or has died as the result of maltreatment" to make a report to the county department of social services. The reporting requirement applies to doctors, social workers, therapists, teachers, law enforcement officers, and others whose professions sometimes involve them directly with problems of abuse, neglect, or dependency. It applies equally, though, to housing inspectors, store clerks, co-workers, friends, relatives, bystanders, and all others.

Confidential and Privileged Communications

With one very small exception for attorneys, which is discussed below, North Carolina law provides that "[n]o privilege shall be grounds for any person or institution failing to report that a juvenile may have been abused, neglected, or dependent, even if the knowledge or suspicion is acquired in an official professional capacity."[1] One of the main

reasons reporting laws were first enacted, after all, was to allow, encourage, or require physicians to report despite the physician–patient privilege and the principle of medical confidentiality.[2]

Attorneys

The Juvenile Code contains only one exception to the otherwise universal duty to report. An attorney is not required to make a report if "the knowledge or suspicion is gained by [the] attorney from that attorney's client during representation only in the abuse, neglect, or dependency case."[3] In any other situation, the law requires attorneys to report like everyone else. If an attorney learns from a parent about that parent's abuse or neglect of a child, or about the parent's inability to care appropriately for the child, while representing the parent in a child support action, a divorce, or any other matter that does not involve the abuse, neglect, or dependency itself, that attorney must make a report to social services.

This legal duty may conflict with a lawyer's ethical duty to maintain a client's confidences.[4] The North Carolina State

Bar, which adopts and interprets Rules of Professional Conduct for the legal profession, gives lawyers broad discretion in deciding how to resolve the conflict. In a 1995 ethics opinion, the State Bar interpreted its rules in relation to the child abuse and neglect reporting law.[5] The opinion concluded that a "lawyer may ethically report information gained during his or her professional relationship with a client to DSS [department of social services] in compliance with the statutory requirement even if to do so may result in substantial harm to the interests of the client." The opinion also states, however, that a lawyer, without violating the Rules of Professional Conduct, "may in good faith conclude that he or she should not reveal confidential information where to do so would substantially undermine the purpose of the representation or substantially damage the interests of his or her client," even where the failure to disclose the information constitutes a violation of the reporting law. The opinion acknowledges that its rules may not protect a lawyer from criminal prosecution for failing to comply with the reporting law.

An attorney weighing compliance with the reporting law and preservation of a client's confidence should consider, among other things, whether making a report would deprive his or her client of a constitutional right—such as the right to effective assistance of counsel in a criminal case. When the two are inconsistent, a client's federal constitutional right may supersede the attorney's duty under state law to report child abuse, neglect, or dependency.[6]

Judges

Like everyone else, judges who have cause to suspect that a child is abused, neglected, or dependent must make reports to departments of social services. A report would be required, for example, if a judge presiding in a child custody or domestic violence case heard evidence that gave the judge cause to suspect that one or both of the parties had disciplined their child in a cruel and harmful way.[7]

A judge may learn of (or develop cause to suspect) abuse, neglect, or dependency during a court proceeding that is required to be strictly confidential. The United States Supreme Court has held that a state may not constitutionally require parental consent for a minor to obtain an abortion unless the state also provides a confidential judicial procedure through which the minor can seek a waiver of the parental consent requirement.[8] North Carolina's so-called judicial bypass statute requires that the court proceeding, records relating to it, and the pregnant minor's identity be kept strictly confidential.[9] The statute also provides, however, that a judge who finds that the minor has been a victim of incest must notify the director of the department of social services "for further action pursuant to [the Juvenile Code provisions relating to abuse and neglect]."[10]

Does the state reporting requirement violate the pregnant minor's constitutional right to a confidential proceeding? The Fourth Circuit Court of Appeals concluded that a party making that argument was not likely to prevail. The court characterized as "unconscionable" the proposition that judges cannot be required to report abuse they learn about in judicial bypass proceedings. The court said:

Appellants would have a judge, who is sworn to uphold the law, withhold vital information regarding rape or incest which would allow state authorities to end the abuse, protect the victim, and punish the abuser. Not only would Appellants' position prevent the judge from helping the victim seeking the abortion, but it would prevent the judge from helping other juveniles in the same household under the same threat of incest. This Court does not believe that the Constitution requires judges to be placed in such an untenable position.[11]

The opinion suggests that the court would apply the same reasoning not only to the specific duty to report incest under the abortion consent waiver statute but also to the duty under the Juvenile Code to report abuse, neglect, and dependency. Quoting with approval from a concurring opinion in a Supreme Court case, the court said: "No one can contend that a minor who is pregnant is somehow less deserving of the State's protection. It is reasonable to provide that any minor who contends that she cannot notify her parent or parents because she is the victim of neglect or abuse must allow the State to use its power to investigate her declaration and protect her from harm."[12]

Religious Officials

Some states' reporting laws explicitly include clergy among the people who are mandated to report child abuse or neglect. In other states clergy are explicitly exempted from the duty to report, at least to the extent that the information they have derives from "pastoral communications."[13] North Carolina's statute has no provision relating

specifically to religious officials and the duty to report; therefore, they apparently are included in the mandate that "any person" with cause to suspect child abuse, neglect, or dependency make a report to the department of social services.[14] A religious official, like everyone else, has a duty to report child abuse, neglect, or dependency regardless of that official's relationship to the child. Whether mistreatment of a child *by* a religious official is abuse or neglect that must be reported to the social services department depends on whether that official is the child's parent, guardian, custodian, or caretaker. (The definition of "caretaker" is discussed in Chapter 4.)

North Carolina law relating to the competence of witnesses to testify in court has long recognized a clergy–communicant privilege.[15] Unlike most other statutory privileges, the clergy–communicant privilege does not include either an exception for child abuse and neglect cases or authority for the court to compel disclosure upon finding that disclosure is necessary to a proper administration of justice.[16] Before July 1, 1999, the Juvenile Code explicitly overrode certain specified privileges—for example, husband–wife and doctor–patient—but not the clergy–communicant privilege. Since July 1, 1999, however, the Juvenile Code has provided unequivocally that no privilege, except the narrow attorney–client privilege, is grounds for failing to report suspected abuse, neglect, or dependency or for excluding evidence in a case involving the abuse, neglect, or dependency of a child.[17]

Confidential communications between a person and his or her rabbi, minister, priest, or other religious confidant might be viewed as part of that individual's exercise of his or her religious freedom. A legal challenge to the application of the reporting law to clergy made on that basis would require a court to balance the individual's interest in exercising that right against the state's objectives in requiring clergy to report.[18]

Researchers

Like many clinicians and practitioners, researchers may find their professional objectives and ethics in conflict with a duty to report suspected child abuse, neglect, or dependency.[19] Especially when the research itself concerns child abuse and neglect, obtaining informed consent from research participants may be hindered by disclosure of the researcher's legal duty to report suspected abuse or neglect. Without the disclosure, on the other hand, the participant's consent is not fully informed if he or she has been told that the information provided will be kept confidential. Even when the research is totally unrelated to abuse or neglect, information the researcher obtains may give that person cause to suspect that a child is abused or neglected.

State law provides no exception or exemption for researchers. Some researchers, however, may obtain a limited exemption under a federal law[20] that allows the federal Secretary of Health and Human Services to issue Certificates of Confidentiality. These certificates are designed to protect "researchers and institutions from being compelled to disclose information that would identify research participants, . . . [to] help achieve

the research objectives and promote participation in studies by assuring privacy to subjects."[21] The Secretary has delegated authority to issue the certificates to the National Institutes of Health (NIH), and applications for certificates go through NIH regardless of whether the research involves NIH funding.[22]

Except for a very limited statutory exception for attorneys, possible constitutional exceptions, and Certificates of Confidentiality for researchers, the law makes no accommodation for professionals who—because of tradition, ethics, or legal obligation—consider confidentiality an essential element of their relationships with clients or patients.

The reporting requirement can raise troublesome issues for these professionals. For example:

- When and how should school guidance counselors, physicians, psychologists, and others inform people who come to them that the law requires confidentiality to be broken if necessary to report child abuse, neglect, or dependency?

- If a school counselor or similar professional assures a young girl that their conversation is confidential, how should that person react when the girl begins to describe the sexual abuse she is suffering at home?

- If students, patients, or clients are informed or reminded that suspected abuse, neglect, or dependency must be reported, will those who need help be discouraged from seeking it?

Questions like these do not have easy answers. The tension between the reporting law and the need to encourage trust and disclosure in order to provide effective services is long-standing and ongoing. Affected professionals—both individually and collectively—struggle to resolve that tension and, no doubt, will continue to do so.[23] Periodically proposals are made to change the law to carve out more exceptions. Unless the law is changed, though, it requires reporting even by those who fear that the report will do more harm than good.

Notes to Chapter 6

1. G.S. 7B-310. State mental health law provides specifically that mental health, developmental disability, and substance abuse facilities must disclose confidential information for purposes of complying with the child abuse, neglect, and dependency reporting law. G.S. 122C-54(h).

2. The terms "privilege" and "confidentiality," although sometimes used interchangeably, do not have exactly the same meaning. "Privilege" generally refers to a statutory rule that allows a person to prevent a court from requiring the disclosure of certain communications in court. "Confidentiality," on the other hand, refers to a broader obligation not to disclose information. Most privileges are statutory. While confidentiality may be based on statute, often it is an ethical duty deriving from professional standards rather than from law. *See, e.g.,* Sultan v. State Bd. of Examiners of Practicing Psychologists, 121 N.C. App. 739, 468 S.E.2d 443 (1996).

State statutes recognize and define the scope of the following types of privileged communications: physician–patient (G.S. 8-53); clergyman–communicant (G.S. 8-53.2); psychologist–client or psychologist–patient (G.S. 8-53.3); school counselor–student (G.S. 8-53.4); marital and family therapist–client (G.S. 8-53.5); husband–wife (G.S. 8-56 and G.S.8-57); certified social worker delivering private social work services–client (G.S. 8-53.7); licensed professional counselor–client (G.S. 8-53.8); optometrist–patient (G.S. 8-53.9); peer counselor–client law enforcement employee (G.S. 8-53.10); journalist–source (G.S. 8-53.11); and employee or agent of a domestic violence or rape crisis center–victim (G.S. 8-53.12).

3. G.S. 7B-310.

4. Rule 1.6 of the Revised Rules of Professional Conduct of the North Carolina State Bar addresses the lawyer's obligation to preserve the confidences of a client. N.C. Admin. Code tit. 27, ch. 2, Rule 1.6 (July 1997). The rule permits a lawyer to disclose confidential information, however, when required to do so "by law or court order."

5. The North Carolina State Bar, "RPC 175 (January 13, 1995)," *The North Carolina State Bar Lawyer's Handbook 2003 (Abridged)* (hereinafter *Handbook*), 205–6. *See also* "RPC 120 (July 17, 1992)," *id.* at 185–86.

6. *See Handbook*, 206. One legal scholar has concluded that "most of the breadth and sweep of the attorney–client privilege is without constitutional protection" and that "a legislature could constitutionally eliminate the protections of the attorney–client privilege except when criminal litigation has been formally initiated." Robert P. Mosteller, "Child Abuse Reporting Laws and Attorney–Client Confidences: The Reality and the Specter of Lawyer as Informant," 42 *Duke Law Journal* 2 (1992): 203, 271–72 .

7. Sometimes a judge hearing a custody dispute between parents will conclude that neither parent is fit to have custody of the child. Although occasionally judges in that situation order that the child be placed in the custody of the department of social services, it is more appropriate for the judge to make a report to the county department of social services. The department can file a juvenile petition and, if necessary, take immediate custody of the child before obtaining a custody order in the juvenile proceeding. G.S. 7B 500.

8. Belloti v. Baird, 443 U.S. 622 (1979).

9. G.S. 90-21.8.

10. G.S. 90-21.8(f).

11. Manning v. Hunt, 119 F.3d 254 (4th Cir. 1997). The court, affirming a judgment of the federal district court, held that the district court had not abused its discretion when it denied a motion for a preliminary injunction and refused to enjoin the enforcement of the state statute. Thus, the court's holding was not that the statute is constitutional, but that the plaintiffs challenging the statute were not likely to prevail on the merits at a trial on that issue.

12. *Id.*, quoting with approval from Justice Kennedy's concurring opinion in *Hodgson v. Minnesota,* 497 U.S. 417, 493–94, 110 S. Ct.

2926, 2967–68 (Kennedy, J., joined by Rehnquist, C.J., White, J., and Scalia, J., concurring).

13. National Clearinghouse on Child Abuse and Neglect Information, "Reporting Laws: Clergy as Mandated Reporters," *Child Abuse and Neglect State Statutes Series* (Washington, D.C.: U.S. Department of Health and Human Services, 2002), 3–4. *See also,* Donald T. Kramer, *Legal Rights of Children,* 2d ed. (Colorado Springs, Colo.: Shepard's/McGraw-Hill, Inc., 1994), 2:63.

14. North Carolina has been described as one of only three states that both mandate reporting by "any person" and deny the clergy–penitent privilege in child abuse cases. National Clearinghouse on Child Abuse and Neglect Information, "Reporting Laws: Clergy as Mandated Reporters," *Child Abuse and Neglect State Statutes Series* (Washington, D.C.: U.S. Department of Health and Human Services, 2002), 3.

15. G.S. 8-53.2 reads as follows: "No priest, rabbi, accredited Christian Science practitioner, or a clergyman or ordained minister of an established church shall be competent to testify in any action, suit or proceeding concerning any information which was communicated to him and entrusted to him in his professional capacity, and necessary to enable him to discharge the functions of his office according to the usual course of his practice or discipline, wherein such person so communicating such information about himself or another is seeking spiritual counsel and advice relative to and growing out of the information so imparted, provided, however,

that this section shall not apply where [the] communicant in open court waives the privilege conferred."

16. When first enacted in 1959, the statute did give the court that authority. In 1967, however, the General Assembly amended the statute to delete that provision. 1967 N.C. Sess. Laws ch. 794. Thereafter the state supreme court held that the amendment indicated "the General Assembly's intent to remove from the trial courts any discretion to compel disclosure when the clergy–communicant's privilege exists." State v. Barber, 317 N.C. 502, 510, 346 S.E.2d 441, 446 (1986).

17. G.S. 7B-310.

18. *See* J. Michael Keel, "Comment: Law and Religion Collide Again: The Priest–Penitent Privilege in Child Abuse Reporting Cases," 28 *Cumberland Law Review* 681 (1997).

19. *See* Rebecca R. S. Socolar, Desmond K. Runyan, and Lisa Amaya-Jackson, "Methodological and Ethical Issues Related to Studying Child Maltreatment," *Journal of Family Issues* 16, no. 5 (September 1995): 565–86.

20. Section 301(d) of the Public Health Service Act (42 U.S.C. 241(d)).

21. Office of Extramural Research, National Institutes of Health, "Certificates of Confidentiality Information: Background Information." Retrieved 8 April 2003 from http://grants1.nih.gov/grants/policy/coc/.

22. *Id.*

23. *See, e.g.,* Seth C. Kalichman, *Mandated Reporting of Suspected Child Abuse: Ethics, Law, & Policy,* 2d ed. (Washington, D.C.: American Psychological Association, 1999).

7

Deciding to Report

Cause to Suspect

What does it mean to have "cause to suspect" that a child is abused, neglected, or dependent? Answering that question means looking at a combination of objective and subjective factors. A mere feeling or suspicion that one cannot connect to something observable, to something the child or someone else has said, or to the child's behavior, probably is not enough to trigger a duty to report. The standard is not just "a suspicion," but "cause to suspect." But a person deciding whether to make a report also must consider a child's statements, appearance, or behavior (or other objective indicators) in light of the person's experience and other available information. This will help the person determine whether he or she has cause to suspect abuse, neglect, or dependency.

A person who has cause to suspect that a child is abused, neglected, or dependent has no duty to conduct an investigation to uncover evidence for the report. He or she is not required to have actual knowledge of abuse, neglect, or dependency, and physical evidence certainly is not required.

When the person considering making a report has a personal or professional relationship with the child's family, that person may want to discuss the suspected problem with the family. That relationship, however, should not be considered grounds for delaying a report. Of course, the reporting law does not permit anyone—professional, friend, or relative— to make an agreement *not* to report in exchange for an assurance that the person suspected of abusing or neglecting a child will seek help or take other actions.

Guidelines

In most situations, someone who has read the Juvenile Code definitions carefully will be able to tell whether one or more of them apply to a particular child. Still, in some respects the definitions leave room for uncertainty. In the absence of formal clarification through legislation, court decisions, or state policy, local guidelines can help relieve this uncertainty and answer questions about the duty to report. Some counties have guidelines (sometimes called "protocols") for cooperation between the county social services department and one or more other county agencies or departments. Ideally, local guidelines should be developed jointly by representatives of the county social services department and other key agencies in the community. Inquiries about local guidelines or protocols should be directed to individual county departments of social services. (See Chapter 14 for an outline of suggested guidelines for cooperation between county departments of social services and local school units.)

With or without local guidelines, there will be circumstances in which individuals and institutions struggle to determine whether the definitions apply and whether a report is required. For example, is a psychologist required to make a report to social services if he or she has cause to suspect that a client's boyfriend or girlfriend is mistreating the client's child? A boyfriend or girlfriend may be in the home frequently but not live there full time. Is the boyfriend or girlfriend a caretaker? Is he or she "responsible for the health and welfare of [the child] in a residential setting"? Is the mistreatment something that constitutes abuse or neglect?

In cases like this and other cases of uncertainty about whether there is a duty to report, the following basic guidelines may be helpful.

1. *Consider the purposes of the reporting law and of the child protective services system, which are to identify and respond to children who may need care, assistance, or protection when the child's parent (or guardian, custodian, or caretaker) either is not providing or cannot provide for those needs.*

Ask yourself whether, in the situation being considered, involuntary intervention by the state (through the county social services department) is consistent with those purposes. Of course, if the definitions clearly apply, a report is required regardless of whether one agrees with those purposes or believes that making a report will help achieve them.

2. *Do not limit your thinking to only one definition.*

If, for example, the mother's boyfriend regularly uses a cruel procedure to discipline the child, but it seems doubtful that he is a caretaker, consider whether the mother herself has placed the child at risk, has allowed the boyfriend to use the cruel procedure, or has failed to provide proper care and supervision. Cause to suspect that she has done any of these would require a report based on the mother's, not the boyfriend's, conduct. If the boyfriend's conduct constitutes an assault or some other crime, a person who knows about it could make a report to law enforcement officials. That report would not relieve the person of the duty to make a report to social services if the boyfriend is a caretaker or if the mother's conduct constitutes abuse or neglect.[1]

3. *Finally, if in doubt, make the report.*

While the legal definitions of "abuse," "neglect," "dependency," "caretaker," and other key terms are important, a person who is concerned about a child but unsure whether the definitions in the law apply should make a report. If the report is made in good faith, there is no liability risk in reporting. (See Chapter 9.) If the child needs help, the department of social services may be able to make appropriate referrals or offer services to the family, even if it turns out that it is not authorized to investigate the matter as a child protective services case.

Note to Chapter 7

1. Reporting to law enforcement officials raises special issues for professionals with a duty of confidentiality, since the report to law enforcement may not be legally required and the person may not have immunity for reporting to law enforcement. (See Chapter 9 for discussion of immunity for making reports to social services.)

8

How to Report

A report to the county department of social services may be made in person, by telephone, or in writing. It must be made to the department of social services in the county where the child lives or is found. Even if a child's legal residence is in another county or state, it is appropriate to make a report to the social services department in the county were the child is physically present. In North Carolina, each of the one hundred counties has a county department of social services or its equivalent.[1] All departments have the capacity to receive and respond to reports twenty-four hours a day, seven days a week. Appendix C lists telephone numbers for making reports in each county. Some of these will change over time. Anyone who does not know how to contact or has trouble contacting the social services department should call 911 or a local law enforcement agency.

The information that must be reported usually will be the same information that creates the person's cause to suspect that a child is abused, neglected, or dependent. The report should include any information that would be helpful in determining whether the department of social services, the court, or both need to take action to protect or assist the child.

What to Include

The report should include as much of the following as the person reporting knows:

- the child's name, age, and address;
- the name and address of the child's parent, guardian, custodian, or care-taker;
- the names and ages of other children in the home;
- the child's location if the child is not at the home address;
- the nature and extent of any injury or condition resulting from abuse, neglect, or dependency; and
- any other information that might help to establish the need for protective services or court intervention.[2]

Anonymous Reports

The law also requires the person who makes a report to give his or her name, address, and telephone number.[3] If the person does not, however, the department of social services still must investigate the report. A person's failure to identify himself or herself when making a report, in addition to violating the reporting law, may prevent the department of social services from obtaining important information. An anonymous report may generate questions about the motivation for the report or doubts as to its reliability. In addition, a person who reports anonymously gives up the right to be notified about how the report is handled and about certain appeal procedures. (See Chapters 9 and 12 for more information on notification and review procedures.)

Reports by Institutions

The duty to report applies to institutions as well as individuals. Hospitals, schools, day care facilities, law enforcement agencies, and similar institutions should develop clear procedures to ensure that reporting occurs when it is required. Some institutions designate a liaison person through whom reports from staff can be channeled to the department of social services. That can be an acceptable way to comply with the law, but only if the following conditions are met:

1. the liaison must serve, in fact, as a channel for conveying reports and not as a screener of reports; and

2. the individual teacher, nurse, or other employee who is the source of the report must have assurance

   ■ that the liaison will convey the report to social services promptly, and

   ■ that he or she also is free to communicate personally with the department of social services.

Notes to Chapter 8

1. Social services and other human services programs are organized somewhat differently in Wake County and Mecklenburg County. *See* G.S. 153A-77.

2. G.S. 7B-301.

3. G.S. 7B-301. *See also* N.C. Admin. Code tit. 10, subchap. 41I, § .0304(a) (September 1994). Occasionally people mistakenly interpret the department's duty to investigate anonymous reports as legal authority for reporting anonymously.

9

Legal Rights of the Reporter

Confidentiality

The law directs county departments of social services to hold "in strictest confidence" the information they receive in reports and during investigations of child abuse, neglect, and dependency. This includes the identity of the reporter.[1]

The confidentiality requirement is not absolute. The department of social services may disclose otherwise confidential information if the disclosure is necessary to carry out the agency's responsibilities. For instance, a reporter's identity might not be protected if he or she had information that had to be presented in court. The reporter could be called as a witness, although ordinarily the reporter would not have to reveal the fact that he or she was the person who made the report. The department of social services also may reveal the reporter's identity to the district attorney or a law enforcement agency investigating the report.[2]

In one situation the law specifically authorizes a judge to require a county social services director to reveal in court the identity of the person who made a report. If someone obstructs or interferes with a department's investigation after a report of suspected abuse, neglect, or dependency, the department may apply to the court for an order directing that person to stop obstructing or interfering with the investigation. At a hearing to determine whether the judge should issue that order, the judge may require the director of social services (or the director's representative) to identify the person who made the report.[3]

The circumstances that give the reporter cause to suspect abuse, neglect, or dependency may make it quite obvious to parents or others where a report originated. For that reason, some people choose to tell the parents (or guardian, custodian, or caretaker) that they are making a report, why they are making it, and something about what the parents can expect to happen as a result of the report. In some situations the person making the report can help the parent understand that the purpose of the report and ensuing investigation is to protect or assist the child. (There is no guarantee, however, that a criminal investigation will not occur.) Some parents may be less likely to confront, accuse, or harbor anger toward the reporter, and may be more cooperative in an investigation, if the

reporter explains his or her actions and the
reasons for them.

Obviously, the reporter should not tell
the parent about the report if there is a
possibility that doing so would lead to the
parent's harming the child or someone
else, or would impede the social services
department's investigation.

Immunity for Reporting, Cooperating, or Testifying

A majority of the reports of suspected
abuse, neglect, and dependency that social
services departments receive prove to be
either unfounded or impossible to
substantiate. In 2000–2001, departments of
social services in North Carolina
substantiated fewer than a third of the
reports they investigated.[4] A person who
has cause to suspect that a child is abused,
neglected, or dependent, but has no proof,
may fear that he or she could be sued for
making a report if it is not substantiated.
The law requires a person in that situation
to make a report and does not require the
person to produce evidence or proof of
any kind. The law does not allow the
person to delay reporting because he or
she is not certain that the child is abused,
neglected, or dependent.

The law encourages prompt reporting
and acknowledges people's concerns about
liability by providing immunity for people
who report in good faith. It also provides
immunity from legal liability to people
who cooperate in a social services
department's investigation (by sharing
information, for example) or who testify in
court actions that result from a report.

Anyone who makes a report pursuant to [the reporting law], cooperates with the county department of

social services in a protective services
inquiry or investigation, testifies in
any judicial proceeding resulting
from a protective services report or
investigation, or otherwise participates in the program authorized by
[the law that provides for reports,
investigations, and the provision of
protective services], is immune from
any civil or criminal liability that
might otherwise be incurred or
imposed for that action provided
that the person was acting in good
faith. In any proceeding involving
liability, good faith is presumed.[5]

This provision was applied in a case in
which a school principal reported to the
department of social services his suspicion
that a substitute teacher had abused
students. The department reported the
information to law enforcement officials,
who conducted an investigation and
charged the teacher with five counts of
assault. After the teacher was found not
guilty of all the charges in criminal court,
he sued the city school system for
malicious prosecution, defamation,
intentional infliction of emotional distress,
and negligence.

Relying on the immunity provision and
the statutory presumption of good faith,
the trial court dismissed the teacher's case
before it even went to trial. The court of
appeals affirmed the trial court's decision.[6]

The principal had reported not only to
the department of social services, but also
to the assistant superintendent for
personnel. The trial court and the court of
appeals applied the immunity provision
and presumption of good faith to that
report as well. The appellate court said:

[A] report made in good faith by the
principal of the school to his or her
superior who is responsible for
school personnel would clearly fall
within the scope of the immunity

contemplated by the statute. To say that the principal was protected in reporting the incident to the Department of Social Services but not in reporting to the Assistant Superintendent would be both contrary to the spirit of the statute and also impractical.[7]

The law cannot prevent irate parents or others from suing people who report suspected child abuse or neglect, testify in court, or cooperate in protective services investigations. The immunity protections in the law, however, make it much less likely that suits will be filed or that a suit, once filed, will succeed. In order to win, the person who sues would have to prove, among other things, that whoever made the report, testified, or cooperated did so "in bad faith"—that is, without any justification other than malice.

The North Carolina Supreme Court has stated that the legislative intent of the immunity provision is to encourage people to "be vigilant in assuring the safety and welfare of the [state's] children"—a policy that "compels a significant evidentiary burden for those who challenge the presumption that people who report . . . abuse or neglect do so in good faith."[8]

Notification and Review

The law and state administrative rules require a county department of social services to give a person who reports suspected abuse, neglect, or dependency certain information about the department's response to the report.[9] Within five days after receiving a report, the department must give the person who made the report written notice of (1) whether the department accepts the report and plans to investigate it and (2) whether the department has referred the report to a state or local law enforcement agency. Every person who makes a report is entitled to this notice unless he or she specifically requests not to receive it.

If the department does accept the report for investigation, the department must give the person who made the report a second written notice within five days after completing the investigation. This notice must tell the reporter (1) whether the department found abuse, neglect, or dependency; (2) what if any action the department is taking to protect the child; (3) whether the department has filed a petition to begin a juvenile court action; and (4) how to request a review of a decision by the department not to file a petition. This notice is required for every report the department accepts for investigation, unless the person who made the report specifically requests not to receive it.

If the department does not accept a report for investigation, the person who made it may request a departmental review of that decision. If the department accepts the report and after the investigation decides not to begin a juvenile court action, the reporter may ask the local prosecutor to review that decision. (Screening of reports is discussed in Chapter 11. Rights of review are described in more detail in Chapter 12.)

Notes to Chapter 9

1. G.S. 7B-302(a). The law does not specify any remedy for a reporter whose identity is disclosed improperly or any penalty for making an improper disclosure.

2. N.C. Admin. Code tit. 10, subchap. 41I, § .0304(c) (September 1994).

3. G.S. 7B-303(e).

4. In fiscal year 2000–2001, county social services departments in North Carolina investigated reports of suspected abuse, neglect, or dependency relating to 102,158 children. Of those, 32,581 were substantiated. Division of Social Services, North Carolina Department of Health and Human Services, "North Carolina Child Abuse Statistics, 1997–2001" (Raleigh, N.C., 2002) (unpublished). These and other child welfare statistics are available through the Web site for the state Division of Social Services. Retrieved 8 April 2003 from http://www.dhhs.state.nc.us/dss/childrensservices/stats/index.htm.

5. G.S. 7B-309.

6. Davis v. Durham City Schools, 91 N.C. App. 520, 372 S.E.2d 318 (1988).

7. *Davis*, 91 N.C. App. at 523, 372 S.E.2d at 320. The parties did not raise, and the court did not discuss, the issues of whether a substitute teacher was a "caretaker" and whether a report to social services had been required. When this case arose, the Juvenile Code definition of "caretaker" did not specify, as it does now, that it refers only to individuals providing care "in a residential setting," and there was some uncertainty as to whether incidents involving school personnel should be reported to social services.

8. Dobson v. Harris, 352 N.C. 77, 530 S.E.2d 829 (2000) (holding that trial court properly dismissed parent's action against a department store and a store employee who made a report to social services after observing the parent yell at the child, pick the child up from a counter, and slam her back down).

9. G.S. 7B-302; N.C. Admin. Code tit. 10, subchap. 41I, §§ .0304(h) and .0308 (September 1994).

10

Consequences of Failing to Report

Unlike many other states, North Carolina has no statute that imposes civil or criminal penalties for failing to report suspected child abuse, neglect, or dependency.[1] Although the General Assembly enacted the state's first mandatory reporting law in 1971 and has amended it several times, it has never provided civil or criminal penalties for *not* making a report when the law requires one.

The committee that drafted the Juvenile Code that was in effect from 1980 to 1999 said in its 1979 report:

> The Committee considered a penalty for not reporting abuse, neglect, or dependency to insure that the administrators of hospitals, schools, and other institutions whose employees may see evidence of abuse, neglect, or dependence develop a mechanism for reporting and encourage their employees to report such incidents as required by law. The Committee, however, concluded that the threat of civil suit for failure to report should be sufficient incentive for institutions to encourage reporting.[2]

Civil Liability

Thus far, the threat of civil suit has materialized rarely. There are no appellate court decisions in North Carolina—and very few nationally—dealing with civil liability for failing to report child abuse, neglect, or dependency.[3] But that does not mean that a person cannot be civilly liable for failing to report child abuse in North Carolina. The issue simply has not come before the courts in this state. Cases from other states and the literature in this area suggest that the potential for civil liability for failing to report is real.[4]

By itself, however, failing to report child abuse, neglect, or dependency is not enough to generate civil liability, even when the law clearly requires a report. Under the general principles of the law of negligence, civil liability is possible if

- someone with a duty to report fails to do so,
- a child is injured or harmed,
- the injury or harm to the child was *caused* by the failure to report, and
- the type of injury or harm the child suffered was a foreseeable consequence of the failure to report.

Proving all of these elements can be difficult. Increased recognition of children's rights, however, may increase the likelihood that liability issues will be examined when children are seriously harmed and people who should have reported their situations did not.

Criminal Prosecution

Criminal prosecutions for failing to report child abuse or neglect have resulted in no appellate court decisions in North Carolina and very few nationally. In at least two cases, however, persons in North Carolina have been prosecuted for violating the reporting law, even though there is no statute making the failure to report a criminal offense. In North Carolina, only appellate court decisions create precedents for other cases, and neither of these cases went to the court of appeals. Still, they are interesting because they illustrate the potential for criminal prosecutions for failing to report.

In 1986, an assistant school superintendent was convicted of a misdemeanor in district court for not reporting suspected sexual abuse of students by a substitute teacher.[5] The defendant did not appeal the conviction. That same year a psychologist was convicted in district court of a misdemeanor for not reporting suspected child abuse. He exercised his right to appeal to superior court, where he could have a new trial before a jury. Before the case went to trial again, however, the superior court judge dismissed the charge. This was partly because, in the judge's view, the General Assembly had not intended criminal consequences for failing to report.[6]

Prosecution of these two cases relied on a seldom-used common-law rule. Common-law rules are derived from ancient English law and past decisions of appellate courts. Under the rule on which these prosecutions were based, if a statute does not specify consequences for failing to perform a duty that the statute creates, a person who fails to perform that duty can be charged with a general misdemeanor.[7]

If this common-law rule applies to the reporting law, the reporting mandate in G.S. 7B-301, combined with the lack of sanctions in the statute for failing to report, makes the failure to report a misdemeanor. There is a strong argument that this common-law rule applies to the reporting requirement.[8] There also is a strong argument, however, that the General Assembly would have spelled out explicit criminal consequences for a failure to report if it had intended them.

Other Consequences of Failing to Report

The most obvious and serious consequence of not reporting suspected child abuse, neglect, or dependency is that a child may suffer unnecessarily. The cost to the child, the family, and ultimately to society may be immense—especially when compared with the small effort required to make a report that may result in protection for the child. In some cases, of course, the consequences of not reporting may be insignificant. The suspicion may be unfounded; the department of social services may be involved already; someone else may have made a report. But there is no way of predicting whether the report will make a difference in a child's life, and the law does not excuse a person from the duty to report for any reason.[9]

North Carolina law relating to civil and criminal liability for failing to report suspected child abuse, neglect, or dependency remains relatively undeveloped. The law relies primarily on the policies that underlie the reporting requirement, the ease of reporting, and the provision of immunity for good faith reporting—rather than fear of civil liability or criminal prosecution—to encourage people to report.

Notes to Chapter 10

1. *See* Seth C. Kalichman, *Mandated Reporting of Suspected Child Abuse: Ethics, Law, & Policy,* 2d ed. (Washington, D.C.: American Psychological Association, 1999), 33–42.

2. Juvenile Code Revision Committee, *The Final Report of the Juvenile Code Revision Committee* (Raleigh, N.C.: North Carolina Department of Crime Control and Public Safety, January 1979), 34–35.

3. A civil action involving allegations that school officials were negligent in failing to report child abuse was filed in Onslow County in 1986. The plaintiff in the case was a student who filed the action after he became eighteen. Hague v. Lloyd (86-CVS-1347, Onslow County Superior Court, complaint filed August 1, 1986). The case was settled before it went to trial.

4. *See, e.g.,* Landeros v. Flood, 17 Cal. 3d 399, 131 Cal. Rptr. 69, 551 P.2d 389 (1976) (doctor and hospital could be liable if their negligent failure to diagnose and report battered-child syndrome resulted in the child's being returned home and receiving further injuries); Note, "Civil Liability for Teachers' Negligent Failure to Report Suspected Child Abuse," *Wayne Law Review* 28 (1981–82): 183–213; Donald T. Kramer, *Legal Rights of Children,* 2d ed. (Colorado Springs, Colo.: Shepard's/McGraw-Hill, Inc., 1994), 2: 64–65; Kalichman, *supra* note 1.

5. State v. Freitag (Wake County District Court, January 31, 1986). *See* "Assistant Superintendent Convicted for Not Reporting Suspected Child Abuse," *School Law Bulletin* 17 (Spring 1986): 46–47. Under current law, a report to the department of social services would not be required in the circumstances of that case, because a teacher is not a "caretaker" as the Juvenile Code defines that term. (See Chapter 4.) Under current law, however, a report to law enforcement officials might be required, at least by the principal, since a principal has a duty to report to law enforcement certain criminal offenses that occur on school property. (See Chapter 14.)

6. State v. Gray (Durham County District Court, February, 1986; Durham County Superior Court, January 14, 1987). *See* "Charges against Chapel Hill Psychologist Dismissed," *Durham Morning Herald,* 15 January 1987, 1A. This case is discussed in Kalichman, 36–37.

7. *See, e.g.,* State v. Parker, 91 N.C. 650 (1884) (statute making it unlawful to sell liquor in specified localities); State v. Bloodworth, 94 N.C. 918 (1886) (statute requiring keeping fence five feet high around cultivated field during crop season); State v. Bishop, 228 N.C. 371 (1947) (statute prohibiting requiring membership in labor union as condition of employment).

8. Neither the courts nor the General Assembly has overturned this rule.

9. *See* White v. North Carolina State Board of Examiners of Practicing Psychologists, 97 N.C. App. 144, 165, 388 S.E.2d 148, 161, *cert. denied,* 326 N.C. 601, 393 S.E.2d 891 (1990). In reviewing the revocation of a psychologist's license based on multiple alleged violations of the Ethical Principles of Psychologists, the court held that the psychologist "technically" had violated both one of the ethical principles and the child abuse reporting law by failing to report suspected child abuse. In response to the psychologist's argument that he had not reported because "he thought the matter was already in the judicial system and the parents and attorneys knew of the alleged sexual abuse," the court of appeals stated that the reporting law "makes no exceptions for extenuating circumstances in reporting suspected child abuse." 97 N.C. App. at 165, 388 S.E.2d at 161.

Part IV

Investigation and Response

11

Social Services Procedures

A report of abuse, neglect, or dependency results in certain actions by the county department of social services. In some cases local law enforcement agencies are involved. The juvenile (district) court may take action, but only when the department of social services determines that a child needs to be removed from the home or that court intervention is needed for some other reason. First, the county social services department receives the report and handles screening, investigation, and, sometimes, protective action.

Screening

When a county department of social services receives a report, it must answer the following question: If the information in the report is true, does the child fit into the Juvenile Code definition of "abused juvenile," "neglected juvenile," or "dependent juvenile"? A report concerning any situation or person not covered by the Code definitions will be screened out, and the department will not investigate the matter. If someone reported that her neighbors were beating their eighteen-year-old daughter, for example, the report

would be screened out because the definition of juvenile does not include someone who is eighteen or older.[1] If an emergency room nurse reported to social services that a fourteen-year-old boy had been stabbed by another student at school, the department would screen the call out because the harm to the child was not caused or allowed by the child's parent, guardian, custodian, or caretaker.[2]

Often screening decisions are less clear-cut, and when they involve interpretations of the Juvenile Code definitions they may be made differently from county to county. This can cause confusion for professionals or institutions, such as hospitals, that make reports to more than one county and receive responses that seem inconsistent. In North Carolina each county department of social services operates its own child protective services program. The state Division of Social Services in the Department of Health and Human Services issues a policy manual,[3] and the state Social Services Commission issues rules[4] for child protective services. Until very recently, however, these have not provided much guidance to counties regarding intake and screening decisions.

Effective June 1, 2003, a lengthy new section of the Division's *Children's Services Manual* established a structured intake process. These new procedures and intake tools emphasize the extreme importance of intake, the need for more consistency in intake decisions, and the importance of focusing early on families' strengths.[5] In some cases these policies provide fairly specific guidance, but they do not answer all of the hard questions. Rather, they include interview and screening tools and suggestions about how to approach the difficult questions in ways that are consistent with the goal of child protection.

As discussed in Chapter 5, cases in which the definitions may be interpreted and applied differently often involve reports that come from schools, hospitals, and other professional settings. Those situations and others that are similarly susceptible to different interpretations underscore both the necessity of interagency coordination at the local level and the value of guidelines developed jointly by social services departments and the agencies and institutions that make reports frequently. If neither the statute nor court opinions nor rules or policies provide an unambiguous "right" answer, then communities need to develop responses to drug-exposed infants, children with basic hygiene and clothing needs, school-attendance problems, and teenagers living apart from their families. Responses that make the best use of resources and provide the best protection for children might look different in different counties.

Any decision to screen out a report of suspected abuse, neglect, or dependency

must involve both the social worker and his or her supervisor.[6] If a report is screened out, the county social services department often will try to refer the reporter to an appropriate agency or resource.

Notification after a Report Is Made

NOTIFYING THE REPORTER[7]

Within five working days after receiving a report, the department of social services must give the person who made the report written notice of

1. whether the report has been accepted for investigation, and
2. whether the report has been referred to the appropriate state or local law enforcement agency.

This notice is required after every report of suspected abuse, neglect, or dependency, unless the person who made the report specifically asks the department not to give the notice. In addition, in any case in which the department does not accept a report for investigation, the notice must inform the reporter of

1. the fact that the department will not conduct an investigation,
2. the basis for that decision, and
3. the reporter's right to ask for a review of the decision and the procedures for making that request.

A person whose report is accepted for investigation is entitled to a second notification when the investigation is completed. (See "Notification Requirements at Conclusion of Investigation," below.)

Review Process[8]

If a county department of social services screens out a report, the reporter is entitled to an agency review of that decision. For example, if a principal reports that a nine-year-old child has excessive absences from school, a county social services department may decline to accept the report and investigate the matter on the ground that the situation, even if exactly as described by the principal, does not constitute neglect. If the principal disagrees and thinks that the child's absences are due to a lack of proper care and supervision by the child's parent, the principal may request a review of the decision. In most cases the principal first would talk informally with people at the department of social services.

It is up to each county department of social services to establish a process for reviewing screening decisions. At a minimum, the process must include

1. notifying the reporter, as described above;
2. designating the persons within the agency who will conduct the reviews; and
3. specifying the manner in which the reviews will be conducted.[9]

Notifying Law Enforcement[10]

In some cases, after screening a report out, the social services director must make an immediate oral report, followed by a written report within forty-eight hours, to both the district attorney and an appropriate local law enforcement agency. These reports are required any time the information in the report indicates that a child may have been physically harmed, in violation of any criminal law, by someone

other than the child's parent, guardian, custodian, or caretaker. The social services department, for example, would not investigate a report that a camp counselor had molested a child. The department would be required, however, to notify the district attorney and law enforcement authorities immediately.

The law enforcement agency must begin a criminal investigation immediately (and in no event more than forty-eight hours after being notified). After the investigation, the district attorney decides whether any criminal charges should be filed. (See "Law Enforcement's Role," below, for discussion of other kinds of notification to law enforcement officials.)

Notification in Day Care Cases[11]

If a report relates to possible abuse or neglect of a child in a day care or other child care facility, the social services director must notify the state Department of Health and Human Services within twenty-four hours after receiving the report. If the report involves possible sexual abuse of a child in a child care setting, the director also must notify the State Bureau of Investigation.

Social Services Investigation

Purpose of Investigation

The purpose of the social services department's investigation is to determine the extent of any abuse or neglect, the risk of harm to the child, whether the child and family need protective services, what services would be most helpful, and whether a petition should be filed to take the matter to juvenile court.[12]

Although nothing in the statute or regulations suggests that investigations should be accusatory or adversarial, those who are the subjects of reports and investigations often perceive them that way. Social workers may do so as well. Significant trends, both nationally and in North Carolina, are to decrease these perceptions and to change the laws, policies, and practices that generate them. Social services departments are involving families and their relatives and communities more directly in planning and evaluating services. Some departments are responding to reports differently based on the nature and seriousness of each report.[13] In some places alternatives to traditional court proceedings, such as mediation and family conferencing, are being implemented as well.[14]

These trends and innovations are more evident in some parts of the state than others, and for the most part they are not yet reflected in the Juvenile Code. The following sections describe primarily the procedures that are set out in the Code.

STARTING THE INVESTIGATION

The county social services director, acting primarily through the local social services staff, is required to make a prompt and thorough investigation of every abuse, neglect, and dependency report that the department does not screen out.[15] If the report alleges abuse, the investigation must start immediately—in no event more than twenty-four hours after the department receives the report. An investigation of a neglect or dependency report must begin within seventy-two hours, unless the report alleges abandonment, in which case the investigation must begin

immediately.[16] Every investigation must include a visit to the place where the child lives. At the request of a county social services director, state or local law enforcement officers must assist with the investigation and with an evaluation of the seriousness of a report of abuse or neglect.

STEPS IN AN INVESTIGATION

The first step in an investigation is to make face-to-face contact with the child, when that is possible.[17] An investigation also includes

- checking county and state records to determine whether other reports have been made concerning the same child or other children in the family;
- interviewing family members and others who might have relevant information;
- seeing any other children who live in the home; and, when possible,
- interviewing the person who is reported to have abused or neglected the child.

The department uses structured decision-making tools to determine whether to substantiate the report and what action to take if the report is substantiated. These tools include assessments that the department conducts with the family to evaluate safety and risks, to identify the family's strengths and needs, and to formulate an initial case plan.[18]

The law requires the department of social services to make a prompt and thorough investigation, but it does not specify any length of time within which the department must complete the investigation.[19] At the conclusion of an investigation, the department classifies the report as either substantiated or unsubstantiated. These terms are not defined in state law, policy, or regulations. Presumably a report is substantiated if the social services investigation reveals facts or evidence sufficient to establish that a child is abused, neglected, or dependent, as the Juvenile Code defines those terms. It is not clear, however, what standard the department should apply in determining whether the evidence and facts are sufficient.[20]

CONFIDENTIAL INFORMATION
In conducting an investigation, the director of the county department of social services (or the director's representative) may ask the reporter for additional information or records. The law authorizes the director to obtain, from the reporter or anyone else, information that the director considers relevant to a case, even if the information otherwise would be confidential.[21] Anyone who receives a social services director's written demand for records or information must provide the director with the information and with access to and copies of any records. Three kinds of information are excluded from this rule:

1. information that is protected by the attorney–client privilege;
2. any information that federal laws or regulations prohibit the person from disclosing;[22] and
3. criminal investigative records.

The third exception applies, however, only if disclosure would jeopardize the investigation or trial of a criminal matter and the custodian of the records applies to the court for an order preventing disclosure.[23]

INVESTIGATING A DEATH
When the department of social services receives a report that a child has died as a result of suspected maltreatment, it must

1. determine immediately whether other children are in the home and, if so,
2. conduct an immediate investigation to determine whether those children need services or need to be removed from the home for their protection.

The department takes action as if a report of possible abuse, neglect, or dependency has been made regarding any other children in the same home.

INVESTIGATION IN AN INSTITUTIONAL SETTING
When a social services department receives a report about a child or children in an institutional setting, such as a residential school or treatment facility, the department must immediately determine whether other children are in the facility and are subject to the care and supervision of the alleged perpetrator. The investigation must include an assessment of the safety of those children as well as that of any child who was the subject of the report.

Law Enforcement's Role
In any case, the department of social services may consult with and seek assistance from a law enforcement agency. If asked to do so by the director, the law enforcement agency must assist in the investigation and an evaluation of the seriousness of any report of abuse, neglect, or dependency.[24]

Whenever an investigation by a social services department reveals that a child may have been abused, the director of social services must make an oral report immediately and a written report within forty-eight hours to both the district attorney and the appropriate local law enforcement agency.[25] The law enforcement agency must begin a criminal investigation immediately (and in no event more than forty-eight hours after being notified) and must coordinate its investigation with the protective services investigation being done by social services. When the criminal investigation is complete, the district attorney decides whether any criminal charges should be filed.

Social Services Action

IMMEDIATE REMOVAL OF CHILD

If the department substantiates that a child is abused, neglected, or dependent, the director must assess whether the child will be safe if left in the home. Sometimes the parent will consent to the child's placement with a relative or even in foster care. Unless a parent consents, the department ordinarily must file a petition and get a court order before assuming custody of a child.

If it appears that the time it would take to get a court order might result either in injury to the child or in the department's inability to take the child into custody later, then a law enforcement officer or social services worker may take the child into temporary physical custody immediately, without a court order. If that is done and the social services department determines that the child should remain in custody for more than twelve hours (twenty-four hours if any of the first twelve-hour period falls on a weekend or

holiday), then within that time the department must file a petition and obtain a court order. (See Chapter 13.)

PROTECTIVE SERVICES

After substantiating a report, the social services department evaluates the need for protective services and develops a plan for protecting the child and working with the family.[26]

Protective services consist of services to help parents (or guardians, custodians, or caretakers)

- prevent abuse or neglect,
- improve the quality of child care,
- be better parents or caretakers, and
- preserve and stabilize family life.[27]

Subject to the exceptions described above, the director can demand confidential information that would assist at this stage of providing protective services as well as during an investigation. For example, the social worker may need to get information from a parent's psychologist in order to assess the parent's ability to care for the child or the likelihood that the child can remain at home safely.

If the department has not filed a petition to start a juvenile court action in order to obtain a nonsecure custody order, the department will file one at any point it believes that the child should be removed from the home or that the court needs to become involved for any other reason.

KEEPING THE FAMILY TOGETHER

State law and policy reflect the belief that children who can remain safely in or return safely to their own homes almost always are better off with their own families than they are in foster care or other substitute care arrangements. Even when abuse or neglect has occurred, the law requires county departments of social services to make "reasonable efforts" to keep the family together. Originally the phrase "reasonable efforts" referred to the legal duty of a county department of social services to make diligent efforts

- to prevent the need to remove a child from the home or,
- if the child has been removed from the home, to return the child home.

The current definition reflects an additional belief—that children need stable, permanent homes and are harmed by delays in achieving that goal. Now, "reasonable efforts" also refers to a department's duty to make diligent efforts to develop and implement some other permanent plan for a child who is not going to be able to return home within a reasonable period of time. The requirement that social services departments make these efforts is both a funding condition for the state's receipt of federal child welfare funds and a mandate of state law.[28]

The district court judge hearing a juvenile case must make findings about whether the department of social services has made reasonable efforts. The judge must include these findings in any order that places a child, or continues the placement of a child, in the custody or placement responsibility of a county department of social services, including

- any order authorizing continued prehearing custody of the child,
- any dispositional order that provides for the child's placement in the

custody of the department of social services, and

- any review-hearing order that continues a child's placement in the department's custody (see Chapter 13).[29]

In these orders, the judge also may provide for services or other efforts aimed at returning the child to a safe home or at achieving another permanent plan for the child.

If a judge finds that a department of social services has not made reasonable efforts to prevent or eliminate the need for a child's placement, the judge still may enter whatever order is appropriate. For example, even if social services fails to provide services that would enable the child to remain at home safely, the court may order the child's removal from the home if the child's removal is necessary to ensure the child's protection. When a child needs placement because of an immediate threat of harm, it may be reasonable for the social services department to place the child without making any efforts to prevent the need for placement, and the juvenile court may make a finding to that effect.[30]

Making reasonable efforts to prevent or eliminate the need for a child's placement does not mean making every possible effort, and it does not mean making efforts for an indefinite period of time. Parents are responsible for providing a safe home for their children and for correcting conditions that led to a child's removal from the parents' custody. The court may relieve a social services department of the duty to make efforts to eliminate the need for placement if the court finds any of the following:

1. The efforts clearly would be futile.
2. The efforts would be inconsistent with the child's health, safety, and need for a safe, permanent home within a reasonable period of time.
3. The parent's rights to another child have been terminated involuntarily by a court.
4. A court has determined that the parent

   - has committed murder or voluntary manslaughter of another child of the parent;
   - has aided, abetted, attempted, conspired, or solicited to commit murder or voluntary manslaughter of the child or another child of the parent; or
   - has committed a felony assault resulting in serious bodily injury to the child or another child of the parent.[31]

After the court makes this kind of determination, the emphasis in the case shifts. The social services department still must make reasonable efforts, but those efforts are directed toward developing and implementing a permanent plan for the child. That plan might be adoption or the designation of a relative or other appropriate person as the child's guardian or legal custodian.

A parent who fails to respond to a social services department's efforts and fails to make his or her own efforts to provide a safe home for the child within a reasonable period of time risks permanent separation from the child. The court may terminate a parent's rights completely—freeing the child for adoption—if the court finds that the parent has willfully left the child in foster care or other out-of-home placement for a year without showing to the court's satisfaction that the

parent has made reasonable progress in correcting conditions that led to the child's removal.[32]

Confidentiality and Information Sharing
CONFIDENTIALITY RULE

A county social services department is required to hold "in strictest confidence" the information it receives in relation to a child protective services matter.[33] This includes the identity of the reporter. The department also must protect information in its records about children who are in the department's custody[34] and information that would reveal the identity of any juvenile who is the subject of an investigation.[35] Except when disclosure is for purposes directly related to the administration of a social services program or is explicitly authorized by law, it is a misdemeanor for anyone to disclose (or, for that matter, to obtain) information concerning persons who are receiving social services, whether the information is derived from the department's records and files or from communications.[36]

WHEN DISCLOSURE IS ALLOWED

Information in the agency's child protective services records can be disclosed when the judge orders the social services director to disclose it. Without a court order, information from social services' records in a child protective services case can be disclosed

- to a child or the child's attorney or guardian ad litem;
- to agencies or individuals that are helping provide or facilitate the provision of services to the child; and

- to a district attorney who needs access to the information to carry out his or her responsibilities relating to a report of abuse or a director's decision not to file a petition.[37]

After the department of social services files a petition alleging that a child is abused, neglected, or dependent, certain agencies—including social services departments—must share with each other information that is relevant to that case. The Juvenile Code requires the state Department of Juvenile Justice and Delinquency Prevention to designate agencies that are authorized to share information, and the Code requires those agencies to share relevant information, upon request, for as long as the juvenile court case is ongoing.[38] It also imposes certain restrictions. Any otherwise confidential information shared by these designated agencies must remain confidential and be withheld from public inspection. In addition, the information may be used only

- for the protection of the child,
- for the protection of others, or
- to improve the child's educational opportunities.

Rules issued by the state Department of Juvenile Justice and Delinquency Prevention[39] designate the following as agencies authorized to share information:

1. The Department of Juvenile Justice and Delinquency Prevention, which includes local chief juvenile court counselors and their staffs
2. The Office of Guardian Ad Litem Services in the Administrative Office of the Courts, which includes local guardian ad litem programs
3. County departments of social services

4. Area mental health, developmental disability, and substance abuse authorities
5. Local law enforcement agencies
6. District attorneys' offices, which can request information from other agencies but are not required to release or disclose any information
7. County mental health facilities and developmental disabilities and substance abuse programs
8. Local school administrative units
9. Local health departments
10. Any other local agency designated by an administrative order issued by the chief district court judge of the district court district in which the agency is located

Any agency that receives information pursuant to the rules and shares it with another authorized agency must document that redisclosure. If one agency refuses another agency's request for information for any reason, the agency refusing to disclose information must inform the other agency of the specific law or regulation that is the basis for the refusal.[40]

Defining appropriate boundaries for the sharing of information about children and families involved in the juvenile court and social services systems is not easy. Even with the legal and regulatory guidance described here, the exact boundaries are sometimes unclear.[41] The applicable law and rules are likely to be the subject of continued scrutiny and of efforts to reconcile competing interests such as

- the need to share sensitive information in order for agencies and professionals to serve families effectively and to coordinate their involvement with families;
- the desire to respect families', and especially children's, privacy;

- an interest in not having fear of publicity discourage people from involvement in the system;
- the public's interest in knowing how well the child protective services system works and in feeling that it is accountable; and
- people's desire to comply with federal and state confidentiality laws and regulations that often are difficult to interpret or reconcile.

Local guidelines or protocols among agencies can help clarify when, how, and with whom certain kinds of information can be shared. They also can help ensure that the person or agency receiving confidential information continues to protect its confidentiality.

Notification Requirements at Conclusion of Investigation

To Reporter

Within five working days after completing an investigation, the department of social services must give the person who made the report a second written notice, unless the reporter asked specifically not to be notified. (The first notice will have informed the reporter that the report was accepted for investigation. See "Notifying the Reporter," earlier in this chapter.) This notice must state

1. whether the department has made a finding of abuse, neglect, or dependency;
2. whether the department is taking action to protect the child and, if so, what that action is;
3. whether the department has filed a petition to begin a juvenile court proceeding;
4. that if the reporter is not satisfied with the director's decision, then within five working days after receiving the notice, the reporter may ask the prosecutor (the

assistant district attorney who handles juvenile cases) to review the decision; and

5. the procedure for requesting a formal review by the prosecutor (including the prosecutor's address). (See Chapter 12.)

Because of confidentiality requirements, the department ordinarily cannot share much more information than this with the reporter. The notice must be given within five working days after the department completes its investigation, and ordinarily that should not be more than thirty days after the department received the report.[42]

To Parent and Alleged Perpetrator

The social services director also must report the outcome of the investigation to the person who was alleged to have abused or neglected the child and to the parent or other person with whom the child lived when the report was made.[43] (Often these will be the same person.)

Regarding Child Care

If the investigation reveals evidence of abuse or neglect in a child care facility, the director must notify the state Department of Health and Human Services (DHHS) immediately.[44] If the evidence relates to sexual abuse in a child care facility, the director also must notify the State Bureau of Investigation as follows:

- immediately, upon learning of the evidence; and
- at the conclusion of the investigation, in writing, of the results of the investigation.

CENTRAL REGISTRY

Each county department of social services must furnish the state Department of Health and Human Services with data about abuse and neglect reports and investigations (as well as dependency and child death reports and investigations). At the state level, this collection of information is called the Central Registry.[45] Created in 1971, the registry provides data for studying the nature and extent of child abuse, neglect, dependency, and fatalities caused by maltreatment in North Carolina. It also helps identify children and families who are involved in repeated reports or instances of these occurrences.

Registry data are confidential. State rules specify the circumstances in which the data can be used for research and study, and when the Chief Medical Examiner's office and law enforcement officials may use the data to determine whether abuse or neglect should be evaluated as a possible factor in a child's death.[46] The Juvenile Code does not provide any procedure for a parent, guardian, custodian, or caretaker to contest a social services department's substantiation of a report or to request the removal of information from the Central Registry. At least in part for that reason, information in the registry is not available to prospective employers or to anyone else who is conducting a background check of an individual.

Notes to Chapter 11

1. Even if the eighteen-year-old were disabled and dependent on her parents for care, the report would be screened out as a child abuse or neglect report. It would be treated as a report under the Protection of the Abused, Neglected or Exploited Disabled Adult Act (Article 6 of G.S. Chapter 108A), which also includes a mandatory reporting requirement. The person making the report would be referred to the department's adult protective services unit.

2. The department would relay the information to law enforcement authorities as required by G.S. 7B-307(a). In addition, physicians and hospitals have a duty to report to law enforcement certain cases of wounds, injuries, or illnesses. This duty arises with regard to (1) any injury that appears to be caused by discharge of a gun or firearm (bullet wound, gunshot wound, powder burn, etc.); (2) any illness apparently caused by poisoning; (3) any wound or injury that appears to be caused by a knife or a sharp or pointed instrument, if it appears to the treating physician or surgeon that a criminal act was involved; and (4) any wound, injury, or illness in which there is grave bodily harm or grave illness, if it appears to the treating physician or surgeon that the condition resulted from a violent criminal act. G.S. 90-21.20.

3. Policies relating to child protective services appear in Chapter VIII of the division's *Children's Service's Manual*. The manual is available for inspection at any county department of social services during regular office hours and can be accessed through the division's Web site. Retrieved 10 April 2003 from http://info.dhhs.state. nc.us/olm/manuals/dss/.

4. Administrative rules relating to child protective services appear in subchapter 41I of title 10 of the North Carolina Administrative Code. The Administrative Code is available in some libraries and on the Internet. Retrieved 10 April 2003 from http://www.oah.state. nc.us/.

5. North Carolina Division of Social Services, "Structured Intake," *Children's Services Manual*, Ch. VIII (Protective Services), § 1407. Retrieved 1 May 2003 from http://info.dhhs. state.nc.us/olm/manuals/dss/csm-60/man/ CS1407.htm#TopOfPage.

6. N.C. Admin. Code tit. 10, subchap. 41I, § .0304(g) (September 1994).

7. *See* G.S. 7B-302(f); N.C. Admin. Code tit. 10, subchap. 41I, § .0304(h) (September 1994).

8. *See* N.C. Admin. Code tit. 10, subchap. 41I, § .0304 (September 1994).

9. N.C. Admin. Code tit. 10, subchap. 41I, § .0304(h) (September 1994).

10. *See* G.S. 7B-307(a).

11. *See* G.S. 7B-307(a).

12. G.S. 7B-302; N.C. Admin. Code tit. 10, subchap. 41I, §§ .0303(9) (July 1993) and .0305 (February 1995).

13. Ten North Carolina counties are piloting the Multiple Response System, in which social workers assign cases to the traditional "investigative track" or to an "assessment track." The first category includes cases that present serious safety issues, possible criminal charges, or both. In cases on the assessment track, the department focuses on helping families address needs in ways that enable them to provide better care for their children. In these cases there may never be a substantiation that labels parents as having abused or neglected their children. *See* North Carolina Division of Social Services and the Family and Children's Resource Program, 7 *Children's Services Practice Notes* 4 (August 2002), which includes several articles about the North Carolina pilot program and the trend generally toward multiple-response systems and family-centered practice. The ten North Carolina pilot counties are Alamance, Bladen, Buncombe, Caldwell, Craven, Franklin, Guilford, Mecklenburg, Nash, and Transylvania.

14. *See, e.g.,* Judge Louis A. Trosch, Jr., Linda Thomas Sanders, J.D., and Sharon Kugelmass, Ph.D., "Child Abuse, Neglect, and Dependency Mediation Pilot Project," 53 *Juvenile and Family Court Journal* 4 (Fall 2002): 67–77; Judge Steven D. Robinson, Melissa Litchfield, Sophia Gatowski, Ph.D., and Shirley Dobbin, Ph.D., "Family Conferencing: A Success for Our Children," 53 *Juvenile and Family Court Journal* 4 (Fall 2002): 43–48.

15. The director must refer a report to another county for investigation if the report involves a county social services employee, foster parent, or board member, and may do so any time the agency might be perceived as having a conflict of interest. N.C. Admin. Code tit. 10, subchap. 41I, § .0103 (September 1994).

16. G.S. 7B-302 and 7B-500; N.C. Admin. Code tit. 10, subchap. 41I, § .0304(d) (September 1994).

17. N.C. Admin. Code tit. 10, subchap. 41I, § .0304(d) (September 1994). *See also* North Carolina Division of Social Services, *Children's*

Services Manual, Ch. VIII (Protective Services), § 1408 III. Retrieved 10 April 2003 from http://info.dhhs.state.nc.us/olm/manuals/dss/.

18. North Carolina Division of Social Services and the Family and Children's Resource Program, "North Carolina Adopts New Approach to CPS: Multiple Response," 7 *Children's Services Practice Notes* 4 (August 2002): 4.

19. State policy is that an investigation should be completed within thirty days or the record should include documentation of the reason it could not be completed within that time. *See* North Carolina Division of Social Services, *Children's Services Manual,* Ch. VIII (Protective Services), § 1408 III. Retrieved 10 April 2003 from http://info.dhhs.state.nc.us/olm/manuals/dss/.

20. If a social services department takes a case to court, it has the burden of proving by "clear and convincing evidence" that the child is abused, neglected, or dependent. G.S. 7B-805. Arguably, a department should not substantiate a report unless it believes it could satisfy that burden if the case goes to court.

Some states do define these terms, and some provide additional categories for disposing of reports, such as "indicated" (possible or likely harm or risk, but evidentiary standard not met) or "closed without a finding." John D. Fluke, Cynthia F. Parry, Patricia Shapiro, Dana Hollinshead, and Vicky Bollenbacher, "The Case on Unsubstantiated Cases," 60 *Policy & Practice of Public Human Services* 3 (September 2002): 16–20, 21. *See also* Karen C. Tumlin and Rob Geen, *The Decision to Investigate: Understanding State Child Welfare Screening Policies and Practices* (Washington, D.C.: The Urban League, 2002). Retrieved 10 April 2003 from http://www.urban.org/.

21. G.S. 7B-302(e).

22. The federal laws and regulations that prohibit disclosure of such information include the Family Educational Rights and Privacy Act (FERPA) (20 U.S.C. § 1232g; 34 C.F.R. Part 99), which protects the privacy of student education records. The Public Health Service Act (42 U.S.C. § 290dd-2; 42 C.F.R. Part 2) restricts the disclosure of drug and alcohol abuse patient records. These restrictions do not apply to reporting suspected child abuse under state reporting

laws, but they appear to apply at any stage after reporting, i.e., during an investigation or the provision of protective services.

23. G.S. 7B-302(e).
24. G.S. 7B-302(e).
25. G.S. 7B-307.
26. N.C. Admin. Code tit. 10, subchap. 41I, § .0306 (September 1994).
27. G.S. 7B-300; N.C. Admin. Code tit. 10, subchap. 35E, § .0317 (July 1984).
28. *See* 42 U.S.C. § 671; G.S. 7B-101(18); and G.S. 7B-507.
29. G.S. 7B-507. These requirements also apply in cases of delinquent or undisciplined juveniles who are placed by the court in the custody of a county department of social services. *See* G.S. 7B-2506(1)b.
30. G.S. 7B-507(a).
31. G.S. 7B-507(b).
32. G.S. 7B-1111(a)(2). This is just one of nine statutory grounds for terminating a parent's rights. The other grounds are:

1. The parent has abused or neglected the child.
2. The parent has willfully failed to pay child support for six months while the child is placed away from home.
3. The parent has willfully failed to pay child support for one year, as required by a court order or custody agreement, when the other parent has custody.
4. The child was born out of wedlock, and the putative father has failed to

   - establish his paternity in court or by affidavit,
   - legitimate the child or file a petition for that purpose,
   - marry the child's mother, or
   - provide substantial financial support or consistent care for the child and mother.

5. The parent is incapable of providing for the child's proper care and supervision, so that the child is a "dependent juvenile," and there is a reasonable probability that the parent's incapability will continue for the foreseeable future.
6. The parent has willfully abandoned the child for at least six months immediately before a petition is filed or for at least sixty days after voluntarily abandoning the child during the first seven days of the child's life.
7. The parent has committed any one of several serious criminal offenses against the child, another child of the parent, or another child residing in the home.
8. A court has terminated the parent's rights with respect to another child, against the parent's wishes, and the parent lacks the ability or willingness to establish a safe home.

Even if one or more grounds exist, the court may not terminate a parent's rights if it finds that doing so would be contrary to the child's best interest. G.S. 7B-1110 and 7B-1111.

33. G.S. 7B-302(a).
34. G.S. 7B-2901(b).
35. G.S. 7B-3100(b).
36. G.S. 108A-80.
37. N.C. Admin. Code tit. 10, subchap. 41I, § .0313 (September 1991).
38. G.S. 7B-3100(a). The sharing of school information must be in accordance with the Family Educational Rights and Privacy Act, 20 U.S.C. § 1232g.
39. N.C. Admin. Code tit. 28, subchap. 01A (July 2002).
40. Id.
41. For an excellent discussion of confidentiality concepts and issues, *see* John L. Saxon, "Confidentiality and Social Services (Part I): What Is Confidentiality?" *Social Services Law Bulletin* No. 30 (February 2001); "Confidentiality and Social Services (Part II): Where Do Confidentiality Rules Come From?" *Social Services Law Bulletin* No. 31 (May 2001); "Confidentiality and Social Services (Part III): A Process for Analyzing Issues Involving Confidentiality," *Social Services Law Bulletin* No. 35 (April 2002); "Confidentiality and Social Services (Part IV): An Annotated Index of Federal and State Confidentiality Laws," *Social Services Law Bulletin* No. 37 (Oct. 2002) (Chapel Hill, NC: Institute of Government, The University of North Carolina at Chapel Hill). For ordering information, call (919) 966-4119 or see http://www.iog.unc.edu/.
42. North Carolina Division of Social Services, *Children's Services Manual*, Ch. VIII

(Protective Services), § 1408 III. Retrieved 10 April 2003 from http://info.dhhs.state.nc.us/olm/manuals/dss/.

43. N.C. Admin. Code tit. 10, subchap. 41I, § .0306 (February 1995) and .0307 (July 1993). If the report was substantiated, the notification must be in writing.

44. G.S. 7B-307. For provisions relating to the authority of the state Department of Health and Human Services to investigate reports of child abuse or neglect in child care settings and to impose administrative sanctions, see N.C. Admin. Code tit. 10, subchap. 3U, § .1900 (April 2001).

45. G.S. 7B-307(c); G.S. 7B-311.

46. N.C. Admin. Code tit. 10, subchap. 41I, § .0102 (July 1993).

12

Review Procedures

Informal Review of Individual Case Decisions

A person whose report to a department of social services is screened out (that is, not accepted for investigation) is entitled to an agency review of that decision. (See "Notification after a Report Is Made" in Chapter 11.) If the department accepts the report and the person who made it is not satisfied with the outcome of the department's investigation, that person may communicate directly with the social worker handling the case. Sometimes the social worker can provide information about the department's actions that will dispel the reporter's dissatisfaction with the department's response. (Of course, confidentiality may limit the department's ability to give full details of the investigation. See Chapter 11.) Or, the social worker may be able to explain legal or other constraints of which the reporter was unaware. Likewise, the reporter may be able to give the social worker additional information or a perspective that would lead the department to rethink its response.

If this kind of communication does not resolve the reporter's dissatisfaction, the reporter may contact the following persons, preferably in this order:

1. the social worker's supervisor;
2. the head of the child protective services unit in the agency; or
3. the county director of social services.

Formal Review of Case Decisions

In most cases, even if the department substantiates that a child is abused, neglected, or dependent, the department does not file a petition to take the matter to juvenile court. Instead, it provides protective services and develops with the family a plan aimed at ensuring the child's safety. A reporter who disagrees with the department's decision not to file a petition has a right to ask the prosecutor to review that decision.[1]

Requests for prosecutors to review case decisions are not made frequently, but they are the only formal recourse for someone who is dissatisfied with the social services department's response to a report following an investigation. If informal review does not seem effective, this process for external review is an important alternative for someone who knows or strongly suspects that a child is abused, neglected, or dependent and feels that the department's response is inadequate.

REQUESTING A FORMAL REVIEW

The reporter may request a review by the prosecutor within five working days after receiving the second written notice from the department of social services. That is the notice that tells the reporter the outcome of the investigation (including whether the department has filed a petition to take the matter to court) and explains the procedures for requesting a review of a decision not to file a petition. Presumably, if the department does not give the reporter the second written notice as required, the time within which the reporter can request a review is extended to at least five days following the date the reporter learns of the department's decision. Someone who asks to be notified orally rather than in writing probably has five days after the oral notification to request a review, and a reporter who asks not to be notified of the outcome of the investigation risks losing his or her right to request a review. Neither the statute nor administrative rules address these situations specifically.

TIMING OF REVIEW

When the person who made a report requests a review of the department's decision not to file a petition, the prosecutor must notify that person and the social services director of the time and place for the review. The prosecutor must conduct the review within twenty days after the reporter receives notice of the department's decision not to file a petition.[2]

CONTENTS OF REVIEW

In conducting a review, the prosecutor should confer with

- the person who made the report,
- the protective services worker,
- the child (if that is practicable), and
- anyone else who has pertinent information about the child or the child's family.

CONCLUSION OF REVIEW

After the review, the prosecutor may

- affirm the social services director's decision,
- ask the appropriate local law enforcement agency to investigate the allegations in the report, or
- direct the social services director to file a petition in juvenile court.

Review of Agency Practices or Community Issues

The informal channels described above for reviewing case decisions also may be appropriate when an individual, a group, an agency, or an institution has concerns about a social services department's general practices or policies regarding child protective services. Anyone who is concerned about agency practices, or about broader community issues involving child protection, should consult first with the county social services director if that is feasible. Concerns also may be taken to the state Division of Social Services, the county social services board (or its equivalent), or the local community child protection team described below.

COUNTY SOCIAL SERVICES BOARDS

Most counties have a three- or five-member county social services board.[3]

This board's responsibilities include

- hiring the county social services director,
- consulting with the director about problems relating to the director's office,
- helping the director plan the department's budget, and
- advising local authorities about policies and plans to improve social conditions in the community.[4]

The county board of social services does not have a role in making or reviewing decisions in individual cases involving abuse, neglect, or dependency. It should have, however, a strong interest in

- the adequacy of the department's child protective services program in general (including its funding),
- the public's understanding of that program, and
- the larger community's response to the problems of child abuse and neglect.[5]

STATE DIVISION OF SOCIAL SERVICES

Although child protective services programs are administered by the counties, the state also has a role.[6] The Division of Social Services (the Division) in the state Department of Health and Human Services provides county social services departments with

- training, consultation, and technical assistance;
- policy manuals that serve as the day-to-day guide for county social services staff;[7]
- regular periodic program reviews;[8] and, sometimes,
- special reviews of counties' practices or handling of particular cases when especially difficult problems arise or are alleged.

Division staff include eight children's program representatives, each of whom works with a designated group of counties and is available for consultation on issues of policy and practice in child protective services cases. In addition, four assistant attorneys general specializing in child welfare law work with the Division to provide training, consultation, and legal assistance to the county departments. Questions about state policy in the area of child protective services can be directed to the Division's Raleigh office.[9]

COMMUNITY CHILD PROTECTION TEAMS

Every county has an interdisciplinary community child protection team that reviews selected child protective services cases. All teams review child fatality cases in which a child's death is suspected to have resulted from abuse or neglect and

1. a report about the child or the child's family was made to social services within the preceding twelve months, or
2. the child or the child's family received child welfare services within twelve months of the child's death.

Each team can define other categories of cases it wishes to review. In addition, any team member may request review of a specific case, and the county social services director may bring cases to the team for review.

These reviews are not appeals. They are designed to help the team fulfill its broader goals of

- developing a community-wide approach to problems of child abuse and neglect;

- understanding the causes of childhood deaths;
- identifying any gaps or deficiencies in the delivery of services to children and families; and
- making and implementing recommendations for changes to laws, rules, and policies that will support children's safe and healthy development and prevent child abuse and neglect.[10]

The team makes recommendations to the board of county commissioners and promotes agency collaboration to create or improve community resources for children.[11]

The law provides for each local community child protection team to include

- the county social services director and a member of the social services staff,
- a local law enforcement officer,
- an attorney from the district attorney's office,
- a representative of the local community action agency,
- the superintendent or other representative of each local school administrative unit,
- a member of the county social services board,
- a local mental health professional,
- a representative of the local guardian ad litem program,
- the director of the local public health department, and
- a local health care provider.[12]

The board of county commissioners may appoint up to five additional team members. Each local team elects its own chair and meets at least four times a year.

Since information about particular cases is confidential, the parts of team meetings devoted to reviewing individual cases are not open to the public. Parts of the meetings that do not involve confidential information—for example, discussions of general findings, recommendations, or community needs—should be open to the public. Information about a county's community child protection team can be obtained from the county manager's office, from one of the agencies represented on the team, or from the state Division of Social Services, which provides coordination for the community child protection team program.[13]

Notes to Chapter 12

1. G.S. 7B-305. "Prosecutor" refers to the district attorney or assistant district attorney who handles cases in juvenile court. G.S. 7B-101(17). The statute refers to the review in relation to the director's decision not to file a petition in juvenile court. The review clearly is available when the social services department substantiates a report of abuse, neglect, or dependency but does not file a petition. It is not as clear whether it is available when the department does not substantiate the report and therefore obviously is not filing a petition. If review by the prosecutor is not available in that circumstance, however, the Code provides no formal procedure for questioning the adequacy of the department's investigation or its decision not to substantiate a report. It seems unlikely that the legislature intended that result.

2. G.S. 7B-306; N.C. Admin. Code tit. 10, subchap. 41I, § .0308 (September 1994).

3. The exceptions are Mecklenburg County, where the board of county commissioners serves as the social services board, and Wake County, which has a consolidated human services board. *See* G.S. 153A-77. In the other ninety-eight counties, the board of county commissioners and the state Social Services Commission appoint members of the board, then those members appoint the third or fifth member. *See* G.S. 108A-3.

4. G.S. 108A-9.

5. County social services boards meet monthly, and their meetings are open to the public. To learn when and where a board meets or how to contact the board chairman,

a person should call the county department of social services. (*See* Appendix C.)

6. In most states, the state administers social services programs. In North Carolina, the counties perform that role. For a description of the social services system in North Carolina, *see* Janet Mason, "Social Services," in *County Government in North Carolina*, 4th ed., eds. A. Fleming Bell, II, and Warren Jake Wicker (Chapel Hill, N.C.: Institute of Government, The University of North Carolina at Chapel Hill, 1998), 693–740.

7. Manuals are available to the public for inspection during regular office hours at county social services departments and on the Internet. Retrieved 10 April 2003 from http://info.dhhs.state.nc.us/olm/manuals/dss/.

8. The Division conducts biennial reviews of each county's children's services program and gives the county a score for each of several program areas. A low score in any area results in the county's submitting a program improvement plan for that area. Biennial review results are available from the county social services director or the Children's Services Section in the state Division of Social Services (919/733-9461).

9. The main number for the state Division of Social Services is 919/733-3055; the children's services section policy unit can be reached at 919/733-3360.

10. G.S. 7B-1400.

11. G.S. 7B-1406; N.C. Admin. Code tit. 10, subchap. 41I, § .0401 (September 1994). Each county also has a juvenile crime prevention council whose membership and goals may overlap with those of the community child protection team. *See* G.S. 143B-544 and 143B-549.

12. G.S. 7B-1407. Either this team or a separate child fatality prevention team also reviews additional child fatalities in the county. A community child protection team that also reviews additional child fatalities must include an emergency medical services provider or firefighter, a district court judge, a county medical examiner, a representative of a local child care facility or Head Start program, and a parent of a child who died before age eighteen.

13. To contact the Division of Social Services for general information about a community child protection team, call (919) 733-3055.

13

Juvenile Court Procedures

The procedures described in this chapter are those set out in the Juvenile Code. Other laws and different procedures apply to proceedings for adoption, voluntary admissions and involuntary commitments of minors to mental health treatment facilities, and custody disputes between parents.[1]

Petition

Sometimes, after the department of social services substantiates a report of abuse, neglect, or dependency, the parent (or guardian, custodian, or caretaker) refuses to accept services that are needed to ensure the child's safety. Sometimes protective services cannot protect the child adequately unless the child is removed from the home. In these situations, the social services director must sign and file a petition alleging the relevant facts and asking the court to intervene on the child's behalf. The filing of a petition begins a juvenile proceeding in the district court. Only a county director of social services (or the director's representative) can file an abuse, neglect, or dependency petition.

Juvenile proceedings are civil actions (that is, they are not criminal prosecutions).

They focus on the condition and needs of the child, not the guilt or innocence of the parent or anyone else.

County departments of social services file petitions in only a small percentage of the cases in which they substantiate that a child is abused, neglected, or dependent. Usually this is because

- the family accepts services voluntarily,
- the family and the department agree on a "protection plan" that provides for the child to stay with a relative or for other steps to protect the child,
- the person who abused or neglected the child is out of the home, or
- the department's assessment indicates that it is safe for the child to remain in the home.

Prehearing Custody[2]

When the social services department substantiates a report and files a petition alleging that a child is abused, neglected, or dependent, it often asks for a court order authorizing the department to place the child immediately in foster care (or another appropriate setting) without waiting for a full hearing on the petition.[3]

When this custody order is sought, a social services worker or law enforcement officer may already have taken the child into custody without a court order. They are allowed to do this if the child might be harmed or disappear if they attempted to get the court order before taking custody of the child. To keep the child longer than twelve hours (or twenty-four hours if a weekend or holiday is involved), the social services department must file a petition and get a custody order within that time. (See "Immediate Removal of Child," in Chapter 11.)

Before granting a request for a prehearing (nonsecure) custody order, a judge must consider releasing the child to a parent or another responsible adult. To grant the order the judge must find that there is a "reasonable factual basis" for believing

1. that the facts alleged in the petition are true, and
2. that removing the child from the home is the only reasonable way to protect the child, and
3. that one of the following is true:

   - the child has been abandoned; or
   - the child has suffered (or is exposed to a substantial risk of) physical injury or sexual abuse; or
   - the child needs medical treatment for a serious condition, and the parent, guardian, or custodian is either unwilling or unable to provide or consent to the treatment; or
   - a parent, guardian, or custodian consents to the child's removal from the home.

If the judge makes these findings and authorizes the child's removal from the home, the judge may direct a law enforcement officer to assume custody of the child and take the child to the social services office or another specified place,

such as the home of a relative. If the judge cannot make these findings, the child must be left in the home until the case is heard in district (juvenile) court.

Removing the child from the home before there has been a full hearing deprives the parents of custody before they have had a chance to present their side of the case. Until the full hearing, which may take several weeks to schedule, the court must hold periodic hearings to determine whether grounds for keeping the child out of the home still exist.[4] Strict time limits apply to these hearings, as described below.

- If a judge entered the order for the child's placement, the first hearing must be held within seven calendar days after the child is removed from the home. If the order was entered by someone other than a judge, to whom the chief judge had delegated authority, the hearing must be held on the earliest day possible within those seven days. This hearing may not be waived, but it may be continued for up to ten business days.

- If the child is not returned home at the first hearing, the court must hold a second hearing within seven business days after the first hearing. This hearing may be waived.

- For as long as the child is kept out of the home without a full hearing on the petition, the court must continue to hold these hearings at least every thirty calendar days, unless they are waived.

At each of these hearings, the burden is on the department of social services to show by clear and convincing evidence that keeping the child out of the parent's custody pending a hearing on the petition is necessary.

Court Representation

GUARDIAN AD LITEM[5]

Whenever a social services department files a petition alleging that a child is abused or neglected the court must appoint a special representative—a guardian ad litem—to represent the child's interests in the proceeding. A guardian ad litem usually will be a volunteer working under the supervision of the judicial district's guardian ad litem program.[6] If the person appointed is not an attorney, the court also must appoint an attorney advocate to represent the child's legal interests. When a petition alleges only that a child is dependent, the judge is not required to appoint a guardian ad litem and attorney advocate for the child, but may do so.

The guardian ad litem program's overall duty is to protect and promote the child's best interests. Its specific duties include

- investigating to determine the facts, the child's needs, and resources available in the family and community;
- facilitating the settlement of disputed issues;
- offering evidence and examining witnesses in court;
- exploring dispositional options; and
- conducting follow-up investigations and reporting to the court if the child's needs are not being met.[7]

The Juvenile Code authorizes guardians ad litem to obtain any information or reports, including those that are confidential, that the guardian ad litem considers relevant to the case. A guardian ad litem who is exercising this authority should present the court order that appointed him or her as the child's guardian ad litem. The person or agency

from whom the guardian ad litem seeks information may want a copy of the order. The guardian ad litem must protect the confidentiality of any information he or she receives.

A medical or mental health provider, a school, or any other agency or professional from whom a guardian ad litem seeks information should provide the information promptly, unless

- the person seeking the information has neither presented the court order appointing him or her or otherwise established that he or she is the child's guardian ad litem, or
- federal law or regulations prohibit disclosure of the information.[8]

COUNSEL FOR PARENTS

In an abuse, neglect, or dependency case, the child's parents, if they are indigent, are entitled to appointed counsel unless they waive that right.[9]

Stages in Juvenile Cases

Juvenile cases have two primary stages adjudication and disposition.

ADJUDICATION[10]

At the adjudicatory hearing, the judge hears testimony, considers other evidence (such as medical records), and determines (1) whether the facts alleged in the petition are true and (2) whether the facts establish that the child is an abused, neglected, or dependent juvenile within the meaning of the Juvenile Code definitions. This hearing must be held within sixty days after the petition is filed unless the court orders that it be held later. The hearing is fairly formal, and the rules of evidence apply. The judge is not required to exclude the public from the hearing, but may do so after making findings about why that is appropriate. The hearing must be open, however, if the child (through the guardian ad litem or attorney advocate) asks that it be open. Anyone who has relevant information, including the person who made the report, may be subpoenaed to testify at the hearing.[11]

If the court does not find by clear and convincing evidence that the child is abused, neglected, or dependent, the case must be dismissed. The "clear and convincing" evidence standard is stricter than the one that applies in most civil cases but less stringent than the standard that applies in criminal or delinquency cases. (Civil cases are decided by the greater weight, or preponderance, of the evidence. Criminal or delinquency cases require proof beyond a reasonable doubt.)

DISPOSITION[12]

The dispositional hearing occurs only if the judge finds at the adjudication hearing that the child is abused, neglected, or dependent. This hearing may take place immediately following the adjudication or sometime later. The hearing is informal, and the judge may consider written reports and evidence that would not be admissible at the adjudicatory stage.

The first step at this hearing is to identify the child's needs. To that end, the judge may order that the child be examined by a physician, psychiatrist, or other expert. The judge may need to receive written reports or hear testimony about the child's educational, medical, psychological, or social needs. With input from all of the parties, the judge then designs an appropriate plan to meet the child's needs. In order to do this, the judge needs to receive information about available resources and about the parents' ability to meet the child's needs.

The finding that a child is abused, neglected, or dependent does not automatically result in the child's being removed from the parents' custody. The law favors leaving the child at home when the child can be safe there. The judge may dismiss the case or postpone further hearings in order to allow the parents or others to take appropriate action. If the child needs better care or supervision, the judge may order the department of social services to supervise the child in the child's own home, subject to conditions the judge specifies. Or, the judge may order that the child be placed in the custody of a parent, some other suitable person, a private agency, or the county department of social services. In any order removing a child from the home or continuing a child's out-of-home placement, the judge must make findings as to whether the department of social services has made reasonable efforts to prevent or eliminate the need for placement. (See "Keeping the Family Together," in Chapter 11.)

Review Hearings[13]

The child (through the guardian ad litem or attorney advocate) or any other party may file a motion at any time asking the court to review a case. A motion for review results in a hearing at which the judge may modify a dispositional order based on a change of circumstances and the child's best interests. If the dispositional order removes a child from the parent's custody, however, the court must hold review hearings according to the schedule described below.[14]

- The first review hearing must be held within ninety days after the dispositional hearing, and often it will be held earlier than that.
- If the child remains out of the home, a second review hearing must be held within six months after the first one.
- Thereafter, reviews must be held at least every six months for as long as the child remains out of the home.
- Within a year after the child was first removed from the home, the court must hold a review hearing that is designated a "permanency planning hearing," to focus directly on whether the child will be able to return home and, if not, what the alternative permanent plan for the child should be.

The county director of social services is responsible for asking the clerk of superior court to schedule these review hearings. The clerk is responsible for giving fifteen days' notice of a review hearing to the following persons: the child's parents, guardian, or custodian; the child, if he or she is twelve or older; any foster parent, relative, or preadoptive parent providing care for the child; any agency that has custody of the child; the guardian ad litem; and anyone else the court specifies.

Authority over Parents[15]

After making proper findings at a dispositional hearing or any review hearing, the judge may order

1. that a parent participate in medical, psychiatric, psychological, or other treatment that the child needs;[16]

2. that the parent himself or herself comply with a plan of psychiatric, psychological, or other treatment or counseling aimed at correcting behaviors or conditions that contributed to the child's being adjudicated or to the court's decision to remove custody of the child from the parent;[17]

3. that, to the extent the parent is able to do so, the parent pay for any treatment the court orders;[18]

4. that a parent who is able to do so pay a reasonable amount of support for a child who is not in the parent's custody;

5. that a parent attend and participate in parental responsibility classes if those are available in the district where the parent lives;[19]

6. that if the child remains in or is returned to the home, a parent who is able to do so provide transportation for the child to keep appointments for medical, psychiatric, psychological, or other treatment the court orders;[20]

7. that a parent take other reasonable steps to remedy the conditions that led or contributed to the child's adjudication or removal from the home.[21]

A parent or other person who violates the court's orders may be held in contempt.

Notes to Chapter 13

1. *See* G.S. Chapter 48 (adoption); G.S. Chapter 122C, Article 5 (voluntary admissions and involuntary commitments of minors to mental health treatment facilities); and G.S. 50-13.1 through 50-13.8 (custody disputes between parents).

2. The Juvenile Code term for the type of custody order described here is "nonsecure custody." The Code uses this somewhat confusing term in order to distinguish foster care and similar placements from the detention ("secure custody") of children who are delinquent.

3. Ordinarily the order will be entered by a district court judge. The chief district court judge, however, may file an administrative order delegating authority to enter these orders to persons other than district court judges. G.S. 7B-502.

4. *See* G.S. 7B-506.

5. *See* G.S. 7B-601.

6. District guardian ad litem programs are part of the statewide Guardian ad Litem Program, which is administered by the state Administrative Office of the Courts. *See* G.S. Ch. 7B, Art. 12.

7. G.S. 7B-601.

8. *See* Chapter 11, note 22.

9. G.S. 7B-602.

10. *See* G.S. 7B-800 through 7B-808.

11. *See* John Rubin and Mark Botts, "Responding to Subpoenas: A Guide for Mental Health Facilities," 64 *Popular Government* 4 (Summer 1999): 27–38. Retrieved 10 April 2003 from http://ncinfo.iog.unc.edu/pubs/electronicversions/pg/botts.pdf.

12. *See* G.S. 7B-900 through 7B-905.

13. *See* G.S. 7B-906 through 7B-910.

14. *See* G.S. 7B-906 and 7B-907.

15. *See* G.S. 7B-904.

16. The court also may direct this kind of order to a guardian, custodian, stepparent, adult member of the child's household, or adult relative entrusted with the child's care. G.S. 7B-904(b).

17. Instead of directing the parent to undergo treatment, the court may make the parent's receipt of treatment a condition of the parent's having custody of the child. The court also may direct these orders to a guardian, custodian, stepparent, adult member of the child's household, or adult relative entrusted with the child's care. G.S. 7B-904(c).

18. If the parent is unable to pay for the treatment, the court may charge the cost to the county.

19. The court also may direct this kind of order to the child's guardian, custodian, or caretaker if that person has been served with a summons in the juvenile proceeding. G.S. 7B-904(d1).

20. The court also may direct this kind of order to the child's guardian, custodian, or caretaker if that person has been served with a summons in the juvenile proceeding. G.S. 7B-904(d1).

21. The court also may direct this kind of order to the child's guardian, custodian, or caretaker if that person has been served with a summons in the juvenile proceeding. G.S. 7B-904(d1).

Part V
Role of Other Agencies

14

Schools and School Personnel

School personnel are in a unique position to recognize and respond to child abuse, neglect, and dependency. Changes in a child's behavior or appearance, as well as the child's own statements, may draw a teacher's, bus driver's, counselor's, or volunteer's attention to a problem others have not noticed. School personnel tend to be very aware of their reporting duties and are among the most frequent reporters.

Reporting by School Personnel

The Juvenile Code does not include any special provisions relating to schools or school personnel. The General Assembly, however, has emphasized the especially important role of school personnel by repeating the reporting mandate in Chapter 115C of the General Statutes, which addresses elementary and secondary education.

> § 115C-400. School personnel to report child abuse.
> Any person who has cause to suspect child abuse or neglect has a duty to report the case of the child to the Director of Social Services of the county, as provided in [the Juvenile Code].

Cooperative Agreements

In some counties the department of social services and the local school system (and sometimes other agencies as well) have adopted procedures for working together in responding to cases of suspected child abuse, neglect, and dependency. These procedures or protocols can clarify each system's role and expectations in ways that reflect not only legal requirements but also local conditions, resources, and needs. The process of developing the procedures can increase understanding and open lines of communication that have lasting effect. The initiative for developing a local protocol for responding to abuse, neglect, and dependency may come from the school, the department of social services, the community child protection team (see Chapter 12), or elsewhere in the community.

Beginning in 1984, and most recently in 1991, the state Department of Health and Human Services and the state Department of Public Instruction have agreed on recommended procedures to "facilitate maximum cooperation" between local school systems and county social services departments in responding to child abuse and neglect.[1] The procedures have never been mandatory; rather, they provide a starting point for schools and social services departments that want to develop local agreements.

SAMPLE PROVISIONS FOR COOPERATIVE AGREEMENTS

There is no one best policy or set of procedures. Following are examples of kinds of provisions a local agreement might include. Some of them are adapted from the state recommended procedures described above.

1. *Adoption of Policies*

   ▪ Specify the group of people responsible for developing and periodically reviewing the local policies.

   ▪ Describe ways in which input will be sought from others who have an interest in the procedures.

   ▪ Indicate what persons or bodies should formally approve or adopt the policies—for example, the county social services director and local school superinten-dent(s), or the county social services board and the local school board(s).

   ▪ Establish a timetable and proce-dure for periodically reviewing the policies.

   ▪ Describe how the policies will be published and distributed.

2. *Reports by School Personnel to Social Services*

   ▪ Require that all school personnel be informed of their responsibili-ties relating to child abuse, ne-glect, and dependency; the ability of the social services department to receive reports any day and any time of day or night; and how reports should be made.

   ▪ Decide whether each local school may (or shall) designate a contact

person (and a backup) to receive reports from school employees and convey them to the depart-ment of social services. If this policy is adopted, it should also make clear that

   (a) the designated person must transmit any report of suspected abuse or neglect to social services immediately;

   (b) the report must identify the originator of the report and include information about how the department of social services can contact that person;

   (c) if a school employee believes these procedures would create a delay that would be detrimental to the child, the employee should make a report directly to the social services depart-ment and then inform the contact person; and

   (d) every school employee should be informed that he or she is free to contact the department of social services about a report the employee initiated and should be encouraged to cooperate with the department with respect to the report and the investigation.

   ▪ Provide that school personnel should gather only enough information to validate that there is cause to suspect abuse, neglect, or dependency, since it is not the responsibility of school officials or employees to conduct investigations.

   ▪ Describe circumstances, if any, under which a school official, at the request of the department of social services, will photograph a child or take other steps to aid the department in its investigation; also describe any actions school officials should not be asked or expected to take.

3. *Social Services Response*

- Indicate whether the department of social services will designate a contact person (and a backup) to receive inquiries from and convey information to school officials about reported cases of abuse, neglect, or dependency.

- State how and to whom the department will provide the written notices regarding whether a report is accepted for investigation and the outcome of an investigation. (In the alternative, specify when, if ever, the right to receive a written notification is or may be waived or when the notification can be given verbally.)

- Provide that upon beginning an investigation, the child protective services social worker will assess the situation to determine the necessity of involving (or further involving) local school personnel.

- Describe circumstances in which it is appropriate for a social worker to interview the child (or other children in the same family) at school and procedures for a social worker to notify the principal or the school contact person to arrange a mutually convenient time that is least disruptive to the child's schedule and the school generally.

- Establish criteria for determining who should be present when a social worker interviews a child at school, making clear that the social worker always has authority to insist on seeing the child alone.[2]

4. *Cooperation between Schools and Social Services*

- Describe ways in which school personnel will cooperate with the social worker in the investigation, such as

  (a) giving the social worker any information that could help establish whether abuse or neglect has occurred;

  (b) allowing the social worker to interview the child alone;

  (c) allowing the social worker to photograph any evidence, such as marks or bruises;

  (d) allowing the social worker to remove the child from the school if the social worker determines that the child is at immediate risk. (This will require a court order unless the statutory conditions for temporary custody without a court order exist. See "Immediate Removal of Child," in Chapter 11.)

5. *Follow-up*

- Describe procedures to ensure that notifications that the social services department provides to the school contact person are shared with the individual who initiated the report.

- Describe ways in which the two agencies will collaborate in planning consistent services for the child and the child's family.

- Establish policies and procedures to enable a child to remain in the same school, if at all possible, when the child is placed in foster care or other out-of-home placement.

6. *General*

- Provide for joint training and learning opportunities for school personnel and social services personnel, including opportunities for each to become better informed about the role of the other.

- Describe how the department of social services and the school system will use their participation in the community child protection team to improve their responses to child abuse, neglect, and dependency. (See "Community Child Protection Teams," in Chapter 12.)

Administrative Reporting Requirements

A teacher's mistreatment of a child at school is not "abuse" or "neglect" within the Juvenile Code definitions. (See Chapters 4 and 5.) Although social services departments do not have a role in investigating and responding to the mistreatment of children in school, school administrators certainly do.

A rule of the State Board of Public Instruction requires local school administrators to report to the state superintendent of public instruction any time they know, or have substantial reason to believe, that a certified school employee has engaged in behavior that

1. would justify revoking the employee's certificate, and
2. involves physical or sexual abuse of a child.[3]

"Physical abuse" for purposes of this requirement means serious, nonaccidental physical injury, inflicted other than in self-defense. "Sexual abuse" means either committing a sexual act upon a student or causing a student to commit a sexual act. Neither the student's age nor whether the student consented is relevant. A failure to make the required report is, in itself, a ground for suspending or revoking an administrator's certificate. Local school boards may have policies that impose similar administrative reporting requirements on other school personnel.

Reporting Certain Criminal or Delinquent Acts

A school principal is required to report immediately to the appropriate local law enforcement agency whenever the principal has personal knowledge or actual notice from school personnel that any of the following acts has occurred on school property:

- assault resulting in serious personal injury
- sexual assault
- sexual offense
- rape
- kidnapping
- indecent liberties with a minor
- assault involving the use of a weapon
- unlawful possession of a firearm
- unlawful possession of a weapon
- unlawful possession of a controlled substance[4]

This reporting requirement applies regardless of the age or status of the person thought to have committed the act. A report could relate to the conduct of a student, a teacher or other employee, a parent, a trespasser, or anyone else. The report to law enforcement is required, though, only if the act occurs on school property, which includes any public school building, bus, campus, grounds, recreational area, or athletic field in the principal's charge.[5]

A principal who fails to make a required report to law enforcement is guilty of a Class 3 misdemeanor. The General Assembly, in addition to imposing this clear reporting requirement on principals, expresses in the statute its "intent" that the principal notify the superintendent and that the superintendent notify the local school board of any report made to law enforcement pursuant to this requirement.[6]

Notes to Chapter 14

1. Bob Etheridge and David T. Flaherty, untitled agreement between North Carolina Department of Human Resources and North Carolina Department of Public Instruction (November 1, 1991) (hereinafter Etheridge and Flaherty). Copies of the recommended procedures should be available from county departments of social services, the administrative offices of local school systems, the state Department of Public Instruction, or the state Division of Social Services in the Department of Health and Human Services. (*See* Appendix C for telephone numbers of state and local social services offices.)

2. Refusing to allow the social services director (which includes the director's representative) to see a child alone constitutes obstructing or interfering with a protective services investigation. G.S. 7B-303(b).

3. N.C. Admin. Code, tit. 16, subchap. 6C, § .0312(b) (August 2000).

4. G.S. 115C-288(g).

5. *Id.*

6. *Id.*

15

Health Professionals and Hospitals

Reporting

Child abuse and neglect often are identified for the first time when a child is taken to a medical facility for diagnosis or treatment. As discussed in Chapter 2, the very first child abuse reporting laws were designed largely to override doctor–patient confidentiality and allow doctors to disclose information about children they saw who were abused. Although reporting laws have expanded to cover many other professionals—and, in North Carolina, to cover everyone—health care professionals continue to be a key source of reports of child abuse, neglect, and dependency.

Professional Ethics and Reporting Responsibilities[1]

Health care professionals sometimes confront very difficult issues when trying to honor both their statutory duty to report suspected abuse, neglect, and dependency and their professional ethic of confidentiality. Confidentiality refers to the ethical mandate to protect patient and client privacy, and it is considered a cornerstone of the professional, therapeutic relationship. Conflicts may occur, for example, when a psychotherapist becomes aware that a young client or

patient has been victimized or that an adult client or patient may have harmed a child.

Although the statutory requirement to report supersedes confidentiality, the ethical codes of psychologists, physicians, counselors, social workers, and others require that professionals not exceed the reporting that is required by law. Health care professionals, therefore, are sensitive to the fine points of the meaning of key terms like "caretaker," "abuse," "neglect," and "serious physical injury." A health or mental health professional who exceeds his or her reporting responsibilities, thereby violating a patient's or client's confidentiality without statutory authority to do so, risks being sanctioned for an ethics violation within his or her profession.

Health care professionals should contact the ethics bodies of their professional associations or their licensing boards for guidance when conflicts between the duty to report and the obligation to respect confidentiality are difficult to resolve. In keeping with the doctrine of informed consent for the provision of professional services, these professionals also should make clients and patients aware of the exceptions to confidentiality as part of the process of contracting for evaluation and treatment.

Even when it is clear that there is no duty to report to social services— for example, because the person who harmed a child is not a parent, guardian, custodian, or caretaker—health care professionals should consider whether they have an ethical duty to take other action to protect clients, patients, or others from serious and foreseeable harm. Finally, health care professionals who have been trained in other states need to become familiar with the North Carolina statutes. Reporting laws, although universal, differ dramatically from state to state in their specific provisions and definitions.

Emergency Custody in Abuse Cases

PROCEDURES

When someone brings a child to a medical facility for diagnosis or treatment, and someone there has cause to suspect that the child has been abused, that person must make a report to the department of social services. If necessary, a social worker from the county department of social services or a law enforcement officer may assume immediate temporary custody of the child without a court order.[2] Then the department of social services may file a petition and seek a court order for continued custody. Occasionally, however, a parent may attempt to take the child from the medical facility before a social worker or law enforcement officer is available.

In that situation, a physician or an administrator of the facility can keep physical custody of the child and provide necessary treatment by following these procedures:[3]

1. *Certify need to retain custody.*
   A physician who examines the child certifies in writing that

   - the child should remain at the facility for medical treatment, or
   - based on the medical evaluation, it is unsafe for the child to return to the parent, guardian, custodian, or caretaker.

2. *Obtain judicial authority.*
   The physician or administrator contacts and receives authorization (most likely by telephone) from the chief district court judge (or someone the judge has designated to act in his or her place) to retain physical custody of the child in the facility.[4] The date and time that the physician or administrator receives judicial authorization to retain custody must be noted on the physician's written certification.

3. *Notify director of social services.*
   Immediately after receiving judicial authority to retain custody, the physician or administrator (or someone that person designates) notifies the director of the department of social services in the county in which the facility is located. The director will treat the notification as a report of suspected abuse and begin an investigation.

4. *Distribute copies of certification.*
   A copy of the certification is given to the child's parent, guardian, custodian, or caretaker. Copies also are placed in the child's medical and court records.

These procedures are not likely to work well unless both judges and medical professionals are familiar with them before an emergency arises. Medical professionals and facilities need to know

- whom, if anyone, the chief district court judge has designated to act in his or her place in these cases;
- who the chief district court judge is, and how to contact him or her and any designees; and
- whether forms to facilitate the required documentation are available locally—from the court, the medical facility, or the social services department—or need to be developed.

It is important to remember that these procedures apply only in cases of suspected abuse, not in cases in which a child's neglect or dependency is the cause for the medical professional's concern. Even in abuse cases the procedure is not mandatory. The physician or administrator may make the required report to social services about the suspected abuse and rely on a law enforcement officer or social worker to assume temporary custody of the child if that is called for.

TIME LIMITS

Using this procedure, the child can be kept in the facility without the parent's consent or a court order for no more than twelve hours. The department of social services, however, may file a juvenile court petition and obtain a nonsecure custody order authorizing continued custody, as long as it is able to do so within the twelve-hour period. (This period is twenty-four hours if any part of the twelve-hour period falls on a weekend or holiday.) The social services department must file a petition within the twelve (or twenty-four) hours if its preliminary investigation shows that

1. in the certifying physician's opinion, the child needs medical treatment to cure or alleviate physical distress or to prevent the child from suffering serious physical injury; and
2. in the physician's opinion, the child should remain in the custody of the facility for at least twelve hours; and
3. the parent, guardian, custodian, or caretaker either cannot be reached or will not consent to the child's treatment in the facility.

FILING A PETITION

If the case meets the criteria described above, the social services director (or the director's representative) must file a petition, and it will be heard in juvenile court like any other juvenile petition alleging abuse. Only the social services director and the certifying physician, together, can voluntarily dismiss the petition.

If the case does not meet the criteria described above and the social services director decides not to file a petition, the physician or administrator may ask the prosecutor to review the director's decision, as in other reports of abuse, neglect, or dependency. (See "Review Process," in Chapter 11.)

COST OF TREATMENT

Finally, if the court determines that the medical treatment the child received was necessary and appropriate, the court may charge the cost of the treatment to the child's parents, guardian, custodian, or caretaker. If the parents are not able to pay, however, the court may charge the costs of the treatment to the county of the child's residence.

Consent for Emergency Medical Treatment[5]

Depriving a child of necessary medical care is a form of neglect. A physician who believes that a parent is refusing to consent to necessary medical treatment for a child must report that situation to the county department of social services.

A physician may use an additional procedure set out in the Juvenile Code when he or she is barred by the parent's refusal to consent from rendering necessary treatment to a child in an emergency. The physician may ask a district court judge to authorize the treatment. The procedure is as follows:

1. The physician signs a statement (or, in an acute emergency, makes an oral statement to the judge) setting out

   - the needed treatment and the nature of the emergency, and
   - the parent's refusal to consent to the treatment, and
   - the impossibility of contacting a second physician for a concurring opinion on the need for treatment in time to prevent immediate harm to the child.[6]

2. A judge examines the physician's written statement (or considers the physician's oral statement) and finds

   - that it complies with the statute, and
   - that the proposed treatment is necessary to prevent immediate harm to the child.

3. The judge issues written authorization for the proposed treatment or, in an acute emergency, authorizes treatment in person or by telephone.

4. If either the physician's statement or the judge's authorization is oral, it is reduced to writing

as soon as possible. The judge's written authorization for treatment should be issued in duplicate:

   - one copy for the treating physician, and
   - one copy to be attached to the physician's written statement and filed as a juvenile proceeding in the office of the clerk of superior court.

5. After a judge authorizes treatment in this manner, and after proper notice, the judge conducts a hearing on the question of payment for the treatment, with two possible results:

   - the judge may order the parent or other responsible parties to pay for the treatment, or
   - if the judge finds that the parent is not able to pay, the judge may order that the costs of the treatment be charged to the county.

Child Medical/Mental Health Evaluation Program[7]

A thorough investigation and evaluation of suspected abuse or neglect often requires the assistance of a medical or mental health professional.[8] The state Division of Social Services administers the Child Medical/Mental Health Evaluation Program through a contractual arrangement with the Department of Pediatrics at the University of North Carolina at Chapel Hill. The program provides medical and psychological assessments to help county social services departments make decisions in connection with investigations of abuse and neglect cases. (It does not include treatment services.) The program's services are provided by a network of local physicians and mental health examiners and are available to every county.[9]

The program has contributed to improved understanding and coordination between social services and medical professionals, more accurate and timely evaluations of children who may be abused or neglected, better testimony and evidence to establish abuse and neglect in cases that go to court, and increased skills and awareness among large numbers of professionals who are involved in these cases.

The program's staff at the University of North Carolina at Chapel Hill provide training for participating medical and mental health providers and also participate frequently in training for social workers, law enforcement officers, and judges.

Notes to Chapter 15

1. This section is adapted from comments submitted to the author by William V. Burlingame, Ph.D., Clinical Professor of Psychology, The University of North Carolina at Chapel Hill, 3 January 2001.

2. G.S. 7B-500. Ordinarily a child may not be taken into custody without a court order. In order to assume custody immediately the social worker or officer must have reasonable grounds to believe that the child is abused, neglected, or dependent and that the child would be injured or could not be taken into custody if it were necessary to obtain a court order first.

3. G.S. 7B-308. Medical professionals may find, or believe, that it is easier and takes no longer to get a law enforcement officer or a social services worker on the scene than to use the procedures described here. The evolution of this law is interesting. In the early 1970s, former G.S. 110-118(d) gave the physician authority on his or her own to retain temporary physical custody of the child in this cir-

cumstance. It put the burden on the parents to seek a court hearing if they objected. A 1975 amendment added a requirement that the physician who retained custody of a child ask social services to file a petition and seek a court order for temporary custody. In 1977, another amendment added authority for the medical facility to render necessary medical treatment to the child. The requirement that the physician get authorization from a district court judge to retain custody of the child appeared first in the 1979 rewrite of the Juvenile Code, and it has been in the law since then.

4. It seems clear from the wording of the statute that this authority must be sought on a case-by-case basis and that a chief district court judge should not, for example, attempt to use an administrative order or other means to give a facility or physician blanket authority. On the other hand, the statute authorizes the chief district court judge to designate someone to act in his or her place in regard to this procedure and does not limit whom the judge may designate.

5. G.S. 7B-3600.

6. *See* G.S. 90-21.1, which addresses when a physician may treat a minor without the consent of the parent.

7. The manual issued by the State Division of Social Services contains a detailed description of the Child Medical/Mental Health Evaluation Program and its procedures. North Carolina Division of Social Services, *Children's Services Manual*, Ch. VIII (Protective Services), § 1422. Retrieved 10 April 2003 from http://info.dhhs.state.nc.us/olm/manuals/dss/.

8. *See In re* Browning, 124 N.C. App. 190, 476 S.E.2d 465 (1996) (parent's objection to his children's being evaluated, although based in part on his religious beliefs, was not a lawful excuse for interfering with a social services investigation).

9. A medical or mental health professional who wants information about participating in the program should write to the Child Medical Evaluation Program, Division of Community Pediatrics, CB# 3415, The University of North Carolina at Chapel Hill, Chapel Hill, N.C. 27599-3415; telephone (919) 843-9365; or send a fax to (919) 843-9368.

Conclusion

North Carolina law requires anyone who has cause to suspect that a child is abused or neglected to report the child's situation to the county department of social services. The law also requires reports about other children who need assistance or placement and children whose deaths may have been caused by maltreatment.

The protective services system, which includes mandated reporting, exists to carry out the state's policy of taking steps to ensure that every child has at least minimally adequate care. It is a safety net, designed to catch those children who have fallen—or are at risk of falling—below that minimal level. Obviously, people want more than that for their own and other children: protection from all kinds of harm; a level of care that is excellent, not just minimal; and opportunities to grow and develop to their full potential.

Other systems aim higher—education, health care, mental health services, and a host of other preventive and voluntary services. How adequately we provide services in areas like education, health care, child care, housing, substance abuse, and job training affects how many children and families need this safety net. Resource shortages can seriously harm those systems as well as the child protective services system and may be one reason the

protective services system sets a threshold of minimally adequate care. Another reason, though, is philosophical: our society tolerates uninvited state intervention into families' lives only when absolutely necessary.

The definitions that give the reporting law real meaning define the scope of that intervention. Some people consider that threshold and scope insufficient in light of the number of children who are harmed by abuse or neglect. To others, state intervention may seem excessive, especially when based on a report of suspected abuse, neglect, or dependency that turns out to be unfounded.

The system involves a delicate balance of societal values. It does not, and cannot, protect every child from harm or from the deprivations of inadequate care. It cannot operate at all, though, with respect to abused, neglected, and dependent children who never come to the attention of those with the legal authority and professional skills to intervene on their behalf. Having cause to suspect child abuse, neglect, or dependency and not reporting it is to risk pulling the safety net out from under a child. It is also to violate a legal responsibility that the North Carolina General Assembly has placed on every individual and institution in the state.

Appendixes

Appendix A

Selected Portions of the North Carolina Juvenile Code

NORTH CAROLINA GENERAL STATUTES

Chapter 7B. Juvenile Code.

Subchapter I. Abuse, Neglect, Dependency

(As amended through the 2002 Session of the General Assembly)

ARTICLE 1.
Purposes; Definitions.

§ 7B-100. Purpose.

This Subchapter shall be interpreted and construed so as to implement the following purposes and policies:

(1) To provide procedures for the hearing of juvenile cases that assure fairness and equity and that protect the constitutional rights of juveniles and parents;

(2) To develop a disposition in each juvenile case that reflects consideration of the facts, the needs and limitations of the juvenile, and the strengths and weaknesses of the family.

(3) To provide for services for the protection of juveniles by means that respect both the right to family autonomy and the juveniles' needs for safety, continuity, and permanence; and

(4) To provide standards for the removal, when necessary, of juveniles from their homes and for the return of juveniles to their homes consistent with preventing the unnecessary or inappropriate separation of juveniles from their parents.

§ 7B-101. Definitions.

As used in this Subchapter, unless the context clearly requires otherwise, the following words have the listed meanings:

(1) Abused juveniles.—Any juvenile less than 18 years of age whose parent, guardian, custodian, or caretaker:

    a. Inflicts or allows to be inflicted upon the juvenile a serious physical injury by other than accidental means;

    b. Creates or allows to be created a substantial risk of serious physical injury to the juvenile by other than accidental means;

    c. Uses or allows to be used upon the juvenile cruel or grossly inappropriate procedures or cruel or grossly inappropriate devices to modify behavior;

    d. Commits, permits, or encourages the commission of a violation of the following laws by, with, or upon the juvenile: first-degree rape, as provided in G.S. 14-27.2; second degree rape as provided in G.S. 14-27.3; first-degree sexual offense, as provided in G.S. 14-27.4; second degree sexual offense, as provided in G.S. 14-27.5; sexual act by a custodian, as provided in G.S. 14-27.7; crime against nature, as provided in G.S. 14-177; incest, as provided in G.S. 14-178 and G.S. 14-179; preparation of obscene photographs, slides, or motion pictures of the juvenile, as provided in G.S. 14-190.5; employing or permitting the juvenile to assist in a violation of the obscenity laws as provided in G.S. 14-190.6; dissemination of obscene material to the juvenile as provided in G.S. 14-190.7 and G.S. 14-190.8; displaying or disseminating material harmful to the juvenile as provided in G.S. 14-190.14 and G.S. 14-190.15; first and second degree sexual exploitation of the juvenile as provided in G.S. 14-190.16 and G.S. 14-190.17; promoting the prostitution of the juvenile as provided in G.S. 14-190.18; and taking indecent liberties with the juvenile, as provided in G.S. 14-202.1, regardless of the age of the parties;

e. Creates or allows to be created serious emotional damage to the juvenile; serious emotional damage is evidenced by a juvenile's severe anxiety, depression, withdrawal, or aggressive behavior toward himself or others; or

f. Encourages, directs, or approves of delinquent acts involving moral turpitude committed by the juvenile.

(2) Aggravated circumstances.—Any circumstance attending to the commission of an act of abuse or neglect which increases its enormity or adds to its injurious consequences, including, but not limited to, abandonment, torture, chronic abuse, or sexual abuse.

(3) Caretaker.—Any person other than a parent, guardian, or custodian who has responsibility for the health and welfare of a juvenile in a residential setting. A person responsible for a juvenile's health and welfare means a stepparent, foster parent, an adult member of the juvenile's household, an adult relative entrusted with the juvenile's care, any person such as a house parent or cottage parent who has primary responsibility for supervising a juvenile's health and welfare in a residential child care facility or residential educational facility, or any employee or volunteer of a division, institution, or school operated by the Department of Health and Human Services. "Caretaker" also means any person who has the responsibility for the care of a juvenile in a child care facility as defined in Article 7 of Chapter 110 of the General Statutes and includes any person who has the approval of the care provider to assume responsibility for the juveniles under the care of the care provider. Nothing in this subdivision shall be construed to impose a legal duty of support under Chapter 50 or Chapter 110 of the General Statutes. The duty imposed upon a caretaker as defined in this subdivision shall be for the purpose of this Subchapter only.

(4) Clerk.—Any clerk of superior court, acting clerk, or assistant or deputy clerk.

(5) Community-based program.—A program providing nonresidential or residential treatment to a juvenile in the community where the juvenile's family lives. A community-based program may include specialized foster care, family

counseling, shelter care, and other appropriate treatment.

(6) Court.—The district court division of the General Court of Justice.

(7) Court of competent jurisdiction.— A court having the power and authority of law to act at the time of acting over the subject matter of the cause.

(7a) "Criminal history" means a local, State, or federal criminal history of conviction or pending indictment of a crime, whether a misdemeanor or a felony, involving violence against a person.

(8) Custodian.—The person or agency that has been awarded legal custody of a juvenile by a court or a person, other than parents or legal guardian, who has assumed the status and obligation of a parent without being awarded the legal custody of a juvenile by a court.

(9) Dependent juvenile.—A juvenile in need of assistance or placement because the juvenile has no parent, guardian, or custodian responsible for the juvenile's care or supervision or whose parent, guardian, or custodian is unable to provide for the care or supervision and lacks an appropriate alternative child care arrangement.

(10) Director.—The director of the county department of social services in the county in which the juvenile resides or is found, or the director's representative as authorized in G.S. 108A-14.

(11) District.—Any district court district as established by G.S. 7A-133.

(12) Judge.—Any district court judge.

(13) Judicial district.—Any district court district as established by G.S. 7A-133.

(14) Juvenile.—A person who has not reached the person's eighteenth birthday and is not married, emancipated, or a member of the armed forces of the United States.

(15) Neglected juvenile.—A juvenile who does not receive proper care, supervision, or discipline from the juvenile's parent, guardian, custodian, or caretaker; or who has been abandoned; or who is not provided necessary medical care; or who is not provided necessary remedial care; or who lives in an environment injurious to the juvenile's welfare; or who has been placed for care or adoption in violation of law. In determining whether a juvenile is a neglected juvenile, it is relevant whether that juvenile lives in a home where another juvenile has died as a result of suspected abuse or neglect or lives in a home where another juvenile has been subjected to abuse or neglect by an adult who regularly lives in the home.

(16) Petitioner.—The individual who initiates court action, whether by the filing of a petition or of a motion for review alleging the matter for adjudication.

(17) Prosecutor.—The district attorney or assistant district attorney assigned by the district attorney to juvenile proceedings.

(18) Reasonable efforts.—The diligent use of preventive or reunification services by a department of social services when a juvenile's remaining at home or returning home is consistent with achieving a safe, permanent home for the juvenile within a reasonable period of time. If a court of competent jurisdiction determines that the juvenile is not to be returned home, then reasonable efforts means the diligent and timely use of permanency planning services by a department of social services to develop and implement a permanent plan for the juvenile.

(19) Safe home.—A home in which the juvenile is not at substantial risk of physical or emotional abuse or neglect.

(20) Shelter care.—The temporary care of a juvenile in a physically unrestricting facility pending court disposition.

The singular includes the plural, the masculine singular includes the feminine singular and masculine and feminine plural unless otherwise specified.

ARTICLE 2.
Jurisdiction.

§ 7B-200. Jurisdiction.

(a) The court has exclusive, original jurisdiction over any case involving a juvenile who is alleged to be abused, neglected, or dependent. This jurisdiction does not extend to cases involving adult defendants alleged to be guilty of abuse or neglect.

The court also has exclusive original jurisdiction of the following proceedings:

(1) Proceedings under the Interstate Compact on the Placement of Children set forth in Article 38 of this Chapter;

(2) Proceedings involving judicial consent for emergency surgical or medical treatment for a juvenile when the juvenile's parent, guardian, custodian, or other person who has assumed the status and obligation of a parent without being awarded legal custody of the juvenile by a court refuses to consent for treatment to be rendered;

(3) Proceedings to determine whether a juvenile should be emancipated;

(4) Proceedings to terminate parental rights;

(5) Proceedings to review the placement of a juvenile in foster care pursuant to an agreement between the juvenile's parents or guardian and a county department of social services;

(6) Proceedings in which a person is alleged to have obstructed or interfered with an investigation required by G.S. 7B-302;

(7) Proceedings involving consent for an abortion on an unemancipated minor pursuant to Article 1A,

Part 2 of Chapter 90 of the General Statutes; and

(8) Proceedings by an underage party seeking judicial authorization to marry, pursuant to Article 1 of Chapter 51 of the General Statutes.

(b) The court shall have jurisdiction over the parent or guardian of a juvenile who has been adjudicated abused, neglected, or dependent, as provided by G.S. 7B-904, provided the parent or guardian has been properly served with summons pursuant to G.S. 7B-406.

§ 7B-201. Retention of jurisdiction.

When the court obtains jurisdiction over a juvenile, jurisdiction shall continue until terminated by order of the court or until the juvenile reaches the age of 18 years or is otherwise emancipated, whichever occurs first.

ARTICLE 3.
Screening of Abuse and Neglect Complaints.

§ 7B-300. Protective services.

The director of the department of social services in each county of the State shall establish protective services for juveniles alleged to be abused, neglected, or dependent.

Protective services shall include the investigation and screening of complaints, casework, or other counseling services to parents, guardians, or other caretakers as provided by the director to help the parents, guardians, or other caretakers and the court to prevent abuse or neglect, to improve the quality of child care, to be more adequate parents, guardians, or caretakers, and to preserve and stabilize family life.

The provisions of this Article shall also apply to child care facilities as defined in G.S. 110-86.

§ 7B-301. Duty to report abuse, neglect, dependency, or death due to maltreatment.

Any person or institution who has cause to suspect that any juvenile is abused, neglected, or dependent, as defined by G.S. 7B-101, or has died as the result of maltreatment, shall report the case of that juvenile to the director of the department of social services in the county where the juvenile resides or is found. The report may be made orally, by telephone, or in writing. The report shall include information as is known to the person making it including the name and address of the juvenile; the name and address of the juvenile's parent, guardian, or caretaker; the age of the juvenile; the names and ages of other juveniles in the home; the present whereabouts of the juvenile if not at the home address; the nature and extent of any injury or condition resulting from abuse, neglect, or dependency; and any other information which the person making the report believes might be helpful in establishing the need for protective services or court intervention. If the report is made orally or by telephone, the person making the report shall give the person's name, address, and telephone number. Refusal of the person making the report to give a name shall not preclude the department's investigation of the alleged abuse, neglect, dependency, or death as a result of maltreatment.

Upon receipt of any report of sexual abuse of the juvenile in a child care facility, the director shall notify the State Bureau of Investigation within 24 hours or on the next workday. If sexual abuse in a child care facility is not alleged in the initial report, but during the course of the investigation there is reason to suspect that sexual abuse has occurred, the director shall immediately notify the State Bureau of Investigation. Upon notification that sexual abuse may have occurred in a child care facility, the State Bureau of Investigation may form a task force to investigate the report.

§ 7B-302. Investigation by director; access to confidential information; notification of person making the report.

(a) When a report of abuse, neglect, or dependency is received, the director of the department of social services shall make a prompt and thorough investigation in order to ascertain the facts of the case, the extent of the abuse or neglect, and the risk of harm to the juvenile, in order to determine whether protective services should be provided or the complaint filed as a petition. When the report alleges abuse, the director shall immediately, but no later than 24 hours after receipt of the report, initiate the investigation. When the report alleges neglect or dependency, the director shall initiate the investigation within 72 hours following receipt of the report. When the report alleges abandonment, the director shall immediately initiate an investigation, take appropriate steps to assume temporary custody of the juvenile, and take appropriate steps to secure an order for nonsecure custody of the juvenile. The investigation and evaluation shall include a visit to the place where the juvenile resides. When the report alleges abandonment, the investigation shall include a request from the director to law enforcement officials to investigate through the North Carolina Center for Missing Persons and other national and State resources whether the juvenile is a missing child. All information received by the department of social services, including the identity of the reporter, shall be held in strictest confidence by the department.

(b) When a report of a juvenile's death as a result of suspected maltreatment or a report of suspected abuse, neglect, or dependency of a juvenile in a noninstitutional setting is received, the director of the department of social services shall immediately ascertain if other juveniles live in the home, and, if so, initiate an investigation in order to determine whether they require protective services or whether immediate removal of the juveniles from the home is necessary for their protection. When a report of a juvenile's death as a result of maltreatment or a report of suspected abuse, neglect, or dependency of a juvenile in an institutional setting such as a residential child care facility or residential educational facility is received, the director of the department of social services shall immediately ascertain if other juveniles remain in the facility subject to the alleged perpetrator's care or supervision, and, if so, assess the circumstances of those juveniles in order to determine whether they require protective services or whether immediate removal of those juveniles from the facility is necessary for their protection.

(c) If the investigation indicates that abuse, neglect, or dependency has occurred, the director shall decide whether immediate removal of the juvenile or any other juveniles in the home is necessary for their protection. If immediate removal does not seem necessary, the director shall immediately provide or arrange for protective services. If the parent, guardian, custodian, or caretaker refuses to accept the protective services provided or arranged by the director, the director shall sign a complaint seeking to invoke the jurisdiction of the court for the protection of the juvenile or juveniles.

(d) If immediate removal seems necessary for the protection of the juvenile or other juveniles in the home, the director shall sign a complaint which alleges the applicable facts to invoke the jurisdiction of the court. Where the investigation shows that it is warranted, a protective services worker may assume temporary custody of the juvenile for the juvenile's protection pursuant to Article 5 of this Chapter.

(d1) Whenever a juvenile is removed from the home of a parent, guardian, custodian, stepparent, or adult relative entrusted with the juvenile's care due to physical abuse, the director shall conduct a thorough review of the background of the alleged abuser or abusers. This review shall include a criminal history check and a review of any available mental health records. If the review reveals that the alleged abuser or abusers have a history of violent behavior against people, the director shall petition the court to order the alleged abuser or abusers to submit to a complete mental health evaluation by a licensed psychologist or psychiatrist.

(e) In performing any duties related to the investigation of the complaint or the provision or arrangement for protective services, the director may consult with any public or private agencies or individuals, including the available State or local law enforcement officers who shall assist in the investigation and evaluation of the seriousness of any report of abuse, neglect, or dependency when requested by the director. The director or the director's representative may make a written demand for any information or reports, whether or not confidential, that may in the director's opinion be relevant to the investigation of or the provision for protective services. Upon the director's or

the director's representative's request and unless protected by the attorney–client privilege, any public or private agency or individual shall provide access to and copies of this confidential information and these records to the extent permitted by federal law and regulations. If a custodian of criminal investigative information or records believes that release of the information will jeopardize the right of the State to prosecute a defendant or the right of a defendant to receive a fair trial or will undermine an ongoing or future investigation, it may seek an order from a court of competent jurisdiction to prevent disclosure of the information. In such an action, the custodian of the records shall have the burden of showing by a preponderance of the evidence that disclosure of the information in question will jeopardize the right of the State to prosecute a defendant or the right of a defendant to receive a fair trial or will undermine an ongoing or future investigation. Actions brought pursuant to this paragraph shall be set down for immediate hearing, and subsequent proceedings in the actions shall be accorded priority by the trial and appellate courts.

(f) Within five working days after receipt of the report of abuse, neglect, or dependency, the director shall give written notice to the person making the report, unless requested by that person not to give notice, as to whether the report was accepted for investigation and whether the report was referred to the appropriate State or local law enforcement agency.

(g) Within five working days after completion of the protective services investigation, the director shall give subsequent written notice to the person making the report, unless requested by that person not to give notice, as to whether there is a finding of abuse, neglect, or dependency, whether the county department of social services is taking action to protect the juvenile, and what action it is taking, including whether or not a petition was filed. The person making the report shall be informed of procedures necessary to request a review by the prosecutor of the director's decision not to file a petition. A request for review by the prosecutor shall be made within five working days of receipt of the second notification. The second notification shall include notice that, if the person making the report is not satisfied with the director's decision, the person may request review of the decision by the prosecutor within five working days of receipt. The person making the report may waive the person's right to this notification, and no notification is required if the person making the report does not identify himself to the director.

§ 7B-303. Interference with investigation.

(a) If any person obstructs or interferes with an investigation required by G.S. 7B-302, the director may file a petition naming said person as respondent and requesting an order directing the respondent to cease such obstruction or interference. The petition shall contain the name and date of birth and address of the juvenile who is the subject of the investigation, shall specifically describe the conduct alleged to constitute obstruction of or interference with the investigation, and shall be verified.

(b) For purposes of this section, obstruction of or interference with an investigation means refusing to disclose the whereabouts of the juvenile, refusing to allow the director to have personal access to the juvenile, refusing to allow the director to observe or interview the juvenile in private, refusing to allow the director access to confidential information and records upon request pursuant to G.S. 7B-302, refusing to allow the director to arrange for an evaluation of the juvenile by a physician or other expert, or other conduct that makes it impossible for the director to carry out the duty to investigate.

(c) Upon filing of the petition, the court shall schedule a hearing to be held not less than five days after service of the petition and summons on the respondent. Service of the petition and summons and notice of hearing shall be made as provided by the Rules of Civil Procedure on the respondent; the juvenile's parent, guardian, custodian, or caretaker; and any other person determined by the court to be a necessary party. If at the hearing on the petition the court finds by clear, cogent, and convincing evidence that the respondent, without lawful excuse, has obstructed or interfered with an investigation required by G.S. 7B-302, the court may order the respondent to cease

such obstruction or interference. The burden of proof shall be on the petitioner.

(d) If the director has reason to believe that the juvenile is in need of immediate protection or assistance, the director shall so allege in the petition and may seek an ex parte order from the court. If the court, from the verified petition and any inquiry the court makes of the director, finds probable cause to believe both that the juvenile is at risk of immediate harm and that the respondent is obstructing or interfering with the director's ability to investigate to determine the juvenile's condition, the court may enter an ex parte order directing the respondent to cease such obstruction or interference. The order shall be limited to provisions necessary to enable the director to conduct an investigation sufficient to determine whether the juvenile is in need of immediate protection or assistance. Within 10 days after the entry of an ex parte order under this subsection, a hearing shall be held to determine whether there is good cause for the continuation of the order or the entry of a different order. An order entered under this subsection shall be served on the respondent along with a copy of the petition, summons, and notice of hearing.

(e) The director may be required at a hearing under this section to reveal the identity of any person who made a report of suspected abuse, neglect, or dependency as required by G.S. 7B-301.

(f) An order entered pursuant to this section is enforceable by civil or criminal contempt as provided in Chapter 5A of the General Statutes.

§ 7B-304. Evaluation for court.

In all cases in which a petition is filed, the director of the department of social services shall prepare a report for the court containing the results of any mental health evaluation under G.S. 7B-503, a home placement plan, and a treatment plan deemed by the director to be appropriate to the needs of the juvenile. The report shall be available to the court immediately following the adjudicatory hearing.

§ 7B-305. Request for review by prosecutor.

The person making the report shall have five working days, from receipt of the decision of the director of the department of social services not to petition the court, to notify the prosecutor that the person is requesting a review. The prosecutor shall notify the person making the report and the director of the time and place for the review, and the director shall immediately transmit to the prosecutor a copy of the investigation report.

§ 7B-306. Review by prosecutor.

The prosecutor shall review the director's determination that a petition should not be filed within 20 days after the person making the report is notified. The review shall include conferences with the person making the report, the protective services worker, the juvenile, if practicable, and other persons known to have pertinent information about the juvenile or the juvenile's family. At the conclusion of the conferences, the prosecutor may affirm the decision made by the director, may request the appropriate local law enforcement agency to investigate the allegations, or may direct the director to file a petition.

§ 7B-307. Duty of director to report evidence of abuse, neglect; investigation by local law enforcement; notification of Department of Health and Human Services and State Bureau of Investigation.

(a) If the director finds evidence that a juvenile may have been abused as defined by G.S. 7B-101, the director shall make an immediate oral and subsequent written report of the findings to the district attorney or the district attorney's designee and the appropriate local law enforcement agency within 48 hours after receipt of the report. The local law enforcement agency shall immediately, but no later than 48 hours after receipt of the information, initiate and coordinate a criminal investigation with the protective services investigation being conducted by the county department of social services. Upon completion of the investigation,

the district attorney shall determine whether criminal prosecution is appropriate and may request the director or the director's designee to appear before a magistrate.

If the director receives information that a juvenile may have been physically harmed in violation of any criminal statute by any person other than the juvenile's parent, guardian, custodian, or caretaker, the director shall make an immediate oral and subsequent written report of that information to the district attorney or the district attorney's designee and to the appropriate local law enforcement agency within 48 hours after receipt of the information. The local law enforcement agency shall immediately, but no later than 48 hours after receipt of the information, initiate a criminal investigation. Upon completion of the investigation, the district attorney shall determine whether criminal prosecution is appropriate.

If the report received pursuant to G.S. 7B-301 involves abuse or neglect of a juvenile in child care, the director shall notify the Department of Health and Human Services within 24 hours or on the next working day of receipt of the report.

(b) If the director finds evidence that a juvenile has been abused or neglected as defined by G.S. 7B-101 in a child care facility, the director shall immediately so notify the Department of Health and Human Services and, in the case of sexual abuse, the State Bureau of Investigation, in such a way as does not violate the law guaranteeing the confidentiality of the records of the department of social services.

(c) Upon completion of the investigation, the director shall give the Department written notification of the results of the investigation required by G.S. 7B-302. Upon completion of an investigation of sexual abuse in a child care facility, the director shall also make written notification of the results of the investigation to the State Bureau of Investigation.

The director of the department of social services shall submit a report of alleged abuse, neglect, or dependency cases or child fatalities that are the result of alleged maltreatment to the central registry under the policies adopted by the Social Services Commission.

§ 7B-308. Authority of medical professionals in abuse cases.

(a) Any physician or administrator of a hospital, clinic, or other medical facility to which a suspected abused juvenile is brought for medical diagnosis or treatment shall have the right, when authorized by the chief district court judge of the district or the judge's designee, to retain physical custody of the juvenile in the facility when the physician who examines the juvenile certifies in writing that the juvenile who is suspected of being abused should remain for medical treatment or that, according to the juvenile's medical evaluation, it is unsafe for the juvenile to return to the juvenile's parent, guardian, custodian, or caretaker. This written certification must be signed by the certifying physician and must include the time and date that the judicial authority to retain custody is given. Copies of the written certification must be appended to the juvenile's medical and judicial records and another copy must be given to the juvenile's parent, guardian, custodian, or caretaker. The right to retain custody in the facility shall exist for up to 12 hours from the time and date contained in the written certification.

(b) Immediately upon receipt of judicial authority to retain custody, the physician, the administrator, or that person's designee shall so notify the director of social services for the county in which the facility is located. The director shall treat this notification as a report of suspected abuse and shall immediately begin an investigation of the case.

(1) If the investigation reveals (i) that it is the opinion of the certifying physician that the juvenile is in need of medical treatment to cure or alleviate physical distress or to prevent the juvenile from suffering serious physical injury, and (ii) that it is the opinion of the physician that the juvenile should for these reasons remain in the custody of the facility for 12 hours, but (iii) that the juvenile's parent, guardian, custodian, or caretaker cannot be reached or, upon request, will not consent to the treatment within the facility, the director shall within the initial 12-hour period file a juvenile petition alleging abuse and setting forth supporting allegations and shall seek a nonsecure custody order. A petition filed and a non-secure custody order obtained in accordance with this subdivision shall come on for hearing under the regular provisions of this Subchapter unless the director and the certifying physician together voluntarily dismiss the petition.

(2) In all cases except those described in subdivision (1) above, the director shall conduct the investigation and may initiate juvenile proceedings and take all other steps authorized by the regular provisions of this Subchapter. If the director decides not to file a petition, the physician, the administrator, or that person's designee may ask the prosecutor to review this decision according to the provisions of G.S. 7B-305 and G.S. 7B-306.

(c) If, upon hearing, the court determines that the juvenile is found in a county other than the county of legal residence, in accord with G.S. 153A-257, the juvenile may be transferred, in accord with G.S. 7B-903(2), to the custody of the department of social services in the county of residence.

(d) If the court, upon inquiry, determines that the medical treatment rendered was necessary and appropriate, the cost of that treatment may be charged to the parents, guardian, custodian, or caretaker, or, if the parents are unable to pay, to the county of residence in accordance with G.S. 7B-903 and G.S. 7B-904.

(e) Except as otherwise provided, a petition begun under this section shall proceed in like manner with petitions begun under G.S. 7B-302.

(f) The procedures in this section are in addition to, and not in derogation of, the abuse and neglect reporting provisions of G.S. 7B-301 and the temporary custody provisions of G.S. 7B-500. Nothing in this section shall preclude a physician or administrator and a director of social services from following the procedures of G.S. 7B-301 and G.S. 7B-500 whenever these procedures are more appropriate to the juvenile's circumstances.

§ 7B-309. Immunity of persons reporting and cooperating in an investigation.

Anyone who makes a report pursuant to this Article, cooperates with the county department of social services in a protective services inquiry or investigation, testifies in any judicial proceeding resulting from a protective services report or investigation, or otherwise participates in the program authorized by this Article, is immune from any civil or criminal liability that might otherwise be incurred or imposed for that action provided that the person was acting in good faith. In any proceeding involving liability, good faith is presumed.

§ 7B-310. Privileges not grounds for failing to report or for excluding evidence.

No privilege shall be grounds for any person or institution failing to report that a juvenile may have been abused, neglected, or dependent, even if the knowledge or suspicion is acquired in an official professional capacity, except when the knowledge or suspicion is gained by an attorney from that attorney's client during representation only in the abuse, neglect, or dependency case. No privilege, except the attorney–client privilege, shall be grounds for excluding evidence of abuse, neglect, or dependency in any judicial proceeding (civil, criminal, or juvenile) in which a juvenile's abuse, neglect, or dependency is in issue nor in any judicial proceeding resulting from a report submitted under this Article, both as this privilege relates to the competency of the witness and to the exclusion of confidential communications.

§ 7B-311. Central registry.

The Department of Health and Human Services shall maintain a central registry of abuse, neglect, and dependency cases and child fatalities that are the result of alleged maltreatment that are reported under this Article in order to compile data for appropriate study of the extent of abuse and neglect within the State and to identify repeated abuses of the same juvenile or of other juveniles in the same family. This data shall be furnished by county directors of social services to the Department of Health and Human Services and shall be confidential, subject to policies adopted by the Social Services Commission providing for its use for study and research and for other appropriate disclosure. Data shall not be used at any hearing or court proceeding unless based upon a final judgment of a court of law.

ARTICLE 4.
Venue; Petitions.

§ 7B-400. Venue; pleading.

A proceeding in which a juvenile is alleged to be abused, neglected, or dependent may be commenced in the district in which the juvenile resides or is present. When a proceeding is commenced in a district other than that of the juvenile's residence, the court, on its own motion or upon motion of any party, may transfer the proceeding to the court in the district where the juvenile resides. A transfer under this section may be made at any time.

§ 7B-401. Pleading and process.

The pleading in an abuse, neglect, or dependency action is the petition. The process in an abuse, neglect, or dependency action is the summons.

§ 7B-402. Petition.

The petition shall contain the name, date of birth, address of the juvenile, the name and last known address of the juvenile's parent, guardian, or custodian and shall allege the facts which invoke jurisdiction over the juvenile. The petition may contain information on more than one juvenile when the juveniles are from the same home and are before the court for the same reason.

Sufficient copies of the petition shall be prepared so that copies will be available for each parent if living separate and apart, the guardian, custodian, or caretaker, the guardian ad litem, the social worker, and any person determined by the court to be a necessary party.

§ 7B-403. Receipt of reports; filing of petition.

(a) All reports concerning a juvenile alleged to be abused, neglected, or dependent shall be referred to the director of the department of social services for screening. Thereafter, if it is determined by the director that a report should be filed as a petition, the petition shall be drawn by the director, verified before an official authorized to administer oaths, and filed by the clerk, recording the date of filing.

(b) A decision of the director of social services not to file a report as a petition shall be reviewed by the prosecutor if review is requested pursuant to G.S. 7B-305.

§ 7B-404. Immediate need for petition when clerk's office is closed.

(a) When the office of the clerk is closed, a magistrate may be authorized by the chief district court judge to draw, verify, and issue petitions as follows:

(1) When the director of the department of social services requests a petition alleging a juvenile to be abused, neglected, or dependent, or

(2) When the director of the department of social services requests a petition alleging the obstruction of or interference with an investigation required by G.S. 7B-302.

(b) The authority of the magistrate under this section is limited to emergency situations when a petition is required in order to obtain a nonsecure custody order or an order under G.S. 7B-303. Any petition issued under this section shall be delivered to the clerk's office for processing as soon as that office is open for business.

§ 7B-405. Commencement of action.

An action is commenced by the filing of a petition in the clerk's office when that office is open or by the issuance of a juvenile petition by a magistrate when the clerk's office is closed, which issuance shall constitute filing.

§ 7B-406. Issuance of summons.

(a) Immediately after a petition has been filed alleging that a juvenile is abused, neglected, or dependent, the clerk shall issue a summons to the parent, guardian, custodian, or caretaker requiring them to appear for a hearing at the time and place stated in the summons. A copy of the petition shall be attached to each summons. Service of the summons shall be completed as provided in G.S. 7B-407, but the parent of the juvenile shall not be deemed to be under a disability even though the parent is a minor.

(b) A summons shall be on a printed form supplied by the Administrative Office of the Courts and shall include:

(1) Notice of the nature of the proceeding;

(2) Notice of any right to counsel and information about how to seek the appointment of counsel prior to a hearing;

(3) Notice that, if the court determines at the hearing that the allegations of the petition are true, the court will conduct a dispositional hearing to consider the needs of the juvenile and enter an order designed to meet those needs and the objectives of the State; and

(4) Notice that the dispositional order or a subsequent order:

a. May remove the juvenile from the custody of the parent, guardian, or custodian.

b. May require that the juvenile receive medical, psychiatric, psychological, or other treatment and that the parent participate in the treatment.

c. May require the parent to undergo psychiatric, psychological, or other treatment or counseling for the purpose of remedying the behaviors or conditions that are alleged in the petition or that contributed to the removal of the juvenile from the custody of that person.

d. May order the parent to pay for treatment that is ordered for the juvenile or the parent.

e. May, upon proper notice and hearing and a finding based on the criteria set out in G.S. 7B-1111, terminate the parental rights of the respondent parent.

(c) The summons shall advise the parent that upon service, jurisdiction over that person is obtained and that failure to comply with any order of the court pursuant to G.S. 7B-904 may cause the court to issue a show cause order for contempt.

(d) A summons shall be directed to the person summoned to appear and shall be delivered to any person authorized to serve process.

§ 7B-407. Service of summons.

The summons shall be personally served upon the parent, guardian, custodian, or caretaker, not less than five days prior to the date of the scheduled hearing. The time for service may be waived in the discretion of the court.

If the parent, guardian, custodian, or caretaker entitled to receive a summons cannot be found by a diligent effort, the court may authorize service of the summons and petition by mail or by publication. The cost of the service by publication shall be advanced by the petitioner and may be charged as court costs as the court may direct.

If the parent, guardian, custodian, or caretaker is personally served as herein provided and fails without reasonable cause to appear and to bring the juvenile before the court, the parent, guardian, custodian, or caretaker may be proceeded against as for contempt of court.

ARTICLE 5.
Temporary Custody; Nonsecure Custody; Custody Hearings.

§ 7B-500. Taking a juvenile into temporary custody; civil and criminal immunity.

(a) Temporary custody means the taking of physical custody and providing personal care and supervision until a court order for nonsecure custody can be obtained. A juvenile may be taken into temporary custody without a court order by a law enforcement officer or a department of social services worker if there are reasonable grounds to believe that the juvenile is abused, neglected, or dependent and that the juvenile would be injured or could not be taken into custody if it were first necessary to obtain a court order. If a department of social services worker takes a juvenile into temporary custody under this section, the worker may arrange for the placement, care, supervision, and transportation of the juvenile.

(b) The following individuals shall, without a court order, take into temporary custody an infant under seven days of age that is voluntarily delivered to the individual by the infant's parent who does not express an intent to return for the infant:

(1) A health care provider, as defined under G.S. 90-21.11, who is on duty or at a hospital or at a local or district health department or at a nonprofit community health center.

(2) A law enforcement officer who is on duty or at a police station or sheriff's department.

(3) A social services worker who is on duty or at a local department of social services.

(4) A certified emergency medical service worker who is on duty or at a fire or emergency medical services station.

(c) An individual who takes an infant into temporary custody under subsection (b) of this section shall perform any act necessary to protect the physical health and well-being of the infant and shall immediately notify the department of social services or a local law enforcement agency. Any individual who takes an infant into temporary custody under subsection (b) of this section may inquire as to the parents' identities and as to any relevant medical history, but the parent is not required to provide the information. The individual shall notify the parent that the parent is not required to provide the information.

(d) Any adult may, without a court order, take into temporary custody an infant under seven days of age that is voluntarily delivered to the individual by the infant's parent who does not express an intent to return for the infant. Any individual who takes an infant into temporary custody under this section shall perform any act necessary to protect the physical health and well-being of the infant and shall immediately notify the department of social services or a local law enforcement agency. An individual who takes an infant into temporary custody under this subsection may inquire as to the parents' identities and as to any relevant medical history, but the parent is not required to provide the information. The individual shall notify the parent that the parent is not required to provide the information.

(e) An individual described in subsection (b) or (d) of this section is immune from any civil or criminal liability that might otherwise be incurred or imposed as a result of any omission or action taken pursuant to the requirements of subsection (c) or (d) of this section as long as that individual was acting in good faith. The immunity established by this subsection does not extend to gross negligence, wanton conduct, or intentional wrongdoing that would otherwise be actionable.

§ 7B-501. Duties of person taking juvenile into temporary custody.

(a) A person who takes a juvenile into custody without a court order under G.S. 7B-500 shall proceed as follows:

(1) Notify the juvenile's parent, guardian, custodian, or caretaker that the juvenile has been taken into temporary custody and advise the parent, guardian, custodian, or caretaker of the right to be present with the juvenile until a determination is made as to the need for nonsecure custody. Failure to notify the parent that the juvenile is in custody shall not be grounds for release of the juvenile.

(2) Release the juvenile to the juvenile's parent, guardian, custodian, or caretaker if the person having the juvenile in temporary custody decides that continued custody is unnecessary.

(3) The person having temporary custody shall communicate with the director of the department of social services who shall consider prehearing diversion. If the decision is made to file a petition, the director

shall contact the judge or person delegated authority pursuant to G.S. 7B-502 for a determination of the need for continued custody.

(b) A juvenile taken into temporary custody under this Article shall not be held for more than 12 hours, or for more than 24 hours if any of the 12 hours falls on a Saturday, Sunday, or legal holiday, unless:

(1) A petition or motion for review has been filed by the director of the department of social services, and

(2) An order for nonsecure custody has been entered by the court.

§ 7B-502. Authority to issue custody orders; delegation.

In the case of any juvenile alleged to be within the jurisdiction of the court, the court may order that the juvenile be placed in nonsecure custody pursuant to criteria set out in G.S. 7B-503 when custody of the juvenile is necessary.

Any district court judge shall have the authority to issue nonsecure custody orders pursuant to G.S. 7B-503. The chief district court judge may delegate the court's authority to persons other than district court judges by administrative order which shall be filed in the office of the clerk of superior court. The administrative order shall specify which persons shall be contacted for approval of a nonsecure custody order pursuant to G.S. 7B-503.

§ 7B-503. Criteria for nonsecure custody.

(a) When a request is made for nonsecure custody, the court shall first consider release of the juvenile to the juvenile's parent, relative, guardian, custodian, or other responsible adult. An order for nonsecure custody shall be made only when there is a reasonable factual basis to believe the matters alleged in the petition are true, and

(1) The juvenile has been abandoned; or

(2) The juvenile has suffered physical injury or sexual abuse; or

(3) The juvenile is exposed to a substantial risk of physical injury or

sexual abuse because the parent, guardian, custodian, or caretaker has created the conditions likely to cause injury or abuse or has failed to provide, or is unable to provide, adequate supervision or protection; or

(4) The juvenile is in need of medical treatment to cure, alleviate, or prevent suffering serious physical harm which may result in death, disfigurement, or substantial impairment of bodily functions, and the juvenile's parent, guardian, custodian, or caretaker is unwilling or unable to provide or consent to the medical treatment; or

(5) The parent, guardian, custodian, or caretaker consents to the nonsecure custody order; or

(6) The juvenile is a runaway and consents to nonsecure custody.

A juvenile alleged to be abused, neglected, or dependent shall be placed in nonsecure custody only when there is a reasonable factual basis to believe that there are no other reasonable means available to protect the juvenile. In no case shall a juvenile alleged to be abused, neglected, or dependent be placed in secure custody.

(b) Whenever a petition is filed under G.S. 7B-302(d1), the court shall rule on the petition prior to returning the child to a home where the alleged abuser or abusers are or have been present. If the court finds that the alleged abuser or abusers have a history of violent behavior against people, the court shall order the alleged abuser or abusers to submit to a complete mental health evaluation by a licensed psychologist or psychiatrist. The court may order the alleged abuser or abusers to pay the cost of any mental health evaluation required under this section.

§ 7B-504. Order for nonsecure custody.

The custody order shall be in writing and shall direct a law enforcement officer or other authorized person to assume custody of the juvenile and to make due return on the order. A copy of the order shall be given to the juve-

nile's parent, guardian, custodian, or caretaker by the official executing the order.

An officer receiving an order for custody which is complete and regular on its face may execute it in accordance with its terms. The officer is not required to inquire into the regularity or continued validity of the order and shall not incur criminal or civil liability for its due service.

§ 7B-505. Place of nonsecure custody.

A juvenile meeting the criteria set out in G.S. 7B-503 may be placed in nonsecure custody with the department of social services or a person designated in the order for temporary residential placement in:

(1) A licensed foster home or a home otherwise authorized by law to provide such care; or

(2) A facility operated by the department of social services; or

(3) Any other home or facility, including a relative's home approved by the court and designated in the order.

In placing a juvenile in nonsecure custody under this section, the court shall first consider whether a relative of the juvenile is willing and able to provide proper care and supervision of the juvenile in a safe home. If the court finds that the relative is willing and able to provide proper care and supervision in a safe home, then the court shall order placement of the juvenile with the relative unless the court finds that placement with the relative would be contrary to the best interests of the juvenile. In placing a juvenile in nonsecure custody under this section, the court shall also consider whether it is in the juvenile's best interest to remain in the juvenile's community of residence. In placing a juvenile in nonsecure custody under this section, the court shall consider the Indian Child Welfare Act, Pub. L. No. 95-608, 25 U.S.C. §§ 1901, et seq., as amended, and the Howard M. Metzenbaum Multiethnic Placement Act of 1994, Pub. L. No. 103-382, 108 Stat. 4056, as amended, as they may apply. Placement of a juvenile with a relative outside of this State must be in accordance with the Interstate Compact on the Placement of Children, Article 38 of this Chapter.

§ 7B-506. Hearing to determine need for continued nonsecure custody.

(a) No juvenile shall be held under a non-secure custody order for more than seven calendar days without a hearing on the merits or a hearing to determine the need for continued custody. A hearing on nonsecure custody conducted under this subsection may be continued for up to 10 business days with the consent of the juvenile's parent, guardian, custodian, or caretaker and, if appointed, the juvenile's guardian ad litem. In addition, the court may require the consent of additional parties or may schedule the hearing on custody despite a party's consent to a continuance. In every case in which an order has been entered by an official exercising authority delegated pursuant to G.S. 7B-502, a hearing to determine the need for continued custody shall be conducted on the day of the next regularly scheduled session of district court in the city or county where the order was entered if such session precedes the expiration of the applicable time period set forth in this subsection: Provided, that if such session does not precede the expiration of the time period, the hearing may be conducted at another regularly scheduled session of district court in the district where the order was entered.

(b) At a hearing to determine the need for continued custody, the court shall receive testimony and shall allow the guardian ad litem, or juvenile, and the juvenile's parent, guardian, custodian, or caretaker an opportunity to introduce evidence, to be heard in the person's own behalf, and to examine witnesses. The State shall bear the burden at every stage of the proceedings to provide clear and convincing evidence that the juvenile's placement in custody is necessary. The court shall not be bound by the usual rules of evidence at such hearings.

(c) The court shall be bound by criteria set forth in G.S. 7B-503 in determining whether continued custody is warranted.

(c1) In determining whether continued custody is warranted, the court shall consider the opinion of the mental health professional who performed an evaluation under G.S. 7B-503(b) before returning the juvenile to the custody of that individual.

(d) If the court determines that the juvenile meets the criteria in G.S. 7B-503 and should continue in custody, the court shall issue an order to that effect. The order shall be in writing with appropriate findings of fact and signed and entered within 30 days of the completion of the hearing. The findings of fact shall include the evidence relied upon in reaching the decision and purposes which continued custody is to achieve.

(e) If the court orders at the hearing required in subsection (a) of this section that the juvenile remain in custody, a subsequent hearing on continued custody shall be held within seven business days of that hearing, excluding Saturdays, Sundays, and legal holidays, and pending a hearing on the merits, hearings thereafter shall be held at intervals of no more than 30 calendar days.

(f) Hearings conducted under subsection (e) of this section may be waived only with the consent of the juvenile's parent, guardian, custodian, or caretaker, and, if appointed, the juvenile's guardian ad litem.

The court may require the consent of additional parties or schedule a hearing despite a party's consent to waiver.

(g) Reserved.

(h) At each hearing to determine the need for continued custody, the court shall:

(1) Inquire as to the identity and location of any missing parent and as to whether paternity is at issue. The court shall include findings as to the efforts undertaken to locate the missing parent and to serve that parent, as well as efforts undertaken to establish paternity when paternity is an issue. The order may provide for specific efforts aimed at determining the identity and location of any missing parent, as well as specific efforts aimed at establishing paternity.

(2) Inquire as to whether a relative of the juvenile is willing and able to provide proper care and supervision of the juvenile in a safe home. If the court finds that the relative is

willing and able to provide proper care and supervision in a safe home, then the court shall order temporary placement of the juvenile with the relative unless the court finds that placement with the relative would be contrary to the best interests of the juvenile. In placing a juvenile in nonsecure custody under this section, the court shall consider the Indian Child Welfare Act, Pub. L. No. 95-608, 25 U.S.C. §§ 1901, et seq., as amended, and the Howard M. Metzenbaum Multiethnic Placement Act of 1994, Pub. L. No. 103-382, 108 Stat. 4056, as amended, as they may apply. Placement of a juvenile with a relative outside of this State must be in accordance with the Interstate Compact on the Placement of Children set forth in Article 38 of this Chapter; and

(3) Inquire as to whether there are other juveniles remaining in the home from which the juvenile was removed and, if there are, inquire as to the specific findings of the investigation conducted under G.S. 7B-302 and any actions taken or services provided by the director for the protection of the other juveniles.

§ 7B-507. Reasonable efforts.

(a) An order placing or continuing the placement of a juvenile in the custody or placement responsibility of a county department of social services, whether an order for continued nonsecure custody, a dispositional order, or a review order:

(1) Shall contain a finding that the juvenile's continuation in or return to the juvenile's own home would be contrary to the juvenile's best interest;

(2) Shall contain findings as to whether a county department of social services has made reasonable efforts to prevent or eliminate the need for placement of the juvenile, unless the court has previously determined under subsection (b) of this section that such efforts are not required or shall cease;

(3) Shall contain findings as to whether a county department of social services should continue to make reasonable efforts to prevent or eliminate the need for placement of the juvenile, unless the court has previously determined or determines under subsection (b) of this section that such efforts are not required or shall cease;

(4) Shall specify that the juvenile's placement and care are the responsibility of the county department of social services and that the agency is to provide or arrange for the foster care or other placement of the juvenile; and

(5) May provide for services or other efforts aimed at returning the juvenile to a safe home or at achieving another permanent plan for the juvenile.

A finding that reasonable efforts have not been made by a county department of social services shall not preclude the entry of an order authorizing the juvenile's placement when the court finds that placement is necessary for the protection of the juvenile. Where efforts to prevent the need for the juvenile's placement were precluded by an immediate threat of harm to the juvenile, the court may find that the placement of the juvenile in the absence of such efforts was reasonable.

(b) In any order placing a juvenile in the custody or placement responsibility of a county department of social services, whether an order for continued nonsecure custody, a dispositional order, or a review order, the court may direct that reasonable efforts to eliminate the need for placement of the juvenile shall not be required or shall cease if the court makes written findings of fact that:

(1) Such efforts clearly would be futile or would be inconsistent with the juvenile's health, safety, and need

for a safe, permanent home within a reasonable period of time;

(2) A court of competent jurisdiction has determined that the parent has subjected the child to aggravated circumstances as defined in G.S. 7B-101;

(3) A court of competent jurisdiction has terminated involuntarily the parental rights of the parent to another child of the parent; or

(4) A court of competent jurisdiction has determined that: the parent has committed murder or voluntary manslaughter of another child of the parent; has aided, abetted, attempted, conspired, or solicited to commit murder or voluntary manslaughter of the child or another child of the parent; or has committed a felony assault resulting in serious bodily injury to the child or another child of the parent.

(c) At any hearing at which the court finds that reasonable efforts to eliminate the need for the juvenile's placement are not required or shall cease, the court shall direct that a permanency planning hearing as required by G.S. 7B-907 be held within 30 calendar days after the date of the hearing and, if practicable, shall set the date and time for the permanency planning hearing.

(d) In determining reasonable efforts to be made with respect to a juvenile and in making such reasonable efforts, the juvenile's health and safety shall be the paramount concern. Reasonable efforts to preserve or reunify families may be made concurrently with efforts to plan for the juvenile's adoption, to place the juvenile with a legal guardian, or to place the juvenile in another permanent arrangement.

§ 7B-508. Telephonic communication authorized.

All communications, notices, orders, authorizations, and requests authorized or required by G.S. 7B-501, 7B-503, and 7B-504 may be made by telephone when other means of communication are impractical. All written orders pursuant to telephonic communication shall

bear the name and the title of the person communicating by telephone, the signature and the title of the official entering the order, and the hour and the date of the authorization.

ARTICLE 6.
Basic Rights.

§ 7B-600. Appointment of guardian.

(a) In any case when no parent appears in a hearing with the juvenile or when the court finds it would be in the best interests of the juvenile, the court may appoint a guardian of the person for the juvenile. The guardian shall operate under the supervision of the court with or without bond and shall file only such reports as the court shall require. The guardian shall have the care, custody, and control of the juvenile or may arrange a suitable placement for the juvenile and may represent the juvenile in legal actions before any court. The guardian may consent to certain actions on the part of the juvenile in place of the parent including (i) marriage, (ii) enlisting in the armed forces, and (iii) enrollment in school. The guardian may also consent to any necessary remedial, psychological, medical, or surgical treatment for the juvenile. The authority of the guardian shall continue until the guardianship is terminated by court order, until the juvenile is emancipated pursuant to Article 35 of Subchapter IV of this Chapter, or until the juvenile reaches the age of majority.

(b) In any case where the court has determined that the appointment of a relative or other suitable person as guardian of the person for a juvenile is in the best interest of the juvenile and has also made findings in accordance with G.S. 7B-907 that guardianship is the permanent plan for the juvenile, the court may not terminate the guardianship or order that the juvenile be reintegrated into a parent's home unless the court finds that the relationship between the guardian and the juvenile is no longer in the juvenile's best interest, that the guardian is unfit, that the guardian has neglected a guardian's duties, or that the guardian is unwilling or unable to continue assuming a guardian's duties. If a party files a motion or petition under G.S. 7B-906 or G.S. 7B-1000, the court may, prior to conducting a review hearing, do one or more of the following:

(1) Order the county department of social services to conduct an investigation and file a written report of the investigation regarding the performance of the guardian of the person of the juvenile and give testimony concerning its investigation.

(2) Utilize the community resources in behavioral sciences and other professions in the investigation and study of the guardian.

(3) Ensure that a guardian ad litem has been appointed for the juvenile in accordance with G.S. 7B-601 and has been notified of the pending motion or petition.

(4) Take any other action necessary in order to make a determination in a particular case.

§ 7B-601. Appointment and duties of guardian ad litem.

(a) When in a petition a juvenile is alleged to be abused or neglected, the court shall appoint a guardian ad litem to represent the juvenile. When a juvenile is alleged to be dependent, the court may appoint a guardian ad litem to represent the juvenile. The juvenile is a party in all actions under this Subchapter. The guardian ad litem and attorney advocate have standing to represent the juvenile in all actions under this Subchapter where they have been appointed. The appointment shall be made pursuant to the program established by Article 12 of this Chapter unless representation is otherwise provided pursuant to G.S. 7B-1202 or G.S. 7B-1203. The appointment shall terminate when the permanent plan has been achieved for the juvenile and approved by the court. The court may reappoint the guardian ad litem pursuant to a showing of good cause upon motion of any party, including the guardian ad litem, or of the court. In every case where a nonattorney is appointed as a guardian ad litem, an attorney shall be appointed in the case in order to assure protection of the juvenile's legal rights throughout the proceeding. The duties of the guardian ad litem program shall be to make an investigation to determine the facts, the needs of the juvenile, and the available resources within the family and community to meet those needs; to facilitate, when appropriate, the settlement of disputed issues; to offer evidence and examine witnesses at adjudication; to explore options with the court at the dispositional hearing; to conduct follow-up investigations to insure that the orders of the court are being properly executed; to report to the court when the needs of the juvenile are not being met; and to protect and promote the best interests of the juvenile until formally relieved of the responsibility by the court.

(b) The court may authorize the guardian ad litem to accompany the juvenile to court in any criminal action wherein the juvenile may be called on to testify in a matter relating to abuse.

(c) The guardian ad litem has the authority to obtain any information or reports, whether or not confidential, that may in the guardian ad litem's opinion be relevant to the case. No privilege other than the attorney–client privilege may be invoked to prevent the guardian ad litem and the court from obtaining such information. The confidentiality of the information or reports shall be respected by the guardian ad litem, and no disclosure of any information or reports shall be made to anyone except by order of the court or unless otherwise provided by law.

§ 7B-602. Parent's right to counsel; guardian ad litem.

(a) In cases where the juvenile petition alleges that a juvenile is abused, neglected, or dependent, the parent has the right to counsel and to appointed counsel in cases of indigency unless that person waives the right.

(b) In addition to the right to appointed counsel set forth above, a guardian ad litem shall be appointed in accordance with the provisions of G.S. 1A-1, Rule 17, to represent a parent in the following cases:

(1) Where it is alleged that the juvenile is a dependent juvenile within the meaning of G.S. 7B-101 in that the parent is incapable as the result of

substance abuse, mental retardation, mental illness, organic brain syndrome, or any other similar cause or condition of providing for the proper care and supervision of the juvenile; or

(2) Where the parent is under the age of 18 years.

§ 7B-603. Payment of court-appointed attorney or guardian ad litem.

(a) An attorney or guardian ad litem appointed pursuant to G.S. 7B-601 shall be paid a reasonable fee fixed by the court or by direct engagement for specialized guardian ad litem services through the Administrative Office of the Courts.

(b) An attorney appointed pursuant to G.S. 7B-602 or pursuant to any other provision of the Juvenile Code for which the Office of Indigent Defense Services is responsible for providing counsel shall be paid a reasonable fee in accordance with rules adopted by the Office of Indigent Defense Services.

(c) The court may require payment of the attorney or guardian ad litem fee from a person other than the juvenile as provided in G.S. 7A-450.1, 7A-450.2, and 7A-450.3. In no event shall the parent or guardian be required to pay the fees for a court-appointed attorney or guardian ad litem in an abuse, neglect, or dependency proceeding unless the juvenile has been adjudicated to be abused, neglected, or dependent, or, in a proceeding to terminate parental rights, unless the parent's rights have been terminated. A person who does not comply with the court's order of payment may be punished for contempt as provided in G.S. 5A-21.

ARTICLE 7.
Discovery.

§ 7B-700. Regulation of discovery; protective orders.

(a) Upon written motion of a party and a finding of good cause, the court may at any time order that discovery be denied, restricted, or deferred.

(b) The court may permit a party seeking relief under subsection (a) of this section to submit supporting affidavits or statements to the court for in camera inspection. If, thereafter, the court enters an order granting relief under subsection (a) of this section, the material submitted in camera must be available to the Court of Appeals in the event of an appeal.

ARTICLE 8.
Hearing Procedures.

§ 7B-800. Amendment of petition.

The court may permit a petition to be amended when the amendment does not change the nature of the conditions upon which the petition is based.

§ 7B-801. Hearing.

(a) At any hearing authorized or required under this Subchapter, the court in its discretion shall determine whether the hearing or any part of the hearing shall be closed to the public. In determining whether to close the hearing or any part of the hearing, the court shall consider the circumstances of the case, including, but not limited to, the following factors:

(1) The nature of the allegations against the juvenile's parent, guardian, custodian or caretaker;

(2) The age and maturity of the juvenile;

(3) The benefit to the juvenile of confidentiality;

(4) The benefit to the juvenile of an open hearing; and

(5) The extent to which the confidentiality afforded the juvenile's record pursuant to G.S. 132-1.4(l) and G.S. 7B-2901 will be compromised by an open hearing.

(b) No hearing or part of a hearing shall be closed by the court if the juvenile requests that it remain open.

(c) The adjudicatory hearing shall be held in the district at such time and place as the chief district court judge shall designate, but no later than 60 days from the filing of the petition unless the judge pursuant to G.S. 7B-803 orders that it be held at a later time.

§ 7B-802. Conduct of hearing.

The adjudicatory hearing shall be a judicial process designed to adjudicate the existence or nonexistence of any of the conditions alleged in a petition. In the adjudicatory hearing, the court shall protect the rights of the juvenile and the juvenile's parent to assure due process of law.

§ 7B-803. Continuances.

The court may, for good cause, continue the hearing for as long as is reasonably required to receive additional evidence, reports, or assessments that the court has requested, or other information needed in the best interests of the juvenile and to allow for a reasonable time for the parties to conduct expeditious discovery. Otherwise, continuances shall be granted only in extraordinary circumstances when necessary for the proper administration of justice or in the best interests of the juvenile.

§ 7B-804. Rules of evidence.

Where the juvenile is alleged to be abused, neglected, or dependent, the rules of evidence in civil cases shall apply.

§ 7B-805. Quantum of proof in adjudicatory hearing.

The allegations in a petition alleging abuse, neglect, or dependency shall be proved by clear and convincing evidence.

§ 7B-806. Record of proceedings.

All adjudicatory and dispositional hearings shall be recorded by stenographic notes or by electronic or mechanical means. Records shall be reduced to a written transcript only when timely notice of appeal has been given. The court may order that other hearings be recorded.

§ 7B-807. Adjudication.

(a) If the court finds that the allegations in the petition have been proven by clear and convincing evidence, the court shall so state. If the court finds that the allegations have not been proven, the court shall dismiss the petition with prejudice, and if the juvenile is in nonsecure custody, the juvenile shall be released to the parent, guardian, custodian, or caretaker.

(b) The adjudicatory order shall be in writing and shall contain appropriate findings of fact and conclusions of law. The order shall be reduced to writing, signed, and entered no later than 30 days following the completion of the hearing.

§ 7B-808. Predisposition investigation and report.

The court shall proceed to the dispositional hearing upon receipt of sufficient social, medical, psychiatric, psychological, and educational information. No predisposition report shall be submitted to or considered by the court prior to the completion of the adjudicatory hearing. The court shall permit the guardian ad litem or juvenile to inspect any predisposition report to be considered by the court in making the disposition unless the court determines that disclosure would seriously harm the juvenile's treatment or would violate a promise of confidentiality. Opportunity to offer evidence in rebuttal shall be afforded the guardian ad litem or juvenile, and the juvenile's parent, guardian, or custodian at the dispositional hearing. The court may order counsel not to disclose parts of the report to the guardian ad litem or juvenile, or the juvenile's parent, guardian, or custodian if the court finds that disclosure would seriously harm the treatment of the juvenile or would violate a promise of confidentiality given to a source of information.

ARTICLE 9.
Dispositions.

§ 7B-900. Purpose.

The purpose of dispositions in juvenile actions is to design an appropriate plan to meet the needs of the juvenile and to achieve the objectives of the State in exercising jurisdiction. If possible, the initial approach should involve working with the juvenile and the juvenile's family in their own home so that the appropriate community resources may be involved in care, supervision, and treatment according to the needs of the juvenile. Thus, the court should arrange for appropriate community-level services to be provided to the juvenile and the juvenile's family in order to strengthen the home situation.

§ 7B-901. Dispositional hearing.

The dispositional hearing may be informal and the court may consider written reports or other evidence concerning the needs of the juvenile. The juvenile and the juvenile's parent, guardian, or custodian shall have an opportunity to present evidence, and they may advise the court concerning the disposition they believe to be in the best interests of the juvenile. The court may exclude the public from the hearing unless the juvenile moves that the hearing be open, which motion shall be granted.

§ 7B-902. Consent judgment in abuse, neglect, or dependency proceeding.

Nothing in this Article precludes the court from entering a consent order or judgment on a petition for abuse, neglect, or dependency when all parties are present, the juvenile is represented by counsel, and all other parties are either represented by counsel or have waived counsel, and sufficient findings of fact are made by the court.

§ 7B-903. Dispositional alternatives for abused, neglected, or dependent juvenile.

(a) The following alternatives for disposition shall be available to any court exercising jurisdiction, and the court may combine any of the applicable alternatives when the court finds the disposition to be in the best interests of the juvenile:

(1) The court may dismiss the case or continue the case in order to allow the parent, guardian, custodian, caretaker or others to take appropriate action.

(2) In the case of any juvenile who needs more adequate care or supervision or who needs placement, the court may:

    a. Require that the juvenile be supervised in the juvenile's own home by the department of social services in the juvenile's county, or by other personnel as may be available to the court, subject to conditions applicable to the parent, guardian, custodian, or caretaker as the court may specify; or

    b. Place the juvenile in the custody of a parent, relative, private agency offering placement services, or some other suitable person; or

    c. Place the juvenile in the custody of the department of social services in the county of the juvenile's residence, or in the case of a juvenile who has legal residence outside the State, in the physical custody of the department of social services in the county where the juvenile is found so that agency may return the juvenile to the responsible authorities in the juvenile's home state. The director may, unless otherwise ordered by the court, arrange for, provide, or consent to, needed routine or emergency medical or surgical care or treatment. In the case where the parent is unknown, unavailable, or unable to act on behalf of the juvenile, the director may, unless otherwise ordered by the court, arrange for, provide, or consent to any psychiatric, psychological, educational, or other remedial evaluations or treatment for the juvenile placed by a court or the court's designee in the custody or physical custody of a county department of social services under the authority of this or any other Chapter of the General Statutes. Prior to exercising this authority, the director shall make reasonable efforts to obtain consent from a parent or guardian of the affected juvenile. If the director cannot obtain such consent, the director shall promptly notify the parent or guardian that care or treatment has been provided and shall give the parent frequent status reports on the circumstances of the juvenile. Upon request of a parent or guardian of the affected juvenile, the results or records of the aforementioned evaluations, findings, or treatment shall be made available to such parent or guardian by the director unless prohibited by G.S. 122C-53(d). If a juvenile is removed from the home and placed in custody or placement responsibility of a county department of social services, the director shall not allow unsupervised visitation with, or return physical custody of the juvenile to, the parent, guardian, custodian, or caretaker without a hearing at which the court finds that the juvenile will receive proper care and supervision in a safe home.

In placing a juvenile in out-of-home care under this section, the court shall first consider whether a relative of the juvenile is willing and able to provide proper care and supervision of the juvenile in a safe home. If the court finds that the relative is willing and able to provide proper care and supervision in a safe home, then the court shall order placement of the juvenile with the relative unless the court finds that the placement is contrary to the best interests of the juvenile. In

placing a juvenile in out-of-home care under this section, the court shall also consider whether it is in the juvenile's best interest to remain in the juvenile's community of residence. Placement of a juvenile with a relative outside of this State must be in accordance with the Interstate Compact on the Placement of Children.

(3) In any case, the court may order that the juvenile be examined by a physician, psychiatrist, psychologist, or other qualified expert as may be needed for the court to determine the needs of the juvenile:

a. Upon completion of the examination, the court shall conduct a hearing to determine whether the juvenile is in need of medical, surgical, psychiatric, psychological, or other treatment and who should pay the cost of the treatment. The county manager, or such person who shall be designated by the chairman of the county commissioners, of the juvenile's residence shall be notified of the hearing, and allowed to be heard. If the court finds the juvenile to be in need of medical, surgical, psychiatric, psychological, or other treatment, the court shall permit the parent or other responsible persons to arrange for treatment. If the parent declines or is unable to make necessary arrangements, the court may order the needed treatment, surgery, or care, and the court may order the parent to pay the cost of the care pursuant to G.S. 7B-904. If the court finds the parent is unable to pay the cost of treatment, the court shall order the county to arrange for treatment of the juvenile and to pay for the cost of the treatment. The county department of social services shall recommend the facility that will provide the juvenile with treatment.

b. If the court believes, or if there is evidence presented to the effect that the juvenile is mentally ill or is developmentally disabled, the court shall refer the juvenile to the area mental health, developmental disabilities, and substance abuse services director for appropriate action. A juvenile shall not be committed directly to a State hospital or mental retardation center; and orders purporting to commit a juvenile directly to a State hospital or mental retardation center except for an examination to determine capacity to proceed shall be void and of no effect. The area mental health, developmental disabilities, and substance abuse director shall be responsible for arranging an interdisciplinary evaluation of the juvenile and mobilizing resources to meet the juvenile's needs. If institutionalization is determined to be the best service for the juvenile, admission shall be with the voluntary consent of the parent or guardian. If the parent, guardian, custodian, or caretaker refuses to consent to a mental hospital or retardation center admission after such institutionalization is recommended by the area mental health, developmental disabilities, and substance abuse director, the signature and consent of the court may be substituted for that purpose.

In all cases in which a regional mental hospital refuses admission to a juvenile referred for admission by a court and an area mental health, developmental disabilities, and substance abuse director or discharges a juvenile previously admitted on court referral prior to completion of treatment, the hospital shall submit to the court a written report setting out the reasons for denial of admission or discharge and setting out the juvenile's diagnosis, indications of mental illness, indications of need for treatment, and a statement as to the location of any facility known to have a treatment program for the juvenile in question.

(b) When the court has found that a juvenile has suffered physical abuse and that the individual responsible for the abuse has a history of violent behavior against people, the court shall consider the opinion of the mental health professional who performed an evaluation under G.S. 7B-503(b) before returning the juvenile to the custody of that individual.

§ 7B-904. Authority over parents of juvenile adjudicated as abused, neglected, or dependent.

(a) If the court orders medical, surgical, psychiatric, psychological, or other treatment pursuant to G.S. 7B-903, the court may order the parent or other responsible parties to pay the cost of the treatment or care ordered.

(b) At the dispositional hearing or a subsequent hearing if the court finds that it is in the best interests of the juvenile for the parent, guardian, custodian, stepparent, adult member of the juvenile's household, or adult relative entrusted with the juvenile's care to be directly involved in the juvenile's treatment, the court may order the parent, guardian, custodian, stepparent, adult member of the juvenile's household, or adult relative entrusted with the juvenile's care to participate in medical, psychiatric, psychological, or other treatment of the juvenile. The cost of the treatment shall be paid pursuant to G.S. 7B-903.

(c) At the dispositional hearing or a subsequent hearing the court may determine whether the best interests of the juvenile require that the parent, guardian, custodian, stepparent, adult member of the juvenile's household, or adult relative entrusted with the juvenile's care undergo psychiatric, psychological, or other treatment or counseling directed toward remediating or remedying behaviors or conditions that led to or contributed to the juvenile's adjudication or to the court's decision to remove custody of the juvenile from the parent, guardian, custodian, stepparent, adult member of the juvenile's household, or adult relative entrusted with the juvenile's care. If the court finds that the best interests of the juvenile require the parent, guardian, custodian, stepparent, adult member of the juvenile's household, or adult relative entrusted with the juvenile's care undergo treatment, it may order that individual to comply with a plan of treatment approved by the court or condition legal custody or physical placement of the juvenile with the parent, guardian, custodian, stepparent, adult member of the juvenile's household, or adult relative entrusted with the juvenile's care upon that individual's compliance with the plan of treatment. The court may order the parent, guardian, custodian, stepparent, adult member of the juvenile's household, or adult relative entrusted with the juvenile's care to pay the cost of treatment ordered pursuant to this subsection. In cases in which the court has conditioned legal custody or physical placement of the juvenile with the parent, guardian, custodian, stepparent, adult member of the juvenile's household, or adult relative entrusted with the juvenile's care upon compliance with a plan of treatment, the court may charge the cost of the treatment to the county of the juvenile's residence if the court finds the parent, guardian, custodian, stepparent, adult member of the juvenile's household, or adult relative entrusted with the juvenile's care is unable to pay the cost of the treatment. In all other cases, if the court finds the parent, guardian, custodian, stepparent, adult member

of the juvenile's household, or adult relative entrusted with the juvenile's care is unable to pay the cost of the treatment ordered pursuant to this subsection, the court may order that individual to receive treatment currently available from the area mental health program that serves the parent's catchment area.

(d) At the dispositional hearing or a subsequent hearing, when legal custody of a juvenile is vested in someone other than the juvenile's parent, if the court finds that the parent is able to do so, the court may order that the parent pay a reasonable sum that will cover, in whole or in part, the support of the juvenile after the order is entered. If the court requires the payment of child support, the amount of the payments shall be determined as provided in G.S. 50-13.4(c). If the court places a juvenile in the custody of a county department of social services and if the court finds that the parent is unable to pay the cost of the support required by the juvenile, the cost shall be paid by the county department of social services in whose custody the juvenile is placed, provided the juvenile is not receiving care in an institution owned or operated by the State or federal government or any subdivision thereof.

(d1) At the dispositional hearing or a subsequent hearing, the court may order the parent, guardian, custodian, or caretaker served with a copy of the summons pursuant to G.S. 7B-407 to do any of the following:

(1) Attend and participate in parental responsibility classes if those classes are available in the judicial district in which the parent, guardian, custodian, or caretaker resides.

(2) Provide, to the extent that person is able to do so, transportation for the juvenile to keep appointments for medical, psychiatric, psychological, or other treatment ordered by the court if the juvenile remains in or is returned to the home.

(3) Take appropriate steps to remedy conditions in the home that led to or contributed to the juvenile's adjudication or to the court's decision to remove custody of the juvenile from the parent, guardian, custodian, or caretaker.

(e) Upon motion of a party or upon the court's own motion, the court may issue an order directing the parent, guardian, custodian, or caretaker served with a copy of the summons pursuant to G.S. 7B-407 to appear and show cause why the parent, guardian, custodian, or caretaker should not be found or held in civil or criminal contempt for willfully failing to comply with an order of the court. Chapter 5A of the General Statutes shall govern contempt proceedings initiated pursuant to this section.

§ 7B-905. Dispositional order.

(a) The dispositional order shall be in writing, signed, and entered no later than 30 days from the completion of the hearing, and shall contain appropriate findings of fact and conclusions of law. The court shall state with particularity, both orally and in the written order of disposition, the precise terms of the disposition including the kind, duration, and the person who is responsible for carrying out the disposition and the person or agency in whom custody is vested.

(b) A dispositional order under which a juvenile is removed from the custody of a parent, guardian, custodian, or caretaker shall direct that the review hearing required by G.S. 7B-906 be held within 90 days from of the date of the dispositional hearing and, if practicable, shall set the date and time for the review hearing.

(c) Any dispositional order shall comply with the requirements of G.S. 7B-507. Any dispositional order under which a juvenile is removed from the custody of a parent, guardian, custodian, or caretaker, or under which the juvenile's placement is continued outside the home shall provide for appropriate visitation as may be in the best interests of the juvenile and consistent with the juvenile's health and safety. If the juvenile is placed in the custody or placement responsibility of a county department of social services, the court may order the director to arrange, facilitate, and supervise a visitation plan expressly approved by the court. If the director subsequently makes a good faith determination that the visitation plan may not be in the best interests of the juvenile or consistent with the juvenile's

health and safety, the director may temporarily suspend all or part of the visitation plan. The director shall not be subjected to any motion to show cause for this suspension, but shall expeditiously file a motion for review.

§ 7B-906. Review of custody order.

(a) In any case where custody is removed from a parent, guardian, custodian, or caretaker the court shall conduct a review hearing within 90 days from the date of the dispositional hearing and shall conduct a review hearing within six months thereafter. The director of social services shall make a timely request to the clerk to calendar each review at a session of court scheduled for the hearing of juvenile matters. The clerk shall give 15 days' notice of the review and its purpose to the parent, the juvenile, if 12 years of age or more, the guardian, any foster parent, relative, or pre-adoptive parent providing care for the child, the custodian or agency with custody, the guardian ad litem, and any other person or agency the court may specify, indicating the court's impending review. Nothing in this subsection shall be construed to make any foster parent, relative, or preadoptive parent a party to the proceeding solely based on receiving notice and an opportunity to be heard.

(b) Notwithstanding other provisions of this Article, the court may waive the holding of review hearings required by subsection (a) of this section, may require written reports to the court by the agency or person holding custody in lieu of review hearings, or order that review hearings be held less often than every six months, if the court finds by clear, cogent, and convincing evidence that:

(1) The juvenile has resided with a relative or has been in the custody of another suitable person for a period of at least one year;

(2) The placement is stable and continuation of the placement is in the juvenile's best interests;

(3) Neither the juvenile's best interests nor the rights of any party require that review hearings be held every six months;

(4) All parties are aware that the matter may be brought before the

court for review at any time by the filing of a motion for review or on the court's own motion; and

(5) The court order has designated the relative or other suitable person as the juvenile's permanent caretaker or guardian of the person.

The court may not waive or refuse to conduct a review hearing if a party files a motion seeking the review. However, if a guardian of the person has been appointed for the juvenile and the court has also made findings in accordance with G.S. 7B-907 that guardianship is the permanent plan for the juvenile, the court shall proceed in accordance with G.S. 7B-600(b).

(c) At every review hearing, the court shall consider information from the parent, the juvenile, the guardian, any foster parent, relative, or preadoptive parent providing care for the child, the custodian or agency with custody, the guardian ad litem, and any other person or agency which will aid in its review.

In each case the court shall consider the following criteria and make written findings regarding those that are relevant:

(1) Services which have been offered to reunite the family, or whether efforts to reunite the family clearly would be futile or inconsistent with the juvenile's safety and need for a safe, permanent home within a reasonable period of time.

(2) Where the juvenile's return home is unlikely, the efforts which have been made to evaluate or plan for other methods of care.

(3) Goals of the foster care placement and the appropriateness of the foster care plan.

(4) A new foster care plan, if continuation of care is sought, that addresses the role the current foster parent will play in the planning for the juvenile.

(5) Reports on the placements the juvenile has had and any services offered to the juvenile and the parent, guardian, custodian, or caretaker.

(6) An appropriate visitation plan.

(7) If the juvenile is 16 or 17 years of age, a report on an independent living assessment of the juvenile and, if appropriate, an independent living plan developed for the juvenile.

(8) When and if termination of parental rights should be considered.

(9) Any other criteria the court deems necessary.

(d) The court, after making findings of fact, may appoint a guardian of the person for the juvenile pursuant to G.S. 7B-600 or may make any disposition authorized by G.S. 7B-903, including the authority to place the juvenile in the custody of either parent or any relative found by the court to be suitable and found by the court to be in the best interests of the juvenile. The court may enter an order continuing the placement under review or providing for a different placement as is deemed to be in the best interests of the juvenile. The order must be reduced to writing, signed, and entered within 30 days of the completion of the hearing. If at any time custody is restored to a parent, guardian, custodian, or caretaker the court shall be relieved of the duty to conduct periodic judicial reviews of the placement.

(e) Reserved.

(f) The provisions of G.S. 7B-507 shall apply to any order entered under this section.

§ 7B-907. Permanency planning hearing.

(a) In any case where custody is removed from a parent, guardian, custodian, or caretaker, the judge shall conduct a review hearing designated as a permanency planning hearing within 12 months after the date of the initial order removing custody, and the hearing may be combined, if appropriate, with a review hearing required by G.S. 7B-906. The purpose of the permanency planning hearing shall be to develop a plan to achieve a safe, permanent home for the juvenile within a reasonable period of time. Subsequent permanency planning hearings shall be held at least every six months thereafter, or earlier as set by the court, to review the progress made in finalizing the permanent plan for the juvenile, or if necessary, to make a new permanent plan for the juvenile. The Director of Social Services shall make a timely request to the clerk to calendar each permanency planning hearing at a session of court scheduled for the hearing of juvenile matters. The clerk shall give 15 days' notice of the hearing and its purpose to the parent, the juvenile if 12 years of age or more, the guardian, any foster parent, relative, or pre-adoptive parent providing care for the child, the custodian or agency with custody, the guardian ad litem, and any other person or agency the court may specify, indicating the court's impending review. Nothing in this pro-vision shall be construed to make any foster parent, relative, or preadoptive parent a party to the proceeding solely based on receiving notice and an opportunity to be heard.

(b) At any permanency planning review, the court shall consider information from the parent, the juvenile, the guardian, any foster parent, relative or preadoptive parent provid-ing care for the child, the custodian or agency with custody, the guardian ad litem, and any other person or agency which will aid it in the court's review. At the conclusion of the hear-ing, if the juvenile is not returned home, the court shall consider the following criteria and make written findings regarding those that are relevant:

(1) Whether it is possible for the juve-nile to be returned home immedi-ately or within the next six months, and if not, why it is not in the juve-nile's best interests to return home;

(2) Where the juvenile's return home is unlikely within six months, whether legal guardianship or cus-tody with a relative or some other suitable person should be estab-lished, and if so, the rights and responsibilities which should remain with the parents;

(3) Where the juvenile's return home is unlikely within six months, whether adoption should be pur-sued and if so, any barriers to the juvenile's adoption;

(4) Where the juvenile's return home is unlikely within six months, whether the juvenile should remain

in the current placement or be placed in another permanent living arrangement and why;

(5) Whether the county department of social services has since the initial permanency plan hearing made reasonable efforts to implement the permanent plan for the juvenile;

(6) Any other criteria the court deems necessary.

(c) At the conclusion of the hearing, the judge shall make specific findings as to the best plan of care to achieve a safe, permanent home for the juvenile within a reasonable period of time. The judge may appoint a guardian of the person for the juvenile pursuant to G.S. 7B-600 or make any disposition authorized by G.S. 7B-903 including the authority to place the child in the custody of either parent or any relative found by the court to be suitable and found by the court to be in the best interest of the juve-nile. If the juvenile is not returned home, the court shall enter an order consistent with its findings that directs the department of social services to make reasonable efforts to place the juvenile in a timely manner in accordance with the permanent plan, to complete whatever steps are necessary to finalize the permanent placement of the juvenile, and to document such steps in the juvenile's case plan. Any order shall be reduced to writing, signed, and entered no later than 30 days following the completion of the hearing. If at any time custody is restored to a parent, or findings are made in accordance with G.S. 7B-906(b), the court shall be relieved of the duty to conduct periodic judicial reviews of the placement.

If the court continues the juvenile's place-ment in the custody or placement responsibil-ity of a county department of social services, the provisions of G.S. 7B-507 shall apply to any order entered under this section.

(d) In the case of a juvenile who is in the custody or placement responsibility of a county department of social services, and has been in placement outside the home for 12 of the most recent 22 months; or a court of competent jurisdiction has determined that the parent has abandoned the child; or has committed murder or voluntary manslaughter of another child of the parent; or has aided, abetted, attempted, conspired, or solicited to commit murder or voluntary manslaughter of the child or another child of the parent, the director of the department of social services shall initiate a proceeding to terminate the parental rights of the parent unless the court finds:

(1) The permanent plan for the juvenile is guardianship or custody with a relative or some other suitable person;

(2) The court makes specific findings why the filing of a petition for termination of parental rights is not in the best interests of the child; or

(3) The department of social services has not provided the juvenile's family with such services as the department deems necessary, when reasonable efforts are still required to enable the juvenile's return to a safe home.

(e) If a proceeding to terminate the parental rights of the juvenile's parents is necessary in order to perfect the permanent plan for the juvenile, the director of the department of social services shall file a petition to terminate parental rights within 60 calendar days from the date of the permanency planning hearing unless the court makes written findings why the petition cannot be filed within 60 days. If the court makes findings to the contrary, the court shall specify the time frame in which any needed petition to terminate parental rights shall be filed.

§ 7B-908. Post termination of parental rights' placement court review.

(a) The purpose of each placement review is to ensure that every reasonable effort is being made to provide for a permanent placement plan for the juvenile who has been placed in the custody of a county director or licensed child-placing agency, which is consistent with the juvenile's best interests. At each review hearing the court may consider information from the department of social services, the licensed child-placing agency, the guardian ad litem, the child, any foster parent, relative, or preadoptive parent providing care for the child, and any other person or agency the court determines is likely to aid in the review.

(b) The court shall conduct a placement review not later than six months from the date of the termination hearing when parental rights have been terminated by a petition brought by any person or agency designated in G.S. 7B-1103(2) through (5) and a county director or licensed child-placing agency has custody of the juvenile. The court shall conduct reviews every six months thereafter until the juvenile is placed for adoption and the adoption petition is filed by the adoptive parents:

(1) No more than 30 days and no less than 15 days prior to each review, the clerk shall give notice of the review to the juvenile if the juvenile is at least 12 years of age, the legal custodian of the juvenile, any foster parent, relative, or preadoptive parent providing care for the juvenile, the guardian ad litem, if any, and any other person or agency the court may specify. Only the juvenile, if the juvenile is at least 12 years of age, the legal custodian of the juvenile, any foster parent, relative, or preadoptive parent providing care for the juvenile, and the guardian ad litem shall attend the review hearings, except as otherwise directed by the court. Nothing in this subdivision shall be construed to make any foster parent, relative, or preadoptive parent a party to the proceeding solely based on receiving notice and an opportunity to be heard.

(2) If a guardian ad litem for the juvenile has not been appointed previously by the court in the termination proceeding, the court, at the initial six-month review hearing, may appoint a guardian ad litem to represent the juvenile. The court may continue the case for such time as is necessary for the guardian ad litem to become familiar with the facts of the case.

(c) The court shall consider at least the following in its review:

(1) The adequacy of the plan developed by the county department of social services or a licensed child-placing agency for a permanent placement relative to the juvenile's best interests and the efforts of the department or agency to implement such plan;

(2) Whether the juvenile has been listed for adoptive placement with the North Carolina Adoption Resource Exchange, the North Carolina Photo Adoption Listing Service (PALS), or any other specialized adoption agency; and

(3) The efforts previously made by the department or agency to find a permanent home for the juvenile.

(d) The court, after making findings of fact, shall affirm the county department's or child-placing agency's plans or require specific additional steps which are necessary to accomplish a permanent placement which is in the best interests of the juvenile.

(e) If the juvenile has been placed for adoption prior to the date scheduled for the review, written notice of said placement shall be given to the clerk to be placed in the court file, and the review hearing shall be cancelled with notice of said cancellation given by the clerk to all persons previously notified.

(f) The process of selection of specific adoptive parents shall be the responsibility of and within the discretion of the county department of social services or licensed child-placing agency. The guardian ad litem may request information from and consult with the county department or child-placing agency concerning the selection process. If the guardian ad litem requests information about the selection process, the county shall provide the information within five days. Any issue of abuse of discretion by the county department or child-placing agency in the selection process must be raised by the guardian ad litem within 10 days following the date the agency notifies the court and the guardian ad litem in writing of the filing of the adoption petition.

§ 7B-909. Review of agency's plan for placement.

(a) The director of social services or the director of the licensed private child-placing agency shall promptly notify the clerk to calendar the case for review of the department's or agency's plan for the juvenile at a session of court scheduled for the hearing of juvenile matters in any case where:

(1) One parent has surrendered a juvenile for adoption under the provisions of Part 7 of Article 3 of Chapter 48 of the General Statutes and the termination of parental rights proceedings have not been instituted against the nonsurrendering parent within six months of the surrender by the other parent, or

(2) Both parents have surrendered a juvenile for adoption under the provisions of Part 7 of Article 3 of Chapter 48 of the General Statutes and that juvenile has not been placed for adoption within six months from the date of the more recent parental surrender.

(b) In any case where an adoption is dismissed or withdrawn and the juvenile returns to foster care with a department of social services or a licensed private child-placing agency, then the department of social services or licensed child-placing agency shall notify the clerk, within 30 days from the date the juvenile returns to care, to calendar the case for review of the agency's plan for the juvenile at a session of court scheduled for the hearing of juvenile matters.

(c) Notification of the court required under subsection (a) or (b) of this section shall be by a petition for review. The petition shall set forth the circumstances necessitating the review under subsection (a) or (b) of this section. The review shall be conducted within 30 days following the filing of the petition for review unless the court shall otherwise direct. The court shall conduct reviews every six months until the juvenile is placed for adoption and the adoption petition is filed by the adoptive parents. The initial review and all subsequent reviews shall be conducted pursuant to G.S. 7B-908.

§ 7B-910. Review of voluntary foster care placements.

(a) The court shall review the placement of any juvenile in foster care made pursuant to a voluntary agreement between the juvenile's parents or guardian and a county department of social services and shall make findings from evidence presented at a review hearing with regard to:

(1) The voluntariness of the placement;
(2) The appropriateness of the placement;
(3) Whether the placement is in the best interests of the juvenile; and
(4) The services that have been or should be provided to the parents, guardian, foster parents, and juvenile, as the case may be, either (i) to improve the placement or (ii) to eliminate the need for the placement.

(b) The court may approve the continued placement of the juvenile in foster care on a voluntary agreement basis, disapprove the continuation of the voluntary placement, or direct the department of social services to petition the court for legal custody if the placement is to continue.

(c) An initial review hearing shall be held not more than 90 days after the juvenile's placement and shall be calendared by the clerk for hearing within such period upon timely request by the director of social services. An additional review hearing shall be held 90 days thereafter and any review hearings at such times as the court shall deem appropriate and shall direct, either upon its own motion or upon written request of the parents, guardian, foster parents, or director of social services. A juvenile placed under a voluntary agreement between the juvenile's parent or guardian and the county department of social services shall not remain in placement more than six months without the filing of a petition alleging abuse, neglect, or dependency.

(d) The clerk shall give at least 15 days' advance written notice of the initial and subsequent review hearings to the parents or guardian of the juvenile, to the juvenile if 12 or more years of age, to the director of social

services, and to any other persons whom the court may specify.

ARTICLE 10.
Modification and Enforcement of Dispositional Orders; Appeals.

§ 7B-1000. Authority to modify or vacate.

(a) Upon motion in the cause or petition, and after notice, the court may conduct a review hearing to determine whether the order of the court is in the best interests of the juvenile, and the court may modify or vacate the order in light of changes in circumstances or the needs of the juvenile. Notwithstanding the provision of this subsection, if a guardian of the person has been appointed for the juvenile and the court has also made findings in accordance with G.S. 7B-907 that guardianship is the permanent plan for the juvenile, the court shall proceed in accordance with G.S. 7B-600(b).

(b) In any case where the court finds the juvenile to be abused, neglected, or dependent, the jurisdiction of the court to modify any order or disposition made in the case shall continue during the minority of the juvenile, until terminated by order of the court, or until the juvenile is otherwise emancipated.

§ 7B-1001. Right to appeal.

Upon motion of a proper party as defined in G.S. 7B-1002, review of any final order of the court in a juvenile matter under this Article shall be before the Court of Appeals. Notice of appeal shall be given in writing within 10 days after entry of the order. However, if no disposition is made within 60 days after entry of the order, written notice of appeal may be given within 70 days after such entry. A final order shall include:

(1) Any order finding absence of jurisdiction;
(2) Any order which in effect determines the action and prevents a judgment from which appeal might be taken;
(3) Any order of disposition after an adjudication that a juvenile is abused, neglected, or dependent; or

(4) Any order modifying custodial rights.

§ 7B-1002. Proper parties for appeal.

An appeal may be taken by the guardian ad litem or juvenile, the juvenile's parent, guardian, or custodian, the State or county agency.

§ 7B-1003. Disposition pending appeal.

Pending disposition of an appeal, the return of the juvenile to the custody of the parent or guardian of the juvenile, with or without conditions, may issue unless the court orders otherwise. When the court has found that a juvenile has suffered physical abuse and that the individual responsible for the abuse has a history of violent behavior, the court shall consider the opinion of the mental health professional who performed the evaluation under G.S. 7B-503(b) before returning the juvenile to the custody of that individual. For compelling reasons which must be stated in writing, the court may enter a temporary order affecting the custody or placement of the juvenile as the court finds to be in the best interests of the juvenile or the State. The provisions of subsections (b), (c), and (d) of G.S. 7B-905 shall apply to any order entered under this section which provides for the placement or continued placement of a juvenile in foster care.

§ 7B-1004. Disposition after appeal.

Upon the affirmation of the order of adjudication or disposition of the court by the Court of Appeals or by the Supreme Court in the event of an appeal, the court shall have authority to modify or alter the original order of adjudication or disposition as the court finds to be in the best interests of the juvenile to reflect any adjustment made by the juvenile or change in circumstances during the period of time the appeal was pending. If the modifying order is entered ex parte, the court shall give notice to interested parties to show cause within 10 days thereafter as to why the modifying order should be vacated or altered.

[Articles 11 and 12, which are not included here, deal with termination of parental rights and the guardian ad litem program, respectively.]

ARTICLE 13.
Prevention of Abuse and Neglect.

§ 7B-1300. Purpose.

It is the expressed intent of this Article to make the prevention of abuse and neglect, as defined in G.S. 7B-101, a priority of this State and to establish the Children's Trust Fund as a means to that end.

§ 7B-1301. Program on Prevention of Abuse and Neglect.

(a) The State Board of Education, through the Department of Public Instruction, shall implement the Program on Prevention of Abuse and Neglect. The Department of Public Instruction, subject to the approval of the State Board of Education, shall provide the staff and support services for implementing this program.

(b) In order to carry out the purposes of this Article:

(1) The Department of Public Instruction shall review applications and make recommendations to the State Board of Education concerning the awarding of contracts under this Article.

(2) The State Board of Education shall contract with public or private nonprofit organizations, agencies, schools, or with qualified individuals to operate community-based educational and service programs designed to prevent the occurrence of abuse and neglect. Every contract entered into by the State Board of Education shall contain provisions that at least twenty-five percent (25%) of the total funding required for a program be provided by the administering organization in the form of in-kind or other services and that a mechanism for

evaluation of services provided under the contract be included in the services to be performed. In addition, every proposal to the Department of Public Instruction for funding under this Article shall include assurances that the proposal has been forwarded to the local department of social services for comment so that the Department of Public Instruction may consider coordination and duplication of effort on the local level as criteria in making recommendations to the State Board of Education.

(3) The State Board of Education, with the assistance of the Department of Public Instruction, shall develop appropriate guidelines and criteria for awarding contracts under this Article. These criteria shall include, but are not limited to: documentation of need within the proposed geographical impact area; diversity of geographical areas of programs funded under this Article; demonstrated effectiveness of the proposed strategy or program for preventing abuse and neglect; reasonableness of implementation plan for achieving stated objectives; utilization of community resources including volunteers; provision for an evaluation component that will provide outcome data; plan for dissemination of the program for implementation in other communities; and potential for future funding from private sources.

(4) The State Board of Education, with the assistance of the Department of Public Instruction, shall develop guidelines for regular monitoring of contracts awarded under this Article in order to maximize the investments in prevention programs by the Children's Trust Fund and to establish appropriate accountability measures for administration of contracts.

(5) The State Board of Education shall develop a State plan for the prevention of abuse and neglect for submission to the Governor, the President of the Senate, and the Speaker of the House of Representatives.

(c) To assist in implementing this Article, the State Board of Education may accept contributions, grants, or gifts in cash or otherwise from persons, associations, or corporations. All monies received by the State Board of Education from contributions, grants, or gifts and not through appropriation by the General Assembly shall be deposited in the Children's Trust Fund. Disbursements of the funds shall be on the authorization of the State Board of Education or that Board's duly authorized representative. In order to maintain an effective expenditure and revenue control, the funds are subject in all respects to State law and regulations, but no appropriation is required to permit expenditure of the funds.

(d) Programs contracted for under this Article are intended to prevent abuse and neglect of juveniles. Abuse and neglect prevention programs are defined to be those programs and services which impact on juveniles and families before any substantiated incident of abuse or neglect has occurred. These programs may include, but are not limited to:

(1) Community-based educational programs on prenatal care, perinatal bonding, child development, basic child care, care of children with special needs, and coping with family stress; and

(2) Community-based programs relating to crisis care, aid to parents, and support groups for parents and their children experiencing stress within the family unit.

(e) No more than twenty percent (20%) of each year's total awards may be utilized for funding State-level programs to coordinate community-based programs.

§ 7B-1302. Children's Trust Fund.

There is established a fund to be known as the "Children's Trust Fund," in the Department of State Treasurer, which shall be funded by a portion of the marriage license fee under G.S. 161-11.1 and a portion of the special license plate fee under G.S. 20-81.12. The money in the Fund shall be used by the State Board of Education to fund abuse and neglect prevention programs so authorized by this Article.

ARTICLE 14.
North Carolina Child Fatality Prevention System.

§ 7B-1400. Declaration of public policy.

The General Assembly finds that it is the public policy of this State to prevent the abuse, neglect, and death of juveniles. The General Assembly further finds that the prevention of the abuse, neglect, and death of juveniles is a community responsibility; that professionals from disparate disciplines have responsibilities for children or juveniles and have expertise that can promote their safety and well-being; and that multidisciplinary reviews of the abuse, neglect, and death of juveniles can lead to a greater understanding of the causes and methods of preventing these deaths. It is, therefore, the intent of the General Assembly, through this Article, to establish a statewide multidisciplinary, multi-agency child fatality prevention system consisting of the State Team established in G.S. 7B-1404 and the Local Teams established in G.S. 7B-1406. The purpose of the system is to assess the records of selected cases in which children are being served by child protective services and the records of all deaths of children in North Carolina from birth to age 18 in order to (i) develop a communitywide approach to the problem of child abuse and neglect, (ii) understand the causes of childhood deaths, (iii) identify any gaps or deficiencies that may exist in the delivery of services to children and their families by public agencies that are designed to prevent future child abuse, neglect, or death, and (iv) make and implement recommendations for changes to laws, rules, and policies that will support

the safe and healthy development of our children and prevent future child abuse, neglect, and death.

§ 7B-1401. Definitions.

The following definitions apply in this Article:

(1) Additional Child Fatality.—Any death of a child that did not result from suspected abuse or neglect and about which no report of abuse or neglect had been made to the county department of social services within the previous 12 months.

(2) Local Team.—A Community Child Protection Team or a Child Fatality Prevention Team.

(3) State Team.—The North Carolina Child Fatality Prevention Team.

(4) Task Force.—The North Carolina Child Fatality Task Force.

(5) Team Coordinator.—The Child Fatality Prevention Team Coordinator.

§ 7B-1402. Task Force—creation; membership; vacancies.

(a) There is created the North Carolina Child Fatality Task Force within the Department of Health and Human Services for budgetary purposes only.

(b) The Task Force shall be composed of 35 members, 11 of whom shall be ex officio members, four of whom shall be appointed by the Governor, 10 of whom shall be appointed by the Speaker of the House of Representatives, and 10 of whom shall be appointed by the President Pro Tempore of the Senate. The ex officio members other than the Chief Medical Examiner shall be nonvoting members and may designate representatives from their particular departments, divisions, or offices to represent them on the Task Force. The members shall be as follows:

(1) The Chief Medical Examiner;

(2) The Attorney General;

(3) The Director of the Division of Social Services;

(4) The Director of the State Bureau of Investigation;

(5) The Director of the Division of Maternal and Child Health of the Department of Health and Human Services;

(6) The Director of the Governor's Youth Advocacy and Involvement Office;

(7) The Superintendent of Public Instruction;

(8) The Chairman of the State Board of Education;

(9) The Director of the Division of Mental Health, Developmental Disabilities, and Substance Abuse Services;

(10) The Secretary of the Department of Health and Human Services;

(11) The Director of the Administrative Office of the Courts;

(12) A director of a county department of social services, appointed by the Governor upon recommendation of the President of the North Carolina Association of County Directors of Social Services;

(13) A representative from a Sudden Infant Death Syndrome counseling and education program, appointed by the Governor upon recommendation of the Director of the Division of Maternal and Child Health of the Department of Health and Human Services;

(14) A representative from the North Carolina Child Advocacy Institute, appointed by the Governor upon recommendation of the President of the Institute;

(15) A director of a local department of health, appointed by the Governor upon the recommendation of the President of the North Carolina Association of Local Health Directors;

(16) A representative from a private group, other than the North Carolina Child Advocacy Institute, that advocates for children,

appointed by the Speaker of the House of Representatives upon recommendation of private child advocacy organizations;

(17) A pediatrician, licensed to practice medicine in North Carolina, appointed by the Speaker of the House of Representatives upon recommendation of the North Carolina Pediatric Society;

(18) A representative from the North Carolina League of Municipalities, appointed by the Speaker of the House of Representatives upon recommendation of the League;

(19) Two public members, appointed by the Speaker of the House of Representatives;

(20) A county or municipal law enforcement officer, appointed by the President Pro Tempore of the Senate upon recommendation of organizations that represent local law enforcement officers;

(21) A district attorney, appointed by the President Pro Tempore of the Senate upon recommendation of the President of the North Carolina Conference of District Attorneys;

(22) A representative from the North Carolina Association of County Commissioners, appointed by the President Pro Tempore of the Senate upon recommendation of the Association;

(23) Two public members, appointed by the President Pro Tempore of the Senate; and

(24) Five members of the Senate, appointed by the President Pro Tempore of the Senate, and five members of the House of Representatives, appointed by the Speaker of the House of Representatives.

(c) All members of the Task Force are voting members. Vacancies in the appointed membership shall be filled by the appointing officer who made the initial appointment. Terms shall be two years. The members shall elect a chair who shall preside for the duration of the chair's term as member. In the event a vacancy occurs in the chair before the expiration of the chair's term, the members shall elect an acting chair to serve for the remainder of the unexpired term.

§ 7B-1403. Task Force—duties.

The Task Force shall:
(1) Undertake a statistical study of the incidences and causes of child deaths in this State and establish a profile of child deaths. The study shall include (i) an analysis of all community and private and public agency involvement with the decedents and their families prior to death, and (ii) an analysis of child deaths by age, cause, and geographic distribution;
(2) Develop a system for multi-disciplinary review of child deaths. In developing such a system, the Task Force shall study the operation of existing Local Teams. The Task Force shall also consider the feasibility and desirability of local or regional review teams and, should it determine such teams to be feasible and desirable, develop guidelines for the operation of the teams. The Task Force shall also examine the laws, rules, and policies relating to confidentiality of and access to information that affect those agencies with responsibilities for children, including State and local health, mental health, social services, education, and law enforcement agencies, to determine whether those laws, rules, and policies inappropriately impede the exchange of information necessary to protect children from preventable deaths, and, if so, recommend changes to them;
(3) Receive and consider reports from the State Team; and

(4) Perform any other studies, evaluations, or determinations the Task Force considers necessary to carry out its mandate.

§ 7B-1404. State Team—creation; membership; vacancies.

(a) There is created the North Carolina Child Fatality Prevention Team within the Department of Health and Human Services for budgetary purposes only.
(b) The State Team shall be composed of the following 11 members of whom nine members are ex officio and two are appointed:
(1) The Chief Medical Examiner, who shall chair the State Team;
(2) The Attorney General;
(3) The Director of the Division of Social Services, Department of Health and Human Services;
(4) The Director of the State Bureau of Investigation;
(5) The Director of the Division of Maternal and Child Health of the Department of Health and Human Services;
(6) The Superintendent of Public Instruction;
(7) The Director of the Division of Mental Health, Developmental Disabilities, and Substance Abuse Services, Department of Health and Human Services;
(8) The Director of the Administrative Office of the Courts;
(9) The pediatrician appointed pursuant to G.S. 7B-1402(b) to the Task Force;
(10) A public member, appointed by the Governor; and
(11) The Team Coordinator.

The ex officio members other than the Chief Medical Examiner may designate a representative from their departments, divisions, or offices to represent them on the State Team.
(c) All members of the State Team are voting members. Vacancies in the appointed membership shall be filled by the appointing officer who made the initial appointment.

§ 7B-1405. State Team—duties.

The State Team shall:

(1) Review current deaths of children when those deaths are attributed to child abuse or neglect or when the decedent was reported as an abused or neglected juvenile pursuant to G.S. 7B-301 at any time before death;

(2) Report to the Task Force during the existence of the Task Force, in the format and at the time required by the Task Force, on the State Team's activities and its recommendations for changes to any law, rule, and policy that would promote the safety and well-being of children;

(3) Upon request of a Local Team, provide technical assistance to the Team;

(4) Periodically assess the operations of the multidisciplinary child fatality prevention system and make recommendations for changes as needed;

(5) Work with the Team Coordinator to develop guidelines for selecting child deaths to receive detailed, multidisciplinary death reviews by Local Teams that review cases of additional child fatalities; and

(6) Receive reports of findings and recommendations from Local Teams that review cases of additional child fatalities and work with the Team Coordinator to implement recommendations.

§ 7B-1406. Community Child Protection Teams; Child Fatality Prevention Teams; creation and duties.

(a) Community Child Protection Teams are established in every county of the State. Each Community Child Protection Team shall:

(1) Review, in accordance with the procedures established by the director of the county department of social services under G.S. 7B-1409:

a. Selected active cases in which children are being served by child protective services; and

b. Cases in which a child died as a result of suspected abuse or neglect, and

1. A report of abuse or neglect has been made about the child or the child's family to the county department of social services within the previous 12 months, or

2. The child or the child's family was a recipient of child protective services within the previous 12 months.

(2) Submit annually to the board of county commissioners recommendations, if any, and advocate for system improvements and needed resources where gaps and deficiencies may exist.

In addition, each Community Child Protection Team may review the records of all additional child fatalities and report findings in connection with these reviews to the Team Coordinator.

(b) Any Community Child Protection Team that determines it will not review additional child fatalities shall notify the Team Coordinator. In accordance with the plan established under G.S. 7B-1408(1), a separate Child Fatality Prevention Team shall be established in that county to conduct these reviews. Each Child Fatality Prevention Team shall:

(1) Review the records of all cases of additional child fatalities.

(2) Submit annually to the board of county commissioners recommendations, if any, and advocate for system improvements and needed resources where gaps and deficiencies may exist.

(3) Report findings in connection with these reviews to the Team Coordinator.

(c) All reports to the Team Coordinator under this section shall include:

(1) A listing of the system problems identified through the review

process and recommendations for preventive actions;

(2) Any changes that resulted from the recommendations made by the Local Team;

(3) Information about each death reviewed; and

(4) Any additional information requested by the Team Coordinator.

§ 7B-1407. Local Teams; composition.

(a) Each Local Team shall consist of representatives of public and nonpublic agencies in the community that provide services to children and their families and other individuals who represent the community. No single team shall encompass a geographic or governmental area larger than one county.

(b) Each Local Team shall consist of the following persons:

(1) The director of the county department of social services and a member of the director's staff;

(2) A local law enforcement officer, appointed by the board of county commissioners;

(3) An attorney from the district attorney's office, appointed by the district attorney;

(4) The executive director of the local community action agency, as defined by the Department of Health and Human Services, or the executive director's designee;

(5) The superintendent of each local school administrative unit located in the county, or the superintendent's designee;

(6) A member of the county board of social services, appointed by the chair of that board;

(7) A local mental health professional, appointed by the director of the area authority established under Chapter 122C of the General Statutes;

(8) The local guardian ad litem coordinator, or the coordinator's designee;

(9) The director of the local department of public health; and

(10) A local health care provider, appointed by the local board of health.

(c) In addition, a Local Team that reviews the records of additional child fatalities shall include the following five additional members:

(1) An emergency medical services provider or firefighter, appointed by the board of county commissioners;

(2) A district court judge, appointed by the chief district court judge in that district;

(3) A county medical examiner, appointed by the Chief Medical Examiner;

(4) A representative of a local child care facility or Head Start program, appointed by the director of the county department of social services; and

(5) A parent of a child who died before reaching the child's eighteenth birthday, to be appointed by the board of county commissioners.

(d) The Team Coordinator shall serve as an ex officio member of each Local Team that reviews the records of additional child fatalities. The board of county commissioners may appoint a maximum of five additional members to represent county agencies or the community at large to serve on any Local Team. Vacancies on a Local Team shall be filled by the original appointing authority.

(e) Each Local Team shall elect a member to serve as chair at the Team's pleasure.

(f) Each Local Team shall meet at least four times each year.

(g) The director of the local department of social services shall call the first meeting of the Community Child Protection Team. The director of the local department of health, upon consultation with the Team Coordinator, shall call the first meeting of the Child Fatality Prevention Team. Thereafter, the chair of each Local Team shall schedule the time and place of meetings, in consultation with these directors, and shall prepare the agenda. The chair shall schedule Team meetings no less often than once per quarter and often enough to allow adequate review of the cases selected for review. Within three months of election, the chair shall participate in the appropriate training developed under this Article.

§ 7B-1408. Child Fatality Prevention Team Coordinator; duties.

The Child Fatality Prevention Team Coordinator shall serve as liaison between the State Team and the Local Teams that review records of additional child fatalities and shall provide technical assistance to these Local Teams. The Team Coordinator shall:

(1) Develop a plan to establish Local Teams that review the records of additional child fatalities in each county.

(2) Develop model operating procedures for these Local Teams that address when public meetings should be held, what items should be addressed in public meetings, what information may be released in written reports, and any other information the Team Coordinator considers necessary.

(3) Provide structured training for these Local Teams at the time of their establishment, and continuing technical assistance thereafter.

(4) Provide statistical information on all child deaths occurring in each county to the appropriate Local Team, and assure that all child deaths in a county are assessed through the multidisciplinary system.

(5) Monitor the work of these Local Teams.

(6) Receive reports of findings, and other reports that the Team Coordinator may require, from these Local Teams.

(7) Report the aggregated findings of these Local Teams to each Local Team that reviews the records of additional child fatalities and to the State Team.

(8) Evaluate the impact of local efforts to identify problems and make changes.

§ 7B-1409. Community Child Protection Teams; duties of the director of the county department of social services.

In addition to any other duties as a member of the Community Child Protection Team, and in connection with the reviews under G.S. 7B-1406(a)(1), the director of the county department of social services shall:

(1) Assure the development of written operating procedures in connection with these reviews, including frequency of meetings, confidentiality policies, training of members, and duties and responsibilities of members;

(2) Assure that the Team defines the categories of cases that are subject to its review;

(3) Determine and initiate the cases for review;

(4) Bring for review any case requested by a Team member;

(5) Provide staff support for these reviews;

(6) Maintain records, including minutes of all official meetings, lists of participants for each meeting of the Team, and signed confidentiality statements required under G.S. 7B-1413, in compliance with applicable rules and law; and

(7) Report quarterly to the county board of social services, or as required by the board, on the activities of the Team.

§ 7B-1410. Local Teams; duties of the director of the local department of health.

In addition to any other duties as a member of the Local Team and in connection with reviews of additional child fatalities, the director of the local department of health shall:

(1) Distribute copies of the written procedures developed by the Team

Coordinator under G.S. 7B-1408 to the administrators of all agencies represented on the Local Team and to all members of the Local Team;

(2) Maintain records, including minutes of all official meetings, lists of participants for each meeting of the Local Team, and signed confidentiality statements required under G.S. 7B-1413, in compliance with applicable rules and law;

(3) Provide staff support for these reviews; and

(4) Report quarterly to the local board of health, or as required by the board, on the activities of the Local Team.

§ 7B-1411. Community Child Protection Teams; responsibility for training of team members.

The Division of Social Services, Department of Health and Human Services, shall develop and make available, on an ongoing basis, for the members of Local Teams that review active cases in which children are being served by child protective services, training materials that address the role and function of the Local Team, confidentiality requirements, an overview of child protective services law and policy, and Team record keeping.

§ 7B-1412. Task Force—reports.

The Task Force shall report annually to the Governor and General Assembly, within the first week of the convening or reconvening of the General Assembly. The report shall contain at least a summary of the conclusions and recommendations for each of the Task Force's duties, as well as any other recommendations for changes to any law, rule, or policy that it has determined will promote the safety and well-being of children. Any recommendations of changes to law, rule, or policy shall be accompanied by specific legislative or policy proposals and detailed fiscal notes setting forth the costs to the State.

§ 7B-1413. Access to records.

(a) The State Team, the Local Teams, and the Task Force during its existence, shall have access to all medical records, hospital records, and records maintained by this State, any county, or any local agency as necessary to carry out the purposes of this Article, including police investigations data, medical examiner investigative data, health records, mental health records, and social services records. The State Team, the Task Force, and the Local Teams shall not, as part of the reviews authorized under this Article, contact, question, or interview the child, the parent of the child, or any other family member of the child whose record is being reviewed. Any member of a Local Team may share, only in an official meeting of that Local Team, any information available to that member that the Local Team needs to carry out its duties.

(b) Meetings of the State Team and the Local Teams are not subject to the provisions of Article 33C of Chapter 143 of the General Statutes. However, the Local Teams may hold periodic public meetings to discuss, in a general manner not revealing confidential information about children and families, the findings of their reviews and their recommendations for preventive actions. Minutes of all public meetings, excluding those of executive sessions, shall be kept in compliance with Article 33C of Chapter 143 of the General Statutes. Any minutes or any other information generated during any closed session shall be sealed from public inspection.

(c) All otherwise confidential information and records acquired by the State Team, the Local Teams, and the Task Force during its existence, in the exercise of their duties are confidential; are not subject to discovery or introduction into evidence in any proceedings; and may only be disclosed as necessary to carry out the purposes of the State Team, the Local Teams, and the Task Force. In addition, all otherwise confidential information and records created by a Local Team in the exercise of its duties are confidential; are not subject to discovery or introduction into evidence in any proceedings; and may only be disclosed as necessary to carry out the purposes of the Local

Team. No member of the State Team, a Local Team, nor any person who attends a meeting of the State Team or a Local Team, may testify in any proceeding about what transpired at the meeting, about information presented at the meeting, or about opinions formed by the person as a result of the meetings. This subsection shall not, however, prohibit a person from testifying in a civil or criminal action about matters within that person's independent knowledge.

(d) Each member of a Local Team and invited participant shall sign a statement indicating an understanding of and adherence to confidentiality requirements, including the possible civil or criminal consequences of any breach of confidentiality.

(e) Cases receiving child protective services at the time of review by a Local Team shall have an entry in the child's protective services record to indicate that the case was received by that Team. Additional entry into the record shall be at the discretion of the director of the county department of social services.

(f) The Social Services Commission shall adopt rules to implement this section in connection with reviews conducted by Community Child Protection Teams. The Health Services Commission shall adopt rules to implement this section in connection with Local Teams that review additional child fatalities. In particular, these rules shall allow information generated by an executive session of a Local Team to be accessible for administrative or research purposes only.

§ 7B-1414. Administration; funding.

(a) To the extent of funds available, the chairs of the Task Force and State Team may hire staff or consultants to assist the Task Force and the State Team in completing their duties.

(b) Members, staff, and consultants of the Task Force or State Team shall receive travel and subsistence expenses in accordance with the provisions of G.S. 138-5 or G.S. 138-6, as the case may be, paid from funds appropriated to implement this Article and within the limits of those funds.

(c) With the approval of the Legislative Services Commission, legislative staff and space in the Legislative Building and the

Legislative Office Building may be made available to the Task Force.

Subchapter III. Juvenile Records.

ARTICLE 29.
Records and Social Reports of Cases of Abuse, Neglect, and Dependency.

§ 7B-2900. Definitions.

The definitions of G.S. 7B-101 and G.S. 7B-1501 apply to this Subchapter.

§ 7B-2901. Confidentiality of records.

(a) The clerk shall maintain a complete record of all juvenile cases filed in the clerk's office alleging abuse, neglect, or dependency. The records shall be withheld from public inspection and, except as provided in this subsection, may be examined only by order of the court. The record shall include the summons, petition, custody order, court order, written motions, the electronic or mechanical recording of the hearing, and other papers filed in the proceeding. The recording of the hearing shall be reduced to a written transcript only when notice of appeal has been timely given. After the time for appeal has expired with no appeal having been filed, the recording of the hearing may be erased or destroyed upon the written order of the court.

The following persons may examine the juvenile's record maintained pursuant to this subsection and obtain copies of written parts of the record without an order of the court:

(1) The person named in the petition as the juvenile;
(2) The guardian ad litem;
(3) The county department of social services; and
(4) The juvenile's parent, guardian, or custodian, or the attorney for the juvenile or the juvenile's parent, guardian, or custodian.

(b) The Director of the Department of Social Services shall maintain a record of the cases of juveniles under protective custody by the Department or under placement by the court, which shall include family background information; reports of social, medical, psychiatric, or psychological information concerning a juvenile or the juvenile's family; interviews with the juvenile's family; or other information which the court finds should be protected from public inspection in the best interests of the juvenile. The records maintained pursuant to this subsection may be examined only by order of the court except that the guardian ad litem, or juvenile, shall have the right to examine them.

(c) In the case of a child victim, the court may order the sharing of information among such public agencies as the court deems necessary to reduce the trauma to the victim.

(d) The court's entire record of a proceeding involving consent for an abortion on an unemancipated minor under Article 1A, Part 2 of Chapter 90 of the General Statutes is not a matter of public record, shall be maintained separately from any juvenile record, shall be withheld from public inspection, and may be examined only by order of the court, by the unemancipated minor, or by the unemancipated minor's attorney or guardian ad litem.

§ 7B-2902. Disclosure in child fatality or near fatality cases.

(a) The following definitions apply in this section:

(1) Child fatality.—The death of a child from suspected abuse, neglect, or maltreatment.

(2) Findings and information.—A written summary, as allowed by subsections (c) through (f) of this section, of actions taken or services rendered by a public agency following receipt of information that a child might be in need of protection. The written summary shall include any of the following information the agency is able to provide:

    a. The dates, outcomes, and results of any actions taken or services rendered.

    b. The results of any review by the State Child Fatality Prevention Team, a local child fatality prevention team, a local community child protection team, the Child Fatality Task Force, or any public agency.

    c. Confirmation of the receipt of all reports, accepted or not accepted by the county department of social services, for investigation of suspected child abuse, neglect, or maltreatment, including confirmation that investigations were conducted, the results of the investigations, a description of the conduct of the most recent investigation and the services rendered, and a statement of basis for the department's decision.

(3) Near fatality.—A case in which a physician determines that a child is in serious or critical condition as the result of sickness or injury caused by suspected abuse, neglect, or maltreatment.

(4) Public agency.—Any agency of State government or its subdivisions as defined in G.S. 132-1(a).

(b) Notwithstanding any other provision of law and subject to the provisions of subsections (c) through (f) of this section, a public agency shall disclose to the public, upon request, the findings and information related to a child fatality or near fatality if:

(1) A person is criminally charged with having caused the child fatality or near fatality; or

(2) The district attorney has certified that a person would be charged with having caused the child fatality or near fatality but for that person's prior death.

(c) Nothing herein shall be deemed to authorize access to the confidential records in the custody of a public agency, or the disclosure to the public of the substance or content of any psychiatric, psychological, or therapeutic evaluations or like materials or information pertaining to the child or the child's family unless directly related to the cause of the child fatality or near fatality, or the disclosure of information that would reveal the identities of persons who provided information related to the suspected abuse, neglect, or maltreatment of the child.

(d) Within five working days from the receipt of a request for findings and information related to a child fatality or near fatality, a public agency shall consult with the appropriate district attorney and provide the findings and information unless the agency has a reasonable belief that release of the information:

(1) Is not authorized by subsections (a) and (b) of this section;

(2) Is likely to cause mental or physical harm or danger to a minor child residing in the deceased or injured child's household;

(3) Is likely to jeopardize the State's ability to prosecute the defendant;

(4) Is likely to jeopardize the defendant's right to a fair trial;

(5) Is likely to undermine an ongoing or future criminal investigation; or

(6) Is not authorized by federal law and regulations.

(e) Any person whose request is denied may apply to the appropriate superior court for an order compelling disclosure of the findings and information of the public agency. The application shall set forth, with reasonable particularity, factors supporting the application. The superior court shall have jurisdiction to issue such orders. Actions brought pursuant to this section shall be set down for immediate hearing, and subsequent proceedings in such actions shall be accorded priority by the appellate courts. After the court has reviewed the specific findings and information, in camera, the court shall issue an order compelling disclosure unless the court finds that one or more of the circumstances in subsection (d) of this section exist.

(f) Access to criminal investigative reports and criminal intelligence information of public law enforcement agencies and confidential information in the possession of the State Child Fatality Prevention Team, the local teams, and the Child Fatality Task Force, shall be governed by G.S. 132-1.4 and G.S. 7B-1413 respectively.

Nothing herein shall be deemed to require the disclosure or release of any information in the possession of a district attorney.

(g) Any public agency or its employees acting in good faith in disclosing or declining to disclose information pursuant to this section shall be immune from any criminal or civil liability that might otherwise be incurred or imposed for such action.

(h) Nothing herein shall be deemed to narrow or limit the definition of "public records" as set forth in G.S. 132-1(a).

ARTICLE 31.
Disclosure of Juvenile Information.

§ 7B-3100. Disclosure of information about juveniles.

(a) The Department [of Juvenile Justice and Delinquency Prevention], after consultation with the Conference of Chief District Court Judges, shall adopt rules designating certain local agencies that are authorized to share information concerning juveniles in accordance with the provisions of this section. Agencies so designated shall share with one another, upon request, information that is in their possession that is relevant to any case in which a petition is filed alleging that a juvenile is abused, neglected, dependent, undisciplined, or delinquent and shall continue to do so until the juvenile is no longer subject to the jurisdiction of juvenile court. Agencies that may be designated as "agencies authorized to share information" include local mental health facilities, local health departments, local departments of social services, local law enforcement agencies, local school administrative units, the district's district attorney's office, the Department of Juvenile Justice and Delinquency Prevention, and the Office of Guardian ad Litem Services of the Administrative Office of the Courts. Any information shared among agencies pursuant to this section shall remain confidential, shall be withheld from public inspection, and shall be used only for the protection of the juvenile and others or to improve the educational opportunities of the juvenile, and shall be released in accordance with the provisions of the Family Educational and Privacy Rights Act as set forth in 20 U.S.C. § 1232g. Nothing in this section or any other provision of law shall preclude any other necessary sharing of information among agencies. Nothing herein shall be deemed to require the disclosure or release of any information in the possession of a district attorney.

(b) Disclosure of information concerning any juvenile under investigation or alleged to be within the jurisdiction of the court that would reveal the identity of that juvenile is prohibited except that publication of pictures of runaways is permitted with the permission of the parents.

ARTICLE 36.
Judicial Consent for Emergency Surgical or Medical Treatment.

§ 7B-3600. Judicial authorization of emergency treatment; procedure.

A juvenile in need of emergency treatment under Article 1A of Chapter 90 of the General Statutes, whose physician is barred from rendering necessary treatment by reason of parental refusal to consent to treatment, may receive treatment with court authorization under the following procedure:

(1) The physician shall sign a written statement setting out:
   a. The treatment to be rendered and the emergency need for treatment;
   b. The refusal of the parent, guardian, custodian, or person who has assumed the status and obligation of a parent without being awarded legal custody of the juvenile by a court to consent to the treatment; and
   c. The impossibility of contacting a second physician for a concurring opinion on the need for treatment in time to prevent immediate harm to the juvenile.

(2) Upon examining the physician's written statement prescribed in subdivision (1) of this section and finding:
   a. That the statement is in accordance with this Article, and
   b. That the proposed treatment is necessary to prevent immediate harm to the juvenile.
   The court may issue a written authorization for the proposed treatment to be rendered.

(3) In acute emergencies in which time may not permit implementation of the written procedure set out in subdivisions (1) and (2) of this section, the court may authorize treatment in person or by telephone upon receiving the oral statement of a physician satisfying the requirements of subdivision (1) of this section and upon finding that the proposed treatment is necessary to prevent immediate harm to the juvenile.

(4) The court's authorization for treatment overriding parental refusal to consent should not be given without attempting to offer the parent an opportunity to state the reasons for refusal; however, failure of the court to hear the parent's objections shall not invalidate judicial authorization under this Article.

(5) The court's authorization for treatment under subdivisions (1) and (2) of this section shall be issued in duplicate. One copy shall be given to the treating physician and the other copy shall be attached to the physician's written statement and filed as a juvenile proceeding in the office of the clerk of court.

(6) The court's authorization for treatment under subdivision (3) of this section shall be reduced to writing as soon as possible, supported by the physician's written statement as prescribed in subdivision (1) of this section and shall be filed as prescribed in subdivision (5) of this section.

The court's authorization for treatment under this Article shall have the same effect as parental consent for treatment.

Following the court's authorization for treatment and after giving notice to the juvenile's parent, guardian, or custodian the court shall conduct a hearing in order to provide for payment for the treatment rendered. The court may order the parent or other responsible parties to pay the cost of treatment. If the court finds the parent is unable to pay the cost of treatment, the cost shall be a charge upon the county when so ordered.

This Article shall operate as a remedy in addition to the provisions in G.S. 7B-903, 7B-2503, and 7B-2506.

Appendix B

Selected Criminal Offenses Involving Victims Who Are Minors

Author's Note: The following material does not reflect the exact wording of criminal statutes. Rather, it provides a guide to the essential elements of various criminal offenses. The material in this appendix is adapted from the Institute of Government publication *North Carolina Crimes*, 5th ed., 2001, edited and revised by Robert L. Farb. For information about Institute of Government publications, contact the Publications Sales Office, CB# 3330, Knapp Building, The University of North Carolina at Chapel Hill, Chapel Hill, NC 27599-3330; telephone (919) 966-4119; e-mail sales@iogmail.iog.unc.edu; or shop for publications on-line with our secure shopping cart at https://iogpubs.iog.unc.edu/.

Offenses Incorporated into the Juvenile Code Definition of Sexual Abuse [G.S. 7B-101(1)d.]

First-degree forcible rape. G.S. 14-27.2.

Elements

A person guilty of this offense
(1) has vaginal intercourse
(2) with a person
(3) by force
(4) and against that person's will
(5) and the defendant
   (a) used or displayed a dangerous or deadly weapon (or what reasonably appeared to be a dangerous or deadly weapon), or
   (b) inflicted serious personal injury on the victim, or
   (c) inflicted serious personal injury on another person, or
   (d) was aided and abetted by one or more other persons.

Punishment

Class B1 felony

Second-degree forcible rape. G.S. 14-27.3.

Elements

A person guilty of this offense
(1) has vaginal intercourse
(2) with a person
(3) and the intercourse is
   (a) by force and against the person's will, or
   (b) with someone who is
      (i)   mentally disabled, or
      (ii) mentally incapacitated, or
      (iii) physically helpless,
      which is (or should be) known by the defendant.

Punishment

Class C felony

First-degree forcible sexual offense. G.S. 14-27.4(a)(2).

Elements

A person guilty of this offense
(1) engages in a sexual act other than vaginal intercourse
(2) with a person
(3) by force
(4) and against that person's will
(5) and the defendant
   (a) used or displayed a dangerous or deadly weapon (or what reasonably appeared to be a dangerous or deadly weapon), or
   (b) inflicted serious personal injury on the victim, or
   (c) inflicted serious personal injury on another person, or
   (d) was aided and abetted by one or more other persons.

Punishment

Class B1 felony

First-degree statutory sexual offense. G.S. 14-27.4(a)(1).

Elements

A person guilty of this offense
(1) engages in a sexual act other than vaginal intercourse
(2) with a child under the age of 13 years
(3) who is at least four years younger than the defendant
(4) and the defendant is at least 12 years old.

Punishment

Class B1 felony

Second-degree sexual offense. G.S. 14-27.5.

Elements

A person guilty of this offense
(1) engages in a sexual act other than vaginal intercourse
(2) with a person
(3) and the act is
   (a) by force and against the person's will or

   (b) with someone who is
      (i) mentally disabled, or
      (ii) mentally incapacitated, or
      (iii) physically helpless,
      which is (or should be) known by the defendant.

Punishment

Class C felony

Sexual activity by a substitute parent. G.S. 14-27.7.

Elements

A person guilty of this offense
(1) assumes the position of a parent in the home of a person less than 18 years old
(2) and has vaginal intercourse or engages in a sexual act
(3) with a person less than 18 years old residing in the home.

Punishment

Class E felony

Sexual activity by a custodian. G.S. 14-27.7.

Elements

A person guilty of this offense
(1) has custody of the victim or is an agent or employee of a person or institution having custody of the victim
(2) and has vaginal intercourse or engages in a sexual act
(3) with the person who is in custody.

Punishment

Class E felony

Sexual activity with student by teacher, school administrator, student teacher, or coach (felony). G.S. 14-27.7(b).

Elements

A person guilty of this offense
(1) is a teacher, school administrator, student teacher, or coach
(2) and has vaginal intercourse or engages in a sexual act

(3) with a student

(4) and the person and the student are at the same school.

Punishment

Class G felony

Sexual activity with student by school personnel other than teacher, school administrator, or student teacher (felony). G.S. 14-27.7(b).

Elements

A person guilty of this offense

(1) is school personnel other than a teacher, school administrator, or student teacher

(2) and has vaginal intercourse or engages in a sexual act

(3) with a student

(4) and is at least four years older than the student

(5) and the person and the student are at the same school.

Punishment

Class G felony

Sexual activity with student by school personnel other than teacher, school administrator, or student teacher. (misdemeanor). G.S. 14-27.7(b).

Elements

A person guilty of this offense

(1) is school personnel other than a teacher, school administrator, or student teacher

(2) and has vaginal intercourse or engages in a sexual act

(3) with a student

(4) and is less than four years older than the student

(5) and the person and student are at the same school.

Punishment

Class A1 misdemeanor

Crime against nature. G.S. 14-177.

Elements

A person guilty of this offense commits the crime against nature.

Notes

The crime against nature is defined only by case law, not by statute. According to appellate court decisions, each of the following acts is an example of "the crime against nature": the taking by a male of the sexual organ of another male into his mouth; the inserting, by a male, of his sexual organ into the mouth or anus of another male or a female; the receiving by a male or female of the sexual organ of a male into his or her mouth or anus; fellatio (oral stimulation of the male sexual organ) by a female; cunnilingus (penetration of the female sexual organ by the tongue); and analingus (penetration of the anus by the tongue).

Punishment

Class I felony

Incest between certain near relatives. G.S. 14-178.

Elements

A person guilty of this offense

(1) has sexual intercourse with his or her

(2) (a) grandparent or grandchild, or

   (b) parent or child or stepchild or legally adopted child, or

   (c) brother or sister of the half or whole blood, or

   (d) uncle, aunt, nephew, or niece

(3) and the person knows of that relationship.

Punishment

(1) Class B1 felony if

   (a) the victim is under the age of 13, and the defendant is at least 12 years old and at least four years older than the victim; or

   (b) the victim is 13, 14, or 15 and the

defendant is at least six years older than the victim.

(2) Class C felony if the victim is 13, 14, or 15 and the defendant is more than four but less than six years older than the victim.

(3) Class F felony in all other cases.

Definitions for certain offenses concerning minors. G.S. 14-190.13.

[*Note:* The following definitions apply to obscenity, exploitation, and prostitution offenses outlined below.]

(1) Harmful to Minors.—That quality of any material or performance that depicts sexually explicit nudity or sexual activity and that, taken as a whole, has the following characteristics:

  a. The average adult person applying contemporary community standards would find that the material or performance has a predominant tendency to appeal to a prurient interest of minors in sex; and

  b. The average adult person applying contemporary community standards would find that the depiction of sexually explicit nudity or sexual activity in the material or performance is patently offensive to prevailing standards in the adult community concerning what is suitable for minors; and

  c. The material or performance lacks serious literary, artistic, political, or scientific value for minors.

(2) Material.—Pictures, drawings, video recordings, films or other visual depictions or representations but not material consisting entirely of written words.

(3) Minor.—An individual who is less than 18 years old and is not married or judicially emancipated.

(4) Prostitution.—Engaging or offering to engage in sexual activity with or for another in exchange for anything of value.

(5) Sexual Activity.—Any of the following acts:

  a. Masturbation, whether done alone or with another human or an animal.

  b. Vaginal, anal, or oral intercourse, whether done with another human or with an animal.

  c. Touching, in an act of apparent sexual stimulation or sexual abuse, of the clothed or unclothed genitals, pubic area, or buttocks of another person or the clothed or unclothed breasts of a human female.

  d. An act or condition that depicts torture, physical restraint by being fettered or bound, or flagellation of or by a person clad in undergarments or in revealing or bizarre costume.

  e. Excretory functions; provided, however, that this subdivision shall not apply to G.S. 14-190.17A.

  f. The insertion of any part of a person's body, other than the male sexual organ, or of any object into another person's anus or vagina, except when done as part of a recognized medical procedure.

(6) Sexually Explicit Nudity.—The showing of:

  a. Uncovered, or less than opaquely covered, human genitals, pubic area, or buttocks, or the nipple or any portion of the areola of the human female breast, except as provided in G.S. 14-190.9(b); or

  b. Covered human male genitals in a discernibly turgid state.

Preparing obscene photographs, slides, and motion pictures.

Elements

I. Photographing—G.S. 14-190.5(1).

A person guilty of this offense
(1) knowingly
(2) photographs
(3) himself, herself, or another person
(4) for purposes of preparing an obscene film or photograph or negative or slide or motion picture
(5) for the purpose of dissemination.

II. Assisting the Photographer—G.S. 14-190.5(2).

A person guilty of this offense
(1) knowingly

(2) models or poses or acts or otherwise assists in the preparation of
(3) an obscene film or photograph or negative or slide or motion picture
(4) for the purpose of dissemination.

Punishment

Class 1 misdemeanor

Employing or permitting minor to assist in obscenity offense. G.S. 14-190.6.

Elements

A person guilty of this offense
(1) is 18 years of age or older and
(2) intentionally
(3) hires or employs or uses or permits
(4) a minor under the age of 16
(5) to do or assist in doing
(6) any act or thing
(7) constituting an offense under Article 26 of G.S. Chapter 14
(8) involving any obscene material, or act, or thing
(9) that the person knows or reasonably should know
(10) is obscene within the meaning of G.S. 14-190.1.

Punishment

Class I felony

Dissemination of obscenity to minors under the age of 16 years. G.S. 14-190.7.

Elements

A person guilty of this offense
(1) is 18 years of age or older and
(2) knowingly
(3) disseminates
(4) to a minor under the age of 16 years
(5) obscene material
(6) that the person knows or reasonably should know
(7) is obscene within the meaning of G.S. 14-190.1.

Punishment

Class I felony

Dissemination of obscenity to minors under the age of 13 years. G.S. 14-190.8.

Elements

A person guilty of this offense
(1) is 18 years of age or older and
(2) knowingly
(3) disseminates
(4) to a minor under the age of 13 years
(5) obscene material
(6) that the person knows or reasonably should know
(7) is obscene within the meaning of G.S. 14-190.1.

Punishment

Class I felony

Displaying material harmful to minors. G.S. 14-190.14.

Elements

A person guilty of this offense
(1) displays
(2) material
(3) that is harmful to minors
(4) at a commercial establishment
(5) so that it is open to view by minors as part of the invited general public, and
(6) has custody, control, or supervision
(7) of the commercial establishment, and
(8) knows the material's character or content.

Punishment

Class 2 misdemeanor. Each day's violation is a separate offense.

Disseminating harmful material to minors; exhibiting harmful performances to minors. G.S. 14-190.15(a).

Elements

I. Furnishing the Material— G.S. 14-190.15(a)(1).

A person guilty of this offense
(1) sells or furnishes or presents or distributes

(2) material
(3) that is harmful to minors
(4) to a minor
(5) with knowledge of the material's character or content.

II. Permitting Browsing—G.S. 14-190.15(a)(2).

A person guilty of this offense
(1) allows
(2) a minor
(3) to review or peruse
(4) material
(5) that is harmful to minors
(6) with knowledge of the material's character or content.

Punishment

Class 1 misdemeanor

Exhibiting Harmful Performances to Minors (part of "Disseminating Harmful Material to Minors"). G.S. 14-190.15(b).

Elements

A person guilty of this offense
(1) allows
(2) a minor
(3) to view
(4) a live performance
(5) that is harmful to minors
(6) with knowledge of the performance's character or content.

Punishment

Class 1 misdemeanor

First-degree sexual exploitation of a minor. G.S. 14-190.16.

Elements

I. Facilitating Production—G.S. 14-190.16(a)(1).

A person guilty of this offense
(1) uses or employs or induces or coerces or encourages or facilitates

(2) a minor
(3) to engage in or to assist others to engage in
(4) sexual activity
(5) for a live performance or for the purpose of producing material that contains a visual representation depicting sexual activity
(6) with knowledge of the character or content
(7) of the performance or material.

II. Permitting Sexual Activity for Production—G.S. 14-190.16(a)(2).

A person guilty of this offense
(1) permits
(2) a minor
(3) under the person's custody or control
(4) to engage in sexual activity
(5) for a live performance or for the purpose of producing material that contains a visual representation depicting sexual activity
(6) with knowledge of the character or content
(7) of the performance or material.

III. Transporting Minor for Production—G.S. 14-190.16(a)(3).

A person guilty of this offense
(1) transports or finances the transportation of
(2) a minor
(3) through North Carolina or across North Carolina
(4) with the intent that the minor engage in sexual activity
(5) for a live performance or for the purpose of producing material that contains a visual representation depicting sexual activity
(6) with knowledge of the character or content
(7) of the performance or material.

IV. Producing Material Commercially—G.S. 14-190.16(a)(4).

A person guilty of this offense
(1) records or photographs or films or develops or duplicates
(2) for sale or pecuniary gain

(3) material that contains a visual representation depicting a minor engaged in sexual activity
(4) with knowledge of the material's character or content.

Punishment

Class D felony

Second-degree sexual exploitation of a minor. G.S. 14-190.17.

Elements

I. Producing Material Noncommercially—G.S. 14-190.17(a)(1).

A person guilty of this offense
(1) records or photographs or films or develops or duplicates
(2) material that contains a visual representation of a minor engaged in sexual activity
(3) with knowledge of the material's character or content.

II. Circulating Material—G.S. 14-190.17(a)(2).

A person guilty of this offense
(1) distributes or transports or exhibits or receives or sells or purchases or exchanges or solicits
(2) material that contains a visual representation of a minor engaged in sexual activity
(3) with knowledge of the material's character or content.

Punishment

Class F felony

Promoting prostitution of a minor. G.S. 14-190.18.

Elements

I. Facilitating Minor's Prostitution— G.S. 14-190.18(a)(1).

A person guilty of this offense
(1) knowingly
(2) entices or forces or encourages or otherwise facilitates

(3) a minor
(4) to participate in prostitution.

II. Protecting Minor's Prostitution— G.S. 14-190.18(a)(2).

A person guilty of this offense
(1) knowingly
(2) supervises or supports or advises or protects
(3) the prostitution
(4) of a minor or by a minor.

Punishment

Class D felony

Taking indecent liberties with children. G.S. 14-202.1.

Elements

A person guilty of this offense
(1) is at least 16 years old and
(2) (a) (i) for the purpose of arousing or gratifying sexual desire
        (ii) willfully takes or attempts to take an indecent liberty with, or
    (b) willfully commits or attempts to commit a lewd or lascivious act upon the body of
(3) a child under the age of 16 years and
(4) the child is five or more years younger than the defendant.

Punishment

Class F felony

Additional Offenses Involving Victims Who Are Minors

Participating in prostitution of a minor. G.S. 14-190.19.

Elements

I. Soliciting—G.S. 14-190.19(a)(1).

A person guilty of this offense
(1) solicits or requests
(2) a minor
(3) to participate in prostitution
(4) when the person soliciting or requesting is not a minor.

II. Paying/Agreeing to Pay— G.S. 14-190.19(a)(2).

A person guilty of this offense
(1) pays or agrees to pay
(2) a minor
(3) to participate in prostitution
(4) when the person who pays or agrees to pay is not a minor.

III. Paying Afterward under Prior Agreement—G.S. 14-190.19(a)(3).

A person guilty of this offense
(1) pays
(2) a minor
(3) for having participated in prostitution
(4) pursuant to a prior agreement
(5) when the person who pays is not a minor.

Punishment

Class F felony

Third-degree sexual exploitation of a minor. G.S. 14-190.17A.

Elements

A person guilty of this offense
(1) possesses
(2) material that contains a visual representation of a minor engaged in sexual activity
(3) with knowledge of the material's character or content.

Punishment

Class I felony

Assault on child under 12. G.S. 14-33(c)(3).

Elements

A person guilty of this offense
(1) commits an assault
(2) on a child under the age of 12 years.

Punishment

Class A1 misdemeanor

Misdemeanor child abuse. G.S. 14-318.2.

Elements

A person guilty of this offense
(1) (a) is a parent of a child less than 16 years of age, or
    (b) is a person providing care or supervision of a child less than 16 years of age, and
(2) (a) inflicts physical injury on, or
    (b) allows physical injury to be inflicted on, or
    (c) creates or allows to be created a substantial risk of physical injury to
(3) that child
(4) other than by accident.

Punishment

Class 1 misdemeanor

Felony child abuse. G.S. 14-318.4.

Elements

A person guilty of this offense
(1) (a) is a parent of a child less than 16 years of age, or
    (b) is a person providing care or supervision to a child less than 16 years of age, and
(2) (a) intentionally inflicts on or to the child, or
    (b) intentionally commits an assault on the child which results in
(3) serious physical injury.

Punishment

Class E felony

Child abuse—prostitution (felony). G.S. 14-318.4(a1).

Elements

A person guilty of this offense
(1) (a) is a parent of a child less than 16 years of age, or
    (b) is a person providing care or supervision to a child less than 16 years of age, and
(2) commits or permits or encourages
(3) an act of prostitution with or by the child.

Punishment

Class E felony

Child abuse—sexual act (felony). G.S. 14-318.4(a2).

Elements

A person guilty of this offense
(1) is a parent or legal guardian of a child less than 16 years of age, and
(2) (a) commits a sexual act upon the juvenile, or
    (b) allows another to commit a sexual act upon the juvenile.

Punishment

Class E felony

Felony child abuse—serious bodily injury or impairment. G.S. 14-318.4(a3).

Elements

A person guilty of this offense
(1) (a) is a parent of a child less than 16 years of age, or
    (b) is a person providing care or supervision to a child less than 16 years of age, and
(2) (a) intentionally inflicts on or to the child, or
    (b) intentionally commits an assault on the child which results in
(3) (a) serious bodily injury[1] to the child, or

    (b) permanent or protracted loss or impairment of any mental or emotional function of the child.

Punishment

Class C felony

Contributing to a juvenile's being delinquent, undisciplined, abused, or neglected. G.S. 14-316.1.

Elements

A person guilty of this offense
(1) is at least 16 years old and
(2) knowingly or willfully
(3) causes or encourages or aids
(4) a juvenile within the jurisdiction of the court
(5) (a) to be in a place or condition or
    (b) to commit an act
(6) whereby the juvenile could be adjudicated
    (a) delinquent or
    (b) undisciplined or
    (c) abused or
    (d) neglected
    as defined in G.S. 7B-101 and G.S. 7B-1501.

Punishment

Class 1 misdemeanor

First-degree statutory rape. G.S. 14-27.2(a)(1).

Elements

A person guilty of this offense
(1) has vaginal intercourse
(2) with a child under the age of 13 years
(3) who is at least four years younger than the defendant
(4) and the defendant is at least 12 years old.

Punishment

Class B1 felony

---

1. For purposes of this offense, serious bodily injury is "bodily injury that creates a substantial risk of death, or that causes serious permanent disfigurement, coma, a permanent or protracted condition that causes extreme pain, or permanent or protracted loss or impairment of the function of any bodily member or organ, or that results in prolonged hospitalization." G.S. 14-318.4(a3).

Statutory rape of person who is 13, 14, or 15 years old. G.S. 14-27.7A.

A. Statutory Rape of Person Who Is 13, 14, or 15 Years Old by a Defendant Who Is at Least Six Years Older than the Victim.

Elements

A person guilty of this offense
(1) has vaginal intercourse
(2) with a child who is 13, 14, or 15 years old, and
(3) the defendant is at least six years older than the child.

Punishment

Class B1 felony

B. Statutory Rape of Person Who Is 13, 14, or 15 Years Old by a Defendant Who Is More than Four but Less than Six Years Older than the Victim.

Elements

A person guilty of this offense
(1) has vaginal intercourse
(2) with a child who is 13, 14, or 15 years old, and
(3) the defendant is more than four but less than six years older than the child.

Punishment

Class C felony

Statutory sexual offense against person who is 13, 14, or 15 years old. G.S. 14-27.7A.

A. Statutory Sexual Offense against Person Who Is 13, 14, or 15 Years Old by a Defendant Who Is at Least Six Years Older than the Victim.

Elements

A person guilty of this offense
(1) engages in a sexual act other than vaginal intercourse
(2) with a child who is 13, 14, or 15 years old, and
(3) the defendant is at least six years older than the child.

Punishment

Class B1 felony

B. Statutory Sexual Offense against Person Who Is 13, 14, or 15 Years Old by a Defendant Who Is More than Four but Less than Six Years Older than the Victim.

Elements

A person guilty of this offense
(1) engages in a sexual act other than vaginal intercourse
(2) with a child who is 13, 14, or 15 years old, and
(3) the defendant is more than four but less than six years older than the child.

Punishment

Class C felony

Appendix C

County Departments of Social Services

County	Main Agency	Child Protective Services Regular Hours	After Hours
Alamance	(336) 570-6532	(336) 229-2908	(336) 229-2908
Alexander	(828) 632-1080	(828) 632-1080	(828) 632-4658
Alleghany	(336) 372-2411	(336) 372-1445	(336) 372-5676
Anson	(704) 694-9351	(704) 694-9351	(704) 694-4188 (county)
			(704) 694-2167 (city)
Ashe	(336) 219-2700	(336) 219-2734	(336) 219-2600
Avery	(828) 733-8230	(828) 733-8230	(828) 733-5855
Beaufort	(252) 975-5500	(252) 975-5500 or	(252) 946-0101
		(252) 940-6026	
Bertie	(252) 794-5320	(252) 794-5370	(252) 794-5330
Bladen	(910) 862-6800	(910) 862-6800	(910) 862-8141
Brunswick	(910) 253-2077	(910) 253-2077	911
Buncombe	(828) 250-5500	(828) 250-5900	211
Burke	(828) 439-2000	(828) 439-2003	(828) 438-5500
Cabarrus	(704) 920-1400	(704) 920-1400	(704) 920-3000
Caldwell	(828) 426-8200	(828) 426-8257	(828) 758-2324
Camden	(252) 331-4787	(252) 331-4787	(252) 331-1500
Carteret	(252) 728-3181	(252) 728-3181	(252) 504-4800
Caswell	(336) 694-4141	(336) 694-4141	(336) 694-9311
Catawba	(828) 695-5600	(828) 324-9111	(828) 324-9111
Chatham	(919) 542-2759	(919) 542-2759	(919) 542-2911
Cherokee	(828) 837-7455	(828) 837-7455	(828) 837-2589
Chowan	(252) 482-7441	(252) 482-7441	(252) 482-4445
Clay	(828) 389-6301	(828) 389-6301	(828) 389-6354
Cleveland	(704) 487-0661	(704) 487-0661	(704) 484-4822
Columbus	(910) 642-2800	(910) 641-3225	(910) 642-2800
Craven	(252) 636-4900	(252) 636-4948	(252) 636-6620

		Child Protective Services	
County	Main Agency	Regular Hours	After Hours
Cumberland	(910) 323-1540	(910) 677-2450	(910) 323-1500
Currituck	(252) 232-3083	(252) 232-3083	(252) 232-3083 or (252) 232-2216
Dare	(252) 475-5500	(252) 475-5500	(252) 473-3444
Davidson	(336) 242-2500	(336) 242-2500	(336) 249-0131
Davie	(336) 751-8800	(336) 751-8800	(336) 751-6238
Duplin	(910) 296-2200	(910) 296-2293	(910) 296-2150
Durham	(919) 560-8000	(919) 560-8424	911
Edgecombe	(252) 641-7611	(252) 641-7611	(252) 641-7611
Forsyth	(336) 727-8311	(336) 727-8351	(336) 727-8351
Franklin	(919) 496-5721	(919) 496-5721	(919) 496-2511
Gaston	(704) 862-7500	(704) 862-7530	(704) 862-7555
Gates	(252) 357-0075	(252) 357-0075	(252) 357-0210
Graham	(828) 479-7911	(828) 479-7911	(828) 479-3352
Granville	(919) 693-1511	(919) 693-1511	(919) 690-0444
Greene	(252) 747-5932	(252) 747-5932	(252) 747-3411
Guilford	(336) 641-3071	(336) 641-3795	1-800-378-5315
Halifax	(252) 536-2511	(252) 536-6500	(252) 536-6500
Harnett	(910) 893-7500	(910) 893-7500	(910) 893-9111 or (910) 893-7599
Haywood	(828) 452-6620	(828) 452-6620	(828) 456-6666
Henderson	(828) 697-5500	(828) 697-5572	(828) 697-4911
Hertford	(252) 358-7830	(252) 358-7830	(252) 358-7800
Hoke	(910) 875-8725	(910) 875-8725, ext. 275	(910) 875-2135 or 1-800-842-9111
Hyde	(252) 926-4199	(252) 926-4476	(252) 926-3171
Iredell	(704) 873-5631	(704) 873-5631	(704) 878-3100
Jackson	(828) 586-5546	(828) 586-5546	(828) 586-1911 or 911
Johnston	(919) 989-5300	(919) 989-5300	(919) 989-5000
Jones	(252) 448-2581	(252) 448-2581	(252) 448-7091
Lee	(919) 718-4690	(919) 718-4690	(919) 775-5531 (county) (919) 775-8268 (city)
Lenoir	(252) 559-6400	(252) 559-8331	(252) 559-6118
Lincoln	(704) 732-0738	(704) 736-8678 or (704) 732-9018	911
Macon	(828) 349-2124	(828) 349-2124	(828) 349-2061 or 911
Madison	(828) 649-2711	(828) 649-9498	(828) 649-2721
Martin	(252) 809-6400	(252) 809-6403	(252) 792-8151 or (252) 792-2868
McDowell	(828) 652-3355	(828) 652-3355	(828) 652-4000

County	Main Agency	Child Protective Services Regular Hours	After Hours
Mecklenburg	(704) 336-2273	(704) 336-2273	(704) 336-2273
Mitchell	(828) 688-2175	(828) 688-2175	(828) 688-9110
Montgomery	(910) 576-6531	(910) 576-6531	(910) 572-1313
Moore	(910) 947-2436	(910) 947-5683	911
Nash	(252) 459-9818	(252) 459-1293	(252) 459-1293
New Hanover	(910) 341-4700	(910) 341-4722	911
Northampton	(252) 534-5811	(252) 534-1773	(252) 534-1773 or (252) 534-2611
Onslow	(910) 989-0230	(910) 938-5460	(910) 455-3113
Orange	(919) 732-8181	(919) 968-2000	(919) 968-8368
Pamlico	(252) 745-4086	(252) 745-4086	(252) 745-3101
Pasquotank	(252) 338-2126	(252) 338-2126	(252) 331-1500
Pender	(910) 259-1240	(910) 259-1240	(910) 259-1212
Perquimans	(252) 426-7373	(252) 426-1806	(252) 426-5615
Person	(336) 599-8361	(336) 599-8361	(336) 597-0500
Pitt	(252) 902-1111	(252) 902-1111	(252) 830-4141
Polk	(828) 859-5825	(828) 859-5825	(828) 894-3001
Randolph	(336) 683-8000	(336) 683-8000	(336) 318-6929
Richmond	(910) 997-8400	(910) 997-8415	(910) 997-8283
Robeson	(910) 671-3500	(910) 671-3770	(910) 671-6217
Rockingham	(336) 342-1394	(336) 342-3537	911
Rowan	(704) 633-4921	(704) 638-3175	911
Rutherford	(828) 287-6165	(828) 287-6165	(828) 287-6165
Sampson	(910) 592-7131	(910) 592-4200	911
Scotland	(910) 277-2500	(910) 277-2500	(910) 277-2580 (county) (910) 276-3211 (Laurinburg)
Stanly	(704) 982-6100	(704) 982-6100	(704) 986-3700
Stokes	(336) 593-2861	(336) 593-2861	1-800-672-2851
Surry	(336) 401-8700	(336) 401-8800	(336) 374-3000
Swain	(828) 488-6921	(828) 488-2197	(828) 488-4844
Transylvania	(828) 884-3174	(828) 884-3174	(828) 884-3188
Tyrrell	(252) 796-3421	(252) 796-3421	(252) 796-2251
Union	(704) 296-4300	(704) 296-4300	(704) 289-1591
Vance	(252) 492-5001	(252) 436-0407	(252) 436-0407
Wake	(919) 212-7000	(919) 212-7430 or (919) 212-7000	(919) 212-7430 or 911
Warren	(252) 257-5000	(252) 257-5002	(252) 257-3364
Washington	(252) 793-4041	(252) 793-4041	(252) 793-2422
Watauga	(828) 265-8100	(828) 265-8100	(828) 264-3761

		Child Protective Services	
County	Main Agency	Regular Hours	After Hours
Wayne	(919) 580-4034	(919) 705-1774	(919) 705-1774
Wilkes	(336) 651-7400	(336) 667-5437	(336) 667-5437
Wilson	(252) 206-4000	(252) 206-4000	(252) 237-8300
Yadkin	(336) 679-4210	(336) 679-4210	(336) 679-4217
Yancey	(828) 682-6148	(828) 682-2470	(828) 682-2124

A person making a call outside regular office hours should ask for the on-call social worker. Some of the after-hours numbers are dispatch numbers for local law enforcement agencies. **In an emergency, anyone who cannot reach either the department of social services or the on-call social worker should call 911.**

Appendix D
Selected Web Sites of Interest

This nonexhaustive list contains some useful governmental, private nonprofit, and advocacy resources. Many of these Web sites include links to numerous related sites.

North Carolina

Center for Child and Family Policy, Terry Sanford Institute of Public Policy, Duke University: www.pubpol.duke.edu/centers/child/

Covenant With North Carolina's Children: www.ncchild.org/covhome.htm

Division of Social Services, North Carolina Department of Health and Human Services: www.dhhs.state.nc.us/dss/c_srv/cserv_protect.htm

   Children's Services: www.dhhs.state.nc.us/dss/childrensservices/index.htm

   Children Services Manuals and Other On-Line Publications: http://info.dhhs.state.nc.us/olm/manuals/dss/

   Directory of County Departments of Social Services: www.dhhs.state.nc.us/dss/cty_cnr/dir.htm

Guardian ad Litem Program, North Carolina Administrative Office of the Courts: www.nccourts.org/Citizens/GAL/Default.asp

Institute of Government, The University of North Carolina at Chapel Hill: www.sog.unc.edu/

Jordan Institute for Families, School of Social Work, The University of North Carolina at Chapel Hill: http://ssw.unc.edu/jif/

North Carolina Child Advocacy Institute: www.ncchild.org/

Prevent Child Abuse North Carolina: www.childabusenc.org/

National

Administration for Children and Families, Children's Bureau, United States Department of Health and Human Services: www.acf.dhhs.gov/programs/cb/

American Academy of Pediatrics, Section on Child Abuse and Neglect: www.aap.org/sections/scan/resources.htm

American Bar Association Center on Children and the Law: www.abanet.org/child/home.html

American Humane Association: www.americanhumane.org/site/PageServer

American Professional Society on the Abuse of Children: www.apsac.org/

Child Abuse Prevention Network: www.child-abuse.com/

Children Now: www.childrennow.org/

Children's Defense Fund: www.childrensdefense.org/index.htm

National Association of Counsel for Children: www.naccchildlaw.org/

National CASA (Court Appointed Special Advocate): www.casanet.org/index.htm and http://nationalcasa.org/

National Center for Youth Law: www.youthlaw.org/

National Clearinghouse on Child Abuse and Neglect Information: www.calib.com/nccanch/

National Council of Juvenile and Family Court Judges: www.ncjfcj.org/

National Data Archive on Child Abuse and Neglect, Family Life Development Center, College of Human Ecology, Cornell University: www.ndacan.cornell.edu/

National Indian Child Welfare Association: www.nicwa.org/

National Resource Center on Child Maltreatment: www.gocwi.org/nrccm/

Prevent Child Abuse America: www.preventchildabuse.org/

through Fri the rest of the year. Admission is by a small donation. For more information call (208) 359-3063.

While in Rexburg, don't miss the *Idaho Centennial Carousel,* located in Porter Park. The merry-go-round was built in 1926 by the Spillman Engineering Company of North Tonawanda, New York, and brought to Rexburg in 1952. By the late 1970s the old carousel had been severely damaged by vandalism and the Teton Dam floodwaters, but it was completely restored and is one of fewer than 175 still in operation. Sherrell Anderson, a master carver, replaced more than fifty broken legs and ten tails for the carousel's horses, then created twelve new horses that match the originals in style but are festooned with symbols of Idaho, making it truly one of a kind.

The lead horse, "Centennial," is decorated with the state tree (white pine), the state bird (mountain bluebird), the state flower (syringa), the state gemstone (star garnet), and the state seal. On the opposite side, the "Chief Joseph" horse is a gray Appaloosa (Idaho's state horse) fitted with ornamentation including a bear-claw necklace and a shield bearing the portrait of the great Nez Perce leader. The carousel's center is decorated with pictures and symbols from all over the Gem State, including scenes of Hells Canyon, Balanced Rock, and Harriman State Park, as well as a moose, grizzly bear, and white-tailed deer. The Idaho Centennial Carousel is open for rides (which cost $1) from noon to 7 p.m. Mon through Sat during the summer months (except on days with bad weather). It can be reserved for group use; for more information call (208) 359-3020.

The *Menan Buttes,* rising southwest of Rexburg, are another National Natural Landmark and offer a fun spot for even the littlest hikers (although steep and challenging treks are available for those who want more adventure). The two 10,000-year-old buttes are composed of glassy basalt lava, found in only a few places in the world. The buttes are 800 and 500 feet high, with

Global Hoedown

Rexburg, Idaho, is more globally minded than most towns of 26,000. Mormon-owned Brigham Young University–Idaho has several hundred international students and many American students who have served church missions all over the planet. But for one week during midsummer each year, Rexburg really starts to resemble a mini–United Nations. That's when about 300 folks from scores of foreign lands arrive to take part in the *Idaho International Summerfest.* Formerly known as the *Idaho International Dance and Music Festival,* it's sort of an Olympics for the arts. Past festivals have attracted performers from Slovakia, India, Sweden, Malaysia, China, Russia, and dozens of other nations. In addition to lots of dancing, events include a parade, street festival, art show, battle of the bands, and more. Get the details at idahosummerfest.com.

craters that measure a half-mile wide and about 300 feet deep. The buttes are north of the small town of Menan, or they may be reached by taking Highway 33 west of Rexburg.

St. Anthony, northeast of Rexburg on US 20, is famous for the sand dunes north of town. Like the dunes at Bruneau in Southwestern Idaho, the *St. Anthony Sand Dunes* are among the highest in the United States, but the St. Anthony complex is much larger than that at Bruneau—about 150 square miles total. The St. Anthony dunes are particularly popular with all-terrain vehicle enthusiasts. Small, rolling hills (open year-round) are suitable for beginners, and hills up to 500 feet in height (open Apr through Dec) offer challenges for more experienced riders. Camping is available. For more information call the Bureau of Land Management (which oversees the dunes) at (208) 524-7500.

Ashton, another 14 miles east of St. Anthony on US 20, is the gateway to the *Mesa Falls Scenic Byway* (Highway 47), a beautiful 25-mile route that runs right by the viewpoints for Lower and Upper Mesa Falls and offers good views of the Teton Range, too. This is one scenic drive that takes barely longer than the more direct highway route, so by all means indulge.

At Lower Mesa Falls, an overlook appropriately dubbed Grandview provides a panorama featuring the Henry's Fork of the Snake River and the 65-foot falls, which are seen at some distance. Upper Mesa Falls, on the other hand, are viewed up close and personal. By descending a series of walkways, it's possible to stand right at the brink of the 114-foot Upper Falls, bask in its thunderous roar, and possibly see a rainbow. Benches offer the traveler an opportunity to sit and reflect on the falls and the tall pines all around. Camping and picnicking are available nearby. Big Falls Inn at Upper Mesa Falls, constructed around the turn of the century and used by travelers en route to Yellowstone National Park, now serves as a visitor information center. From Upper Mesa Falls the byway continues 12 miles to US 20, returning to the main route near Island Park.

Island Park is among Idaho's top recreation areas. Aside from being a town of some 280 people, Island Park is a geological feature—a caldera, or volcanic basin, about 15 miles in diameter. The caldera was created when a volcano originally situated in the area erupted continuously for thousands of years before finally collapsing. This is also the land of the Henry's Fork, considered one of America's premier trout streams. The river was named for Andrew Henry, who passed through the area in 1810 as part of a fur-trapping expedition and established a trading post. These days numerous outfitters offer guide services and equipment for anglers, snowmobilers, and other recreationists.

Big Springs, located northeast of Island Park, is the source of much of the Henry's Fork flow and the home of some truly impressive rainbow trout. A National Natural Landmark, the springs are one of a kind, issuing at the rate of 92,000 gallons per minute from the same rhyolitic lava flows that created the

Yellowstone's Back Door

A side trip from the Mesa Falls Scenic Byway takes travelers into the little-known **Bechler District of Yellowstone National Park**—an isolated area marked by broad meadows and abundant waterfalls. Remarkably, this rich region was almost lost to a reservoir in the early 20th century, when Idaho farmers prevailed on Congressman Addison Smith to seek the Bechler area's removal from Yellowstone National Park so a dam could be built for irrigation water. In hearings, Smith insisted to his peers that the region was nothing more than a swamp. But fortunately naturalist William Gregg got word of the scheme and launched a crusade to save the Bechler district. The dam idea was finally crushed by public outcry.

To detour about 40 miles round-trip to "the Bechler," which sits astride the Idaho-Wyoming border, watch 4 miles outside Marysville (itself just east of Ashton) for the Cave Falls Road (1400 North) and follow it for 19 miles. A Forest Service campground sits just past the Wyoming border. Nearby, a picnic area affords a view of Cave Falls, which drop along the entire width of the Falls River. An easy 1-mile trail leads through the pine forest to Bechler Falls. Longer trails in the region can take you to magnificent meadowlands and dramatic waterfalls, including Union Falls and Albright Falls; check at the Bechler Ranger Station (located at the end of a short spur road off the Cave Falls Road) for details and permits, which are required for overnight treks.

caldera. The Targhee National Forest has a campground at the site. No fishing is allowed at Big Springs, but the trout will happily accept handouts of bread tossed by visitors. The Johnny Sack Cabin, listed on the National Register of Historic Places, sits nearby and is open to visitors mid-June through mid-Sept.

Mack's Inn Resort, on the banks of the Henry's Fork between Island Park and West Yellowstone, Montana, is another spot Idaho families have enjoyed for generations. The resort sports a variety of accommodations ranging from cabins of several sizes to condos, along with an RV park. Recreational amenities include all kinds of boat rentals (including transportation to the Big Springs launch site), miniature golf, basketball, volleyball, horseshoe pits, and more. There's a dinner theater here in summertime, too. Call (208) 558-7272 for more information or see macksinn.com.

Island Park can be a noisy place in winter, what with all the snowmobilers racing across the white fields of snow. But solace isn't hard to find for those seeking a more serene wintertime experience. **Harriman State Park** has some of the state's best cross-country skiing and snowshoeing, and the park is closed to snow machines (though fat bikes can now ply the groomed trails). Winter visitors are likely to catch glimpses of bald eagles, trumpeter swans, sandhill cranes, elk, deer, moose, and coyotes.

Harriman is peaceful in summertime, too. Trails ranging in length from 1 mile to 5.5 miles meander along the Henry's Fork, Silver Lake, and Golden

Lake, or up to the top of a ridge where the Teton Range may be viewed. Again these paths are open only to nonmotorized use by hikers, mountain bicyclists, and horseback riders. Visitors may bring their own horse or take guided trail rides, which are offered June through Oct. Get details from Dry Ridge Outfitters at (208) 558-7433 or dryridge.com. The park is also the setting for Writers at Harriman (a workshop for high school students) and Mountains and Strings, a chamber music camp for teens.

Harriman State Park has no camping, but there are several places to stay within the **Railroad Ranch,** a collection of buildings erected in the early 20th century by investors from the Oregon Short Line Railroad. Over time the ranch became a favorite retreat of prominent American industrialists and their families. It was E. H. Harriman, founder of the Union Pacific Railroad, who envisioned the area as a refuge for wildlife. Ironically, he never really got to enjoy the ranch, but his son and daughter-in-law, E. Roland and Gladys Harriman, spent six weeks of most summers at the ranch, and a cabin remains furnished much as they used it. About forty buildings were constructed at the Railroad Ranch. Most of these original structures still stand; some have been renovated, and many are included in tours given during the summer months. See the "unique overnight stays" page at parksandrecreation.idaho.gov/parks/harriman for information on facilities for families and groups. For reservations, call (888) 922-6743. Harriman State Park also has two yurts adjacent to the trail system. Each can sleep up to six people and they rent year-round for $55 a night.

From Island Park, it's possible to take back roads to the last area of Eastern Idaho on our itinerary, the opal mines of Clark County. A2, a county road, runs from just north of Island Park west to Kilgore and on to Spencer, which sits on I-15. The Spencer area is reportedly the only place in North America where opals are abundant enough to mine commercially. Several businesses in the Spencer-Dubois area sell finished gemstones and opal jewelry. One of them, the Opal Country Cafe and Gift Shop at 27 Opal Ave. in Spencer, is headquarters for **Spencer Opal Mines.** A "mini-mine" behind the cafe is open to everyone for digging from 9 a.m. to 5 p.m. Memorial Day through Labor Day. The cost is $15 per person for one pound of rock. The mine recommends the following tools for working with the opal: rock hammer, bucket, spray bottle, gloves, sturdy shoes or boots, and safety glasses (which are required). For more information call (208) 374-5476 or see spenceropalmines.com.

Whether you've been digging for opals or driving all day, you're going to be hungry. One of the most unexpected restaurants in Idaho is in the little town of Roberts, just off I-15 maybe an hour south of Spencer and about twenty minutes north of Idaho Falls. **BJ's Bayou** marked twenty years in business in 2016, serving Cajun and Creole food. Look for its food trailer at events around Eastern Idaho, too. Laissez les bon temps rouler!

Places to Stay in Eastern Idaho

IDAHO FALLS

Best Western Plus Cottontree Inn
900 Lindsay Blvd.
(208) 523-6000
bestwesternidaho.com
Moderate

Destinations Inn
295 West Broadway
(208) 528-8444
destinationsinn.com
Moderate–Expensive

Hilton Garden Inn
700 Lindsay Blvd.
(208) 522-9500
hilton.com
Expensive

Motel West
1540 West Broadway
(208) 522-1112
motelwestidaho.com
Inexpensive–Moderate

Residence Inn
635 West Broadway
(208) 542-0000
marriott.com
Expensive

Shilo Inn Suites Hotel
780 Lindsay Blvd.
(208) 523-0088
shiloinns.com
Moderate

RIGBY

Blue Heron Inn
706 North Yellowstone Hwy.
(866) 745-9922
idahoblueheron.com
Moderate–Expensive

South Fork Inn Motel
425 Farnsworth Way
(208) 745-8700
Inexpensive

SWAN VALLEY

The Lodge at Palisades Creek
(208) 483-2222
tlapc.com
Very Expensive

Sleepy J Cabins
19 Highway 31
(208) 483-0411
sleepyjcabins.com
Moderate–Expensive

VICTOR

Moose Creek Ranch
2733 Moose Creek Rd.
(208) 787-6078
moosecreekranch.com
Moderate–Expensive

Teton Springs Lodge & Spa
10 Warm Creek Lane
(888) 451-0156
tetonspringslodge.com
Very Expensive

DRIGGS

Best Western Teton West
476 North Main St.
(208) 354-2363
bestwesternidaho.com
Moderate

Grand Targhee Resort
(Alta, Wyoming)
(800) TARGHEE
grandtarghee.com
Moderate–Expensive

Pines Motel–Guest Haus
105 South Main
(800) 354-2778
thepinestetonvalley.com
Inexpensive–Moderate

REXBURG

AmericInn Lodge & Suites
1098 Golden Beauty Dr.
(208) 356-5333
americinn.com
Moderate

Quality Inn
885 West Main St.
(208) 359-1311
choicehotels.com
Moderate–Expensive

SpringHill Suites
1177 South Yellowstone Hwy.
(208) 356-3003
marriott.com
Expensive

ST. ANTHONY

GuestHouse Henry's Fork Inn
115 South Bridge St.
(208) 624-3711
henrysforkinn.com
Moderate

ASHTON

Log Cabin Motel
1001 Main St.
(208) 652-3956
logcabinmotelidaho.com
Inexpensive

Rankin Motel
120 South Yellowstone Hwy.
(208) 652-3570
rankinmotel.com
Moderate

ISLAND PARK

Mack's Inn Resort
US 20
(208) 558-7272
macksinn.com
Inexpensive

Pond's Lodge
(208) 558-7221
pondslodge.com
Moderate–Expensive

Sawtelle Mountain Resort
4133 Quakie Lane
(208) 558-9366
sawtellemountainresort.com
Moderate

Places to Eat in Eastern Idaho

IDAHO FALLS

The Cellar
(fine dining)
3520 East 17th St.
(Ammon)
(208) 525-9300
Expensive

Diablas Kitchen
(New American)
368 A St.
(208) 522-1510
Inexpensive–Moderate

Grandpa's Southern Barbecue
(soul food)
545 Shoup Ave.
(208) 881-5123
Inexpensive–Moderate

Jalisco's Mexican Restaurant
2107 East 17th St.
(208) 552-2021
Inexpensive–Moderate

The Sandpiper
(steaks/seafood)
750 Lindsay Blvd.
(208) 524-3344
Moderate–Expensive

Smitty's Pancake & Steakhouse
(American)
645 West Broadway
(208) 523-6450
Moderate

The Snake Bite
(eclectic)
401 Park Ave.
(208) 525-2522
Inexpensive–Moderate

SWAN VALLEY

Angus Restaurant
(American)
2986 Swan Valley Hwy.
(Irwin)
(208) 483-2666
Inexpensive

VICTOR

Knotty Pine
(American)
58 South Main St.
(208) 787-2866
Moderate

Victor Emporium
(soda fountain/lunch counter)
45 North Main St.
(208) 787-2221
Inexpensive

DRIGGS

The Royal Wolf
(American)
63 Depot St.
(208) 354-8365
Moderate

Warbirds Cafe
(American)
Driggs Reed Memorial Airport
(208) 354-2550
Moderate–Expensive

REXBURG

Da Pineapple Grill
(island fare)
383 South Second West
(208) 356-4398
Moderate

HELPFUL WEBSITES FOR EASTERN IDAHO

Idaho Falls Chamber of Commerce
idahofallschamber.com

Island Park area information
westyellowstonenet.com

Yellowstone National Park
nps.gov/yell

Yellowstone Teton Territory
yellowstoneteton.org

Teton Valley Chamber
discovertetonvalley.com

ALSO WORTH SEEING IN EASTERN IDAHO

Idaho Falls Aquatic Center
Idaho Falls

Idaho's Vietnam Veterans Memorial
Idaho Falls

Kelly Canyon Ski Area
east of Heise

Hess Heritage Museum
near Ashton

Yellowstone Bear World
Rexburg

Flat Ranch Preserve (Nature Conservancy)
Island Park

Frontier Pies
(American)
460 West Fourth South
(208) 356-3600
Inexpensive–Moderate

Pizza Pie Cafe
240 North Second East
(208) 359-1123
Inexpensive–Moderate

ST. ANTHONY

El Jaliciense
(Mexican)
119 Bridge St.
(208) 624-1124
Inexpensive–Moderate

ASHTON

Frostop Drive-In
(fast food)
26 North US 20
(208) 652-7762
Inexpensive

Trails Inn Restaurant
(American)
213 Main
(208) 652-9918
Inexpensive–Moderate

ISLAND PARK

Boondocks Restaurant
(American)
3587 Kilgore-Yale Rd.
(208) 716-3720
Inexpensive–Moderate

Lodgepole Grill
(New American)
3907 Phillips Loop Rd.
(208) 558-0192
Moderate–Expensive

ROBERTS

BJ's Bayou
(Cajun)
655 North 2880 East
(208) 228-2331
Inexpensive–Moderate

Central Idaho

When people think of Idaho, they think of mountains, wild-life, and white water. For many residents and visitors, Central Idaho—blessed with all these natural treasures and more—is the region that most epitomizes the Gem State.

Few highways traverse Central Idaho; those that do are separated and isolated by mountain ranges. We'll explore this region in a counterclockwise fashion, starting on Highway 28 north from the ghost town of Gilmore to Salmon and points north toward the Montana border. From Salmon, we'll head south on US 93, offer a few suggestions for sights in the Lost River Valley, then pick up Highway 75 for its trip to the Saw-tooth National Recreation Area and Sun Valley. We'll finish by crossing the high desert on US 20.

Central Idaho doesn't have a regional tourism office. Your best bet is to contact the Sun Valley/Ketchum Chamber & Visitors Bureau at (866) 265-4197 or see visitsunvalley.com.

Lemhi River Valley

Highway 28 is also known as the *Sacajawea Historic Byway*—so named because the Lemhi River Valley, which

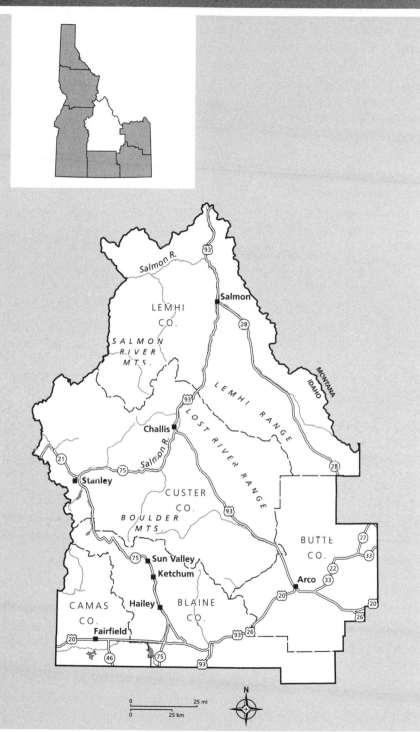

LEMHI CO.

SALMON RIVER MTS.

Salmon R.

Salmon

LEMHI RANGE

MONTANA
IDAHO

Challis

LOST RIVER RANGE

Salmon R.

Stanley

CUSTER CO.

BOULDER MTS.

BUTTE CO.

Sun Valley

Ketchum

Arco

CAMAS CO.

Hailey

BLAINE CO.

Fairfield

0   25 mi
0   25 km

N

Highway 28 parallels from the town of Leadore north to Salmon, was the birthplace of one of America's greatest heroines, Sacajawea. (Although national scholars prefer the spelling "Sacagawea," "Sacajawea" is more popular in Idaho.) This Lemhi-Shoshone Indian woman was an invaluable asset to the Lewis and Clark Expedition two centuries ago, as we shall see.

Central Idaho was the site of a major mining boom in the late 19th and early 20th centuries, and the ghost town of ***Gilmore*** stands in mute testimony to those days. To get there watch for the historical marker telling of Gilmore near milepost 73, then take the road west immediately across the highway. Gilmore sat about a mile and a half west over a gravel, washboarded road, and its two dozen or so remaining buildings come into view almost immediately. "Enjoy but Do Not Destroy," weathered signs warn the visitor. Look for the remnants of an old railroad bed. This was the Gilmore and Pittsburgh Railway—a branch railroad from Montana—which helped Gilmore's mines produce more than $11.5 million in silver and lead before a power plant explosion ended operations in 1929.

A rewarding side trip is possible from Highway 28 to ***Lembi Pass,*** where Meriwether Lewis became the first white American to cross the Continental Divide in August 1805. Traveling ahead of the rest of the Lewis and Clark Expedition, Captain Lewis was searching for the Shoshone Indians in hopes they could provide horses to help the Corps of Discovery travel overland. On August 12, Lewis's party moved west into the mountains from what is now Montana's Clark Canyon Reservoir, following what Lewis called a "large and plain Indian road . . . I therefore did not despair of shortly finding a passage over the mountains and of tasting the waters of the great Columbia this evening." Soon after, Lewis and his men reached a stream that he dubbed "the most distant fountain of the mighty Missouri in search of which we have spent so many toilsome days and restless nights." After pausing for a drink from the stream, Lewis and his men continued to the top of the ridge, where Lewis later wrote he saw "immense ranges of high mountains still to the west of us with their tops partially covered with snow." It was a point of reckoning for the expedition. Lewis had crossed the divide, but the sight of those mountains meant there would be no easy passage to the Columbia.

The day after reaching Lemhi Pass, Lewis and his party came upon several Shoshones, who led the whites to their chief, Cameahwait. Lewis convinced the chief to accompany him back over the pass, where Clark and the rest were waiting with their baggage. It was to be a most extraordinary meeting, for it turned out that Cameahwait was the long-lost brother of Sacajawea, the Shoshone woman who—together with her husband, Charbonneau, and their infant son—had accompanied the Corps of Discovery after their winter stay in

AUTHOR'S FAVORITES IN CENTRAL IDAHO

Lemhi Pass
east of Tendoy

Gold Mine Thrift Shop and Consign
Ketchum

Galena Lodge
north of Ketchum

Sun Valley Summer Symphony
Sun Valley

Silver Creek
west of Picabo

Craters of the Moon National Monument
west of Arco

the Mandan Villages of North Dakota. Because of this family coincidence, the expedition was able to get the horses it needed.

To visit Lemhi Pass turn east at the small settlement of Tendoy. The steep and winding 26-mile loop drive to the pass isn't recommended for large RVs or vehicles towing trailers, but most pickup trucks and passenger vehicles in good shape will make it with no problem. (The Montana approach to the pass is much less steep; apparently a busload of Lewis and Clark buffs made it to the top that way.) Face west at the pass to see the ridge upon ridge of mountains Lewis described. At 7,373 feet, Lemhi Pass is the highest point on the Lewis and Clark Trail and one of the most pristine, too. It's a great place to watch a sunset. The primitive *Agency Creek Recreation Site* sits 7.5 miles from the summit on the Agency Creek Road. Agency Creek, run by the Bureau of Land Management, has a handful of campsites, a vault toilet, and picnic tables. Before returning to the highway, note the grave of Chief Tendoy, a Native American leader who commanded respect and influence. The burial site is sacred to Indians, and visitation by the general public is not considered appropriate. The small store at Tendoy sells gas and food; it's another 20 miles north to Salmon, where all services are available.

River of No Return

Learn more about Idaho's most famous daughter and her people at the *Sacajawea Interpretive, Cultural, and Education Center,* just south of Salmon on Highway 28. The site includes a small visitor center, an outdoor trail with interpretive panels, and several pieces of impressive public art, including a larger-than-life statue of the young Shoshone woman holding her baby, Jean Baptiste Charbonneau, nicknamed "Pomp" by William Clark. (The statue, by Agnes Vincen "Rusty" Talbot, also can be seen in front of the

Idaho Historical Museum in Boise, where its production was funded in part by $8,000 in donations from Idaho schoolchildren.) Agai'dika Heritage Days, held annually in mid-August, feature frontier and Native American living history demonstrations. Outdoor summer concerts are a draw as well. The interpretive center is open 9 a.m. to 5 p.m. Mon through Sat and 12:30 to 5 p.m. Sun late May through early Sept. Admission is $5 per person or $12 for a family, with kids age 6 and under admitted for free. The grounds are open all year during daylight hours. For more information call (208) 756-1188 or see sacajaweacenter.org.

Even though it has just about 3,100 people, Salmon is one of Idaho's busiest recreation gateways. Fishing, hunting, rafting, and mountain biking are all big here, and visitsalmonvalley.com has links to regional outfitters. Salmon's small downtown has several good restaurants to feed hungry outdoors folks and road-weary travelers. *Junkyard Bistro* at 405 Main St. has sandwiches you might not expect to find in a remote Idaho town, including Vietnamese báhn mì and New Orleans–style muffaletta, plus plenty of vegetarian options. *Bertram's Brewery* in a beautiful historic building at 101 South Andrews St. is among Idaho's oldest. It also serves food, and families are welcome.

Twenty-one miles north of Salmon, the hamlet of North Fork is the jumping-off spot for many river trips on the "River of No Return," the Main Salmon, which heads west from here. The gussied-up *Village at North Fork* has put a new shine on the old cafe and general store at the junction, with updated guest rooms, an RV park, and even Wi-Fi among the modern amenities. See thevillage atnorthfork.com and call (208) 865-7001 for reservations.

Even if you're not planning a river trip on the Main Salmon from North Fork, you may want to drive the river road a ways anyhow. The road is paved for about 16 miles, then it's a good packed gravel byway. There's a small settlement at Shoup, which until 1991 had the last hand-cranked telephone system in the United States. Another 2 miles west, the Class III+ to IV *Pine Creek Rapids* are the highlight of most short river trips on this stretch of river. William Clark, making a reconnaissance trip in the area in August 1805, may have seen these rapids from a nearby bluff. The wild river, coupled with the canyon's sheer rock cliffs, convinced Clark he and Lewis would need to find a safer route west.

West of Pine Creek Rapids, a wayside has been built at the *Shoup Rock Shelter,* a site dating from perhaps 8,000 years ago. Pictographs can be seen here. The North Fork Road ends at River Mile 46, where the Corn Creek boat ramp marks the start of the Salmon's federally designated Wild and Scenic stretch. Permits are required to float the 79-mile section from here to Long Tom

TOP ANNUAL EVENTS IN CENTRAL IDAHO

Sun Valley Ice Show
(mid-June through Sept)

**Sawtooth Mountain Mamas Arts
and Crafts Fair**
Stanley (mid-July)

Sun Valley Summer Symphony
(late July–early Aug)

Agai'dika Heritage Days
Salmon (mid-Aug)

Wagon Days
Ketchum (Labor Day weekend)

Trailing of the Sheep
Wood River Valley (early Oct)

Sun Valley Jazz & Music Festival
Sun Valley (mid-Oct)

Bar. Contact the Idaho Outfitters & Guides Association at ioga.org or (208) 342-1438 for more information on floating the Main Salmon.

It's also worth exploring the stretch of US 93 from North Fork toward the Montana border. Three miles from North Fork, **100 Acre Wood Lodge** has bed-and-breakfast accommodations starting at $75, plus a variety of area tours ranging from fishing and float trips to wildlife viewing and a Lewis and Clark back roads journey. See 100acrewoodlodge.com or call (208) 865-2165 for details.

Another 7 miles north at Gibbonsville, just before the highway starts its climb to Lost Trail Pass, **Ramey's Broken Arrow** serves delicious and authentic pork carnitas, enchiladas, tacos, and other Mexican treats. The restaurant is open for dinner Thurs through Sun from Mother's Day weekend through the first weekend in Nov. The Broken Arrow also has rustic cabins and RV spaces for rent. Call (208) 865-2241 or see thebrokenarrow.com for more information.

Twelve miles south of Salmon along US 93, the **Greyhouse Inn Bed and Breakfast** offers welcoming stays right along the river. This beautiful Victorian building was once a hospital in Salmon and was trucked to its current location in the early 1970s. Proprietors Sharon and David Osgood offer guest rooms in the main house, as well as in the Carriage House or several cabins, priced from about $95 to $125. For information call (800) 348-8097 or see greyhouseinn.com.

The Greyhouse also is home base for **Kookaburra Outfitters.** Most raft trips on the River of No Return run for several days, but for people with less time, Kookaburra offers a full-day trip for about $110 for adults and $95 to $100 for kids and teens, including a tasty lunch. The company also offers fishing expeditions. Call (888) 654-4386 or see raft4fun.com.

Goldbug Hot Springs (sometimes called Elk Bend Hot Springs) is the region's most popular soaking spot, accessed via a strenuous 2-mile hike up

Warm Springs Creek from a parking area near the highway about 24 miles south of Salmon. Ask locally for directions, be respectful of the private property along the trail, and plan to spend a day relaxing in the hot and cool pools.

It's 60 miles from Salmon to Challis on US 93, with the road following the Salmon River the whole way. If you're famished after the drive, head for *Antonio's Pizza and Pasta* at Fifth and Main uptown, where the menu also includes calzones, sandwiches, and burgers. You won't leave hungry. At Challis, travelers need to choose between taking US 93 south to Arco or hopping off on Highway 75, which continues along the Salmon River. Either way, the scenery is glorious.

US 93 streaks south through the Lost River Valley. Fourteen miles southeast of Challis at about milepost 150, the road bisects *Grand View Canyon,* a short but impressive gorge forged about 350 million years ago. Another 20 miles south, plan a stop at the *Mount Borah* interpretive area to marvel at Idaho's highest mountain and learn about the 1983 earthquake that struck this area (see sidebar).

South of Mount Borah, watch for the Trail Creek Road sign and turn right for a "shortcut" to Sun Valley. Trail Creek Road (Forest Road 208) is open in the summer months and accessible to passenger vehicles, although the westernmost section descending into Wood River Valley is steep and rocky. It's a good idea to inquire locally or check with the Forest Service in Ketchum (208-622-5371) to assess road conditions.

Halfway to Sun Valley along Trail Creek Road, Forest Road 135 heads south from the byway toward *Wild Horse Creek Ranch,* another classic Idaho guest ranch well suited for family reunions and group retreats. Year-round, the ranch offers a luxurious base camp for mountain activities ranging from fishing and hiking to cross-country skiing and snowmobiling. In addition to accommodations and creature comforts like a pool and hot tub, Wild Horse Creek also can set you up with everything from a one-hour trail ride to an extended big-game hunt. For more information call (208) 588-2575 or see wildhorsecreekranch.net. Past the Wild Horse Creek turnoff, Forest Road 135 follows the East Fork of the Big Lost River to Copper Basin, spectacularly situated between the Pioneer Mountains and the White Knob Mountains.

Back on US 93, it's 26 miles from Mackay to Arco. But we'll now return our attention to Highway 75. Just as US 93 did north of Challis, Highway 75 hugs the Salmon River tightly here, making for slow but stupendously scenic driving. It's easy to spend an entire day lingering here and there along the 55-mile drive from Challis to Stanley. Interesting stopping spots along the way include *Torrey's Resort and RV Park,* which offers food and cozy cabins at a popular float trip takeout west of Clayton, and the **Sunbeam area** with its history, hot springs, and a cool beverage or ice cream on the deck of the **Sunbeam Cafe.**

To many Idahoans unable to take lengthy and often expensive river trips down the Main or Middle forks of the Salmon River, a day float down this stretch of the Salmon is a mini-vacation and a whole lot of fun. Quite a few excursions leave from Sunbeam Village, including those offered by **White Otter Outdoor Adventures.** Whether you want lots of whitewater rapids or a calm scenic float, the Salmon delivers. Fun-seekers have their choice of oar boats, where the guide does all the work; paddle rafts, in which floaters help propel the boat downriver; and one-person inflatable kayaks that can be maneuvered by just about anyone 14 or older. Cost for a half-day float with snack is about $75 per teen or adult and $60 for kids. White Otter also runs scenic floats with no rapids on a quiet stretch of the river near Stanley. Call (208) 726-4331 or see whiteotter.com for reservations or more information.

Several accessible hot springs are located along Highway 75 west of Sunbeam. East to west there's the very visible **Sunbeam Hot Springs,** complete with bathhouse; **Basin Creek Hot Spring,** located near a campground of the same name; **Campground Hot Spring,** actually located in the Basin

The Borah Earthquake

On the morning of October 28, 1983, an earthquake measuring 7.3 on the Richter scale rocked Idaho's Lost River region. This temblor was the strongest in the continental United States in a quarter-century, and it proved more powerful than the two high-profile California earthquakes in 1989 and 1994, which combined killed 123 people. But because Central Idaho is so sparsely populated, the damage was correspondingly less, though not insignificant: Two children were killed in Challis, and area residents lost property valued in the millions.

Geologically, the quake made its mark, too. A side road from US 93 leads to a viewing area where it's easy to see the scarp left in the quake's wake, 21 miles long and 10 to 14 feet high. This rock ledge at the base of the Lost River Range stands in raw testimony to the temblor.

Mount Borah gained 2 feet in elevation during the 1983 quake, which means it now stands at 12,662 feet. The mountain, earlier christened Beauty Peak, was renamed in 1933 for William Borah, the "Lion of Idaho," who served in the US Senate from 1907 to 1940. Experienced mountaineers say Borah Peak can be climbed up and back in a day, but trekkers need to be well prepared mentally and physically for the strenuous, if not technical, ascent. Check with the Forest Service office at 716 West Custer St. in Mackay for more information—and to let them know of your plans. For more information call (208) 588-2224.

Creek Campground (walk into the bushes at Site 4); *Mormon Bend Hot Spring,* good for late-summer soaking (because a river crossing is necessary); and *Elkhorn Hot Spring.* Although these springs are all located near the highway, soakers are apt to feel a million miles away as they lean back and gaze at the blue sky above.

The Stanley Basin

If the Tetons are the West's most magnificent mountain range, Idaho's Sawtooths run a close second. Stanley, situated at the Highway 75–Highway 21 intersection, is the hub of Sawtooth country—in fact, it's the only place in the United States where three National Forest Scenic Byways converge.

Summer in Stanley means camping, fishing, and boating on the Salmon River and at Redfish Lake, and hikes high into the mountains and adjacent wilderness areas. *Redfish Lake Lodge* has a variety of rooms and cabins for rent from late May through early Oct, plus meals, a marina, boat tours, horseback riding, bike rentals, and more. For more info see redfishlake.com. But for many people, winter is prime time in the Stanley Basin because that's when snowmobiling season starts. More than 200 miles of groomed trails and outfitters are poised to help visitors with everything from snow machine rental to lodging and meals. For snowmobile rentals and guides, check with *Williams Motor Sports* at (208) 774-2229 or see snowtracks.com/williams-motor-sports.

Stanley is the departure point for most trips on the *Middle Fork of the Salmon River,* which many people regard among the world's premier whitewater trips. The classic Middle Fork trip covers 105 miles of river over six days, with prices of about $2,000 to $2,300 per person. Many outfitters run the Main Salmon; for help in choosing and booking a trip, check out idahosmiddlefork.com, an excellent site compiled by members of the Middle Fork Outfitters Association.

If you're just passing through Stanley, fortify yourself at the *Stanley Baking Company & Cafe* at 250 Wall St., where there's a line out the door some mornings. It's open daily from 7 a.m. to 2 p.m. mid-May through Oct. The *Sawtooth Hotel* at 755 Ace of Diamonds St. is open for dinner Thurs through Mon and has rooms starting at about at $70. Call (208) 721-2459 or see sawtoothhotel.com.

The *Idaho Rocky Mountain Ranch* south of Stanley ranks among the Gem State's most renowned guest ranches. Built in 1930 and listed on the National Register of Historic Places, and surrounded by more wilderness than anywhere in the continental United States, the ranch offers an abundance of activities (although it sometimes seems visitors are happiest just relaxing on the huge front porch of the central lodge, with its view of the Sawtooth Mountains). On-site diversions include a hot springs swimming pool, horseback riding, fishing in the Salmon River or the stocked catch-and-release pond, exploring the 900-acre property on foot or bike, horseshoes, and wildlife viewing. Rafting, rock climbing, and visits to nearby ghost towns are available as well.

Idaho Rocky Mountain Ranch has cabin and lodge accommodations, all with private baths. A continental breakfast buffet and a hot breakfast menu greet guests each morning, and dinners are served nightly, alternating between multicourse meals in the lodge and outdoor feasts. Rates (including breakfast, a packed picnic lunch, dinner, and use of the ranch facilities) range from $240 to $375 per person double occupancy, depending on accommodations chosen and length of stay. Children's and single occupancy rates are available, with discounts for some dates in June and Sept. For more information or reservations, call (208) 774-3544 or see idahorocky.com.

Stop at the Bethine and Frank Church Overlook on Highway 75 at **Galena Summit** for one of Idaho's best views, including the Sawtooth Mountains and the headwaters of the Salmon River. It's hard to believe the tiny trickle of a stream below here becomes the raging River of No Return, the longest river flowing within one state in the continental United States. The overlook honors the late senator Frank Church and his wife, Bethine, who were both active advocates for wilderness preservation. Church, who served Idaho in the US Senate for nearly a quarter-century, helped pass the national Wilderness Act in 1964 and the Wild and Scenic Rivers Act four years later.

Some of Idaho's best telemark skiing can be found on the Stanley Basin (or Humble Pie) side of Galena. Gentler terrain is available in the vicinity of **Galena Lodge,** situated at the base of the mountain on the Sun Valley side. Galena Lodge serves lunch, and its recreation menu includes cross-country skiing and snowshoeing in winter and mountain biking, barbecue dinner wagon trips, and horseback rides in summer. The lodge also has several ski- or hike-in yurts for rent. In winter, guests can have gourmet meals delivered to the yurts. Get information at galenalodge.com or call (208) 726-4010.

Wood River Valley

The Wood River Valley is more famously known as Sun Valley–Ketchum, site of America's first destination ski resort. In 1935 Union Pacific chief Averell Harriman dispatched Count Felix Schaffgotsch to find the perfect setting for a European-style ski retreat. After scouring the West, the count finally found what he was looking for near the scruffy Idaho mining town of Ketchum. Ironically, when the Sun Valley resort opened in 1936, there was barely enough snow to cover the slopes. But today Sun Valley has state-of-the-art snowmaking capabilities, and it's widely considered one of the best ski areas in North America (though the experience doesn't come cheap; single-day high-season lift tickets top $110).

Skiing is the big draw here, of course, but there are other reasons to visit, too. Eating is another favorite pastime in the Wood River Valley; without a doubt, the area is home to some of the state's best and most creative restaurants. The dining scene is constantly evolving, but a few perennial favorites include the creative **Ketchum Grill,** the casual **Pioneer Saloon,** and **Whiskey Jacques',** which features raucous live entertainment in addition to pizza, sandwiches, and salads. For breakfast, good choices include **The Kneadery** or **Cristina's.**

For an unusual winter dining experience, take a horse-drawn sleigh ride from the Sun Valley Inn to **Trail Creek Cabin.** The sleigh rides run Wed through Sun in winter, and nightly near Christmas and Presidents' Day. Call (208) 622-2135 for more information. In summer, the Sun Valley Lodge offers front-row seats to the **Sun Valley Ice Show** on one of the few year-round outdoor rinks in the United States. The biggest stars in figure skating—including recent Olympic medalists—appear each year. General admission tickets start at about $50; premium tickets with a dinner buffet run about $130. Reserve at sunvalley.ticketfly.com, or call (208) 622-2135 for more information. When there's no show planned, amateur ice skaters can take a spin on the same rink for about $12 for adults, $10 for kids.

Of course, Sun Valley is an excellent base from which to explore the neighboring Pioneer, Boulder, Smoky, Sawtooth, and White Cloud Mountains. **Sun Valley Trekking** has been leading guided summer and winter adventure trips in the region and beyond for decades, and it also rents backcountry huts and yurts. See svtrek.com or call (208) 788-1966.

Fly Sun Valley offers tandem paragliding trips off the resort's Bald Mountain in both summer and winter. No experience is necessary, all ages are welcome, and paragliding is even possible for people with a variety of physical limitations. See more details at flysunvalley.com and call (208) 726-3332 for current pricing.

The Wood River Valley strongly embraces the arts, with numerous galleries, movie theaters, and more. The **Sun Valley Summer Symphony,** the largest free-admission symphony in the United States, features concerts in the Sun Valley Pavilion and various other venues from late July to mid-Aug. Call (208) 622-5607 or see svsummersymphony.org for performance dates and programs.

Ernest Hemingway spent part of his last years in Ketchum, and fans of his writing will find several local spots worth a stop. First there's the **Hemingway Memorial** located along Trail Creek east of town; take Sun Valley Road east from the stoplight in downtown Ketchum, and watch for the sign on your right.

A short path leads to a memorial as spare as Papa's prose, topped by a rugged bust of the author and embellished by this passage Hemingway wrote in 1939 while in Idaho:

Best of all he loved the fall
the leaves yellow on the cottonwoods
leaves floating on the trout streams
and above the hills
the high blue windless skies
. . . now he will be part of them forever.

Hemingway first came to Idaho in 1939 and visited many times over the next two decades. In 1959 he and his wife, Mary, finally bought a home in Ketchum, but by 1961, apparently depressed over his failing health, he was dead, the victim of a self-inflicted shotgun blast. He is buried in the Ketchum Cemetery, located just north of the downtown area. Look for two pine trees growing closely together near the rear of the graveyard; there you'll find the plots of Ernest Miller Hemingway and his last wife, Mary. Like Jim Morrison's grave in Paris, Hemingway's burial site sometimes attracts people who want to spend some time with the writer's spirit. On one visit this author had been preceded by a pilgrim who had left behind a pack of Dutch Masters little cigars—three left out of the box as if in homage—and an empty bottle of Maker's Mark whiskey.

For more local lore, check out the **Sun Valley Museum of History.** Located in the former Civilian Conservation Corps–built Forest Service complex at 180 First St. East in Ketchum, the museum has a big collection of early ski gear and pioneer memorabilia. Hours are 1 to 5 p.m. Tues through Sat, with admission by donation. Call (208) 726-8118 or see comlib.org/museum for more information. Forest Service Park also is the scene for Kech'em Alive, a series of free summer concerts held Tues evenings from mid-June to mid-Aug.

This resort area offers plenty of great shopping and browsing at art galleries and boutiques, but for many savvy visitors, the **Gold Mine Thrift Shop** at 331 Walnut Ave. and **Gold Mine Consign** at 591 Fourth St. East are the mother lodes of great deals in Ketchum. From designer-label sportswear to outdoor gear galore, it's all here, and all purchases benefit the local library. The thrift shop is open daily and the consignment store is open Tues through Sat.

Sun Valley and Ketchum are full of interesting places to stay. If you'd like to sleep where Hemingway and countless other celebrities have slept, check into the venerable **Sun Valley Lodge.** It'll cost you, though; following an extensive renovation that doubled the size of most rooms, rates run $500 or more a night. (They're a little less expensive in the shoulder seasons, as well as at other Sun Valley Resort company properties in the village.) Call (800) 786-8259 or see sunvalley.com for a splurge. For a luxury bed-and-breakfast stay, the European-style **Knob Hill Inn** has twenty-six guest suites and rooms, each with a balcony and mountain views. The location is good, just a short stroll from downtown Ketchum at 960 North Main St., and the rates are slightly less breathtaking than those in Sun Valley. For more information see knobhillinn.com or call (800) 526-8010.

For lower-priced lodging and a more laid-back vibe, it's better to look at Hailey and Bellevue, the two "lower valley" towns. They're much less known than Ketchum and Sun Valley but definitely worth exploring. Dining options in Hailey rival those of Ketchum, with **CK's Real Food** at 320 South Main St. among the area's standouts. Fresh and local are the watchwords here, with lamb dishes as a specialty. Ask to sit on the terrace if the weather's fine. The 1950s-style **Shorty's Diner** at 126 South Main St. is a mainstay for breakfast and lunch.

Company of Fools, based at the Liberty Theatre on Main Street in Hailey, was the first Idaho theater to attain "constituent" status from Theatre Communications Group, which puts it in the same league with such top playhouses as the Guthrie in Minneapolis, Lincoln Center Theater in New York, and the

Preserving the Past

Heroes, rogues, scoundrels, and saints . . . they're all well represented at the **Blaine County Historical Museum,** located at Main and Galena Streets in Hailey. This is the repository for the Joe Fuld Political Button Collection, among the largest of its type in the world. Fuld was an early Hailey businessman who started collecting political memorabilia in the late 19th century and wound up with more than 5,000 items of campaign souvenirs, not just buttons but handkerchiefs, pencils, posters, an ashtray used by Teddy Roosevelt, even the inaugural ball program from 1881.

The museum also has a corner devoted to **Ezra Pound,** the iconoclastic writer born in Hailey in 1885. Pound's parents left Idaho when Ezra was only 15 months old, but the poet seemed ever after to consider himself an Idahoan. Perhaps he felt the state's outpost image was one well suited to his own renegade reputation. Pound went on to pen thousands of poems (including the epic Cantos series), but he outraged many when he embraced fascism and started making anti-American broadcasts from Europe during World War II. Pound later renounced totalitarianism, and he is now best remembered as a champion of other writers, including T. S. Eliot and Ernest Hemingway.

The Blaine County Historical Museum is open Memorial Day weekend through Oct. Hours are from 11 a.m. to 5 p.m. Mon through Sat and 1 to 5 p.m. Sun. Admission is by donation. For more information call (208) 788-1801 or see bchistoricalmuseum.org.

Seattle Rep. (Others are the Boise Contemporary Theater and the Idaho Shakespeare Festival.) It's now under the umbrella of the Sun Valley Center for the Arts. For tickets or information on upcoming shows, call (208) 788-6520 or see the Company of Fools page at sunvalleycenter.org.

Camas Lilies and Lava Beds

South of Bellevue more vehicles topped with ski racks travel the intersection of Highway 75 and US 20 than any other in Idaho. Most are heading north to Sun Valley, of course, but some are destined for **Soldier Mountain** about 10 miles north of Fairfield. Lift tickets at Soldier Mountain cost about a third what they do at Sun Valley, so it's a good family bargain. The skiing's not bad, either, with three dozen runs and 1,400 feet of vertical drop plus backcountry snowcat ski adventures. For more information on current hours and prices, call (208) 764-2526 or see soldiermountain.com.

Fairfield doesn't have much in the way of services, but the **Cliff Bar and Grille** at 503 Soldier Rd. ships in fresh Alaskan seafood for special dinners.

This part of Central Idaho is known as the Camas Prairie for the beautiful blue flowers that were such an important food source for Native Americans. (Yes, part of North Central Idaho near the Nez Perce reservation is known as the Camas Prairie, too.) The week before Memorial Day is generally the best time to see the flowers in midbloom; they're at their best the spring after a wet winter. Drive through the 3,100-acre **Camas Prairie Centennial Marsh Wildlife Management Area** west of Fairfield to see the camas lilies as well as waterfowl and other wildlife.

East of the Highway 75/US 20 junction, drivers soon spy **Silver Creek,** a fly-fishing dream stream. This was Hemingway's favorite fishing hole, and avid anglers say it's one of the best anywhere in the world, period. The Nature Conservancy protects part of Silver Creek with a wonderful preserve that also features a short nature trail and a visitor center. Silver Creek runs close to the little ranching town of Picabo, which some lexicologists say is Native for "silver water." Picabo's namesake is Picabo Street, the now-retired champion Olympic and World Cup skier who grew up plying the slopes at Sun Valley. Picabo actually grew up in another tiny Wood River Valley town, Triumph, and somehow that town's name seems apt for her, too.

US 20 and 26 come together at Carey. From here, it's 25 miles east to **Craters of the Moon National Monument.** From Native Americans to early white explorers to the Apollo astronauts, people long have been fascinated with the strange landscapes of this region. Natives probably never lived on the harsh lava lands, but artifacts found in the area show they visited, probably to hunt and gather tachylite—a kind of basaltic volcanic glass—for arrow points. In the early 20th century, Boisean Robert Limbert extensively explored the lava flows; it was his work and an article he penned in *National Geographic* that led to Craters of the Moon being named a national monument in 1924. In 1969 a group of Apollo astronauts preparing to go to the moon first visited Craters to get a feel for what the lunar landscape might be like.

The same experiences are available today. Though Craters has a popular 7-mile loop drive offering opportunities for several short hikes, it also has a surprisingly accessible designated wilderness area that receives much less use than the rest of the monument. The best time to visit is in the spring, when delicate wildflowers cover the black rock, or in fall after the often-extreme heat of the desert summer abates. In winter the loop road is closed to vehicular traffic but may be enjoyed by cross-country skiers or on snowshoes.

There are two predominant types of lava at Craters: the jagged aa (pronounced "ah-ah," Hawaiian for "hard on the feet") and the smoother pahoehoe (also Hawaiian, meaning "ropey" and pronounced "pa-hoy-hoy"). Both may be seen on the North Crater Flow loop trail, a good introduction to the monument's geology. Also consider an overnight stay in the campground; the sites set amid the lava make an absolutely perfect setting for telling ghost stories (although you'll have to do so without a campfire; no wood fires are permitted, because the only available trees are the ancient and slow-growing limber pines).

Craters of the Moon National Monument's visitor center is open daily from 8 a.m. to 6 p.m. in summer and until 4:30 p.m. in winter. Admission is free and the exhibits are worthwhile, so it makes a good rest stop on desolate US 20/26/93, though Arco is just 18 miles to the east. Beyond the visitor center, admission is $10 per vehicle. For more information call (208) 527-1300 or see nps.gov/crmo.

Arco was the first community in the world to be lit by electricity generated by nuclear power, in July 1955. This sounds like a big deal, except the feat lasted only for about an hour and, then as now, Arco is a little town. Eighteen miles southeast of Arco, a side road off US 20/26 provides access to the **EBR-1 National Historic Landmark,** which offers interesting exhibits on how the Experimental Breeder Reactor No. 1 first generated usable electricity from atomic energy in 1951. (It was the first reactor built in what's now known as the Idaho National Laboratory, a vast scientific reserve that covers nearly 900 square miles of Idaho high desert.) The center also explores later nuclear energy research, including how nuclear power lost favor after the Three Mile Island and Chernobyl accidents, but how it might be a more environmentally sound form of energy than burning fossil fuels. EBR-1 is open from 9 a.m. to 5 p.m. daily Memorial Day weekend through Labor Day weekend. See inl.gov/ebr for more information.

The lava lands surrounding Arco and Craters of the Moon are but a small part of the huge Great Rift section of Idaho, which covers nearly 170,000 acres across the eastern Snake River Plain. For a view of the whole expanse, try a hike or drive up **Big Southern Butte,** the 300,000-year-old monolith towering 2,500 feet above the surrounding landscape. To get to the butte, follow the signs west from Atomic City. The dirt road up Big Southern Butte is steep, with a 2,000-foot elevation gain and some 15+ percent grades. For detailed information on this and many other Idaho treks, check out sagehiker.net, a site from Sheldon Bluestein, the witty and wise author of the classic guidebook *Exploring Idaho's High Desert.*

Places to Stay in Central Idaho

NORTH FORK

One Hundred Acre Wood Bed & Breakfast
north of town on US 93
(208) 865-2165
100acrewoodlodge.com
Inexpensive–Moderate

River's Fork Inn
2036 US 93 North
(208) 865-2301
riversfork.com
Moderate

The Village at North Fork
2046 US 93 North
(208) 865-7001
thevillageatnorthfork.com
Moderate

SALMON

Greyhouse Inn Bed & Breakfast
12 miles south on US 93
(208) 756-3968
greyhouseinn.com
Moderate

Sacajawea Inn
705 South Challis St.
(208) 756-2294
hotelsalmon.com
Inexpensive

Stagecoach Inn
201 Riverfront Dr.
(208) 756-2919
stagecoachinnmotel.com
Moderate

CHALLIS

Northgate Inn Motel
US 93
(208) 879-2490
Inexpensive

Village Inn
310 South US 93
(208) 879-2239
challisvillageinn.com
Inexpensive–Moderate

MACKAY

Bear Bottom Inn
412 West Spruce St.
(208) 588-2483
thebearbottominn.com
Inexpensive

Wild Horse Creek Ranch
4387 Wild Horse Creek Rd.
(20 miles west off of Trail Creek Road)
(208) 588-2575
wildhorsecreekranch.com
Moderate–Expensive

STANLEY

Idaho Rocky Mountain Ranch
south on Highway 75
(208) 774-3544
idahorocky.com
Expensive

Mountain Village Resort
Highways 21 and 75
(800) 843-5475
mountainvillage.com
Moderate–Expensive

Redfish Lake Lodge
(208) 774-3536
redfishlake.com
Moderate–Expensive

Sawtooth Hotel
755 Ace of Diamonds St.
(208) 721-2459
sawtoothhotel.com
Moderate–Expensive

SUN VALLEY/KETCHUM

Bellemont Hotel
600 North Main St.
(Ketchum)
(800) 262-4833
bellemonthotelsunvalley.com
Moderate–Expensive

HELPFUL WEB SITES FOR CENTRAL IDAHO

Idaho Mountain Express (Sun Valley–area newspaper)
sunvalleycentral.com

Sun Valley/Ketchum Chamber of Commerce
visitsunvalley.com

Central Idaho Rockies Association (regional tourism)
centralidahorockies.org

Stanley-Sawtooth Chamber of Commerce
stanleycc.org

Salmon Valley Chamber of Commerce
salmonchamber.com

Craters of the Moon National Monument
nps.gov/crmo

Best Western Plus Kentwood Lodge
180 South Main St. (Ketchum)
(208) 726-4114
bestwesternidaho.com
Expensive

Knob Hill Inn
Highway 75 (Ketchum)
(800) 526-8010
knobhillinn.com
Very Expensive

Sun Valley Resort
(800) 786-8259
sunvalley.com
Expensive–Very Expensive

HAILEY

The Inn at Ellsworth Estate
702 Third Ave. South
(208) 788-6354
ellsworthestate.com
Moderate

Wood River Inn
601 North Main
(208) 578-0600
woodriverinn.com
Expensive

BELLEVUE

High Country Motel
766 Main St. South
(208) 721-0067
highcountrymotelbellevue
.com
Inexpensive–Moderate

FAIRFIELD

The Prairie Inn
US 20
(208) 764-2247
theprairieinn.com
Moderate

Soldier Mountain Ranch and Resort
(208) 764-2506
soldiermountainranch.com
Moderate–Expensive

ARCO

Arco Inn
540 Grand Ave. West
(208) 527-3100
arcomotel.com
Inexpensive

D-K Motel
316 South Front St.
(208) 527-8282
dkmotel.com
Inexpensive

Lost River Motel
405 Highway Dr.
(208) 527-3600
lrmotel.com
Inexpensive

Places to Eat in Central Idaho

SALMON

Bertram's Brewery
(American/microbrewery)
101 South Andrews St.
(208) 756-3391
Inexpensive–Moderate

Junkyard Bistro
(eclectic)
405 Main St.
(208) 756-2466
Inexpensive–Moderate

Shady Nook
(American)
501 Riverfront Dr.
(208) 756-4182
Moderate–Expensive

GIBBONSVILLE

Ramey's Broken Arrow
(Mexican)
US 93
(208) 865-2241
Moderate

NORTH FORK

The Village Grill
(American)
US 93
(208) 865-7001
Inexpensive–Moderate

CHALLIS

Antonio's
(pizza/pasta)
431 East Main Ave.
(208) 879-2210
Inexpensive

MACKAY

Bear Bottom Inn
(eclectic)
412 West Spruce St.
(208) 588-2483
Inexpensive–Moderate

Ken's Club
(steakhouse)
302 South Main Ave.
(208) 588-9983
Moderate–Expensive

STANLEY

Papa Brunee's
(pizza and subs)
Ace of Diamonds Street
(208) 774-2536
Inexpensive–Moderate

Redfish Lake Lodge
(American)
Redfish Lake Rd.
(208) 774-3536
Moderate–Expensive

Sawtooth Hotel
(American)
Ace of Diamonds Street
(208) 721-2459
Moderate

**Stanley Baking
Company & Cafe**
(breakfast)
Wall Street
(208) 774-6573
Inexpensive

SUN VALLEY/KETCHUM

Cristina's Restaurant
(brunch and bakery)
520 Second St. East
(Ketchum)
(208) 726-4499
Moderate

KB's
(Mexican)
260 North Main St.
(208) 928-6955
Inexpensive–Moderate

Ketchum Grill
(contemporary American)
520 East Ave.
(208) 726-4660
Moderate

The Kneadery
(breakfast)
260 Leadville Ave.
(208) 726-9462
Moderate

Perry's
(American)
131 West Fourth St.
(208) 726-7703
Moderate

Pioneer Saloon
(American)
320 North Main St.
(Ketchum)
(208) 726-3139
Moderate–Expensive

**Warfield Distillery &
Brewery**
(eclectic)
280 North Main St.
(208) 726-2739
Moderate–Expensive

HAILEY

CK's Real Food
(Northwest)
320 South Main St.
(208) 788-1223
Moderate–Expensive

ALSO WORTH SEEING IN CENTRAL IDAHO

Challis Hot Springs
east of Challis

Land of the Yankee Fork State Park
near Challis

Sawtooth National Fish Hatchery
near Stanley

Easley Hot Springs
north of Ketchum

Magic Lantern Cinemas
Ketchum

DaVinci's
(Italian)
17 West Bullion St.
(208) 788-7699
Moderate

Shorty's Diner
(American)
126 South Main St.
(208) 578-1293
Inexpensive

**Sun Valley
Brewing Company**
(eclectic)
202 North Main St.
(208) 788-0805
Moderate

Zou 75
(French Asian)
416 North Main St.
(208) 788-3310
Moderate–Expensive

FAIRFIELD

Cliff Bar and Grille
(American)
503 Soldier Rd.
(208) 764-2543
Moderate

ARCO

Deli Sandwich Shop
(pizza, shakes, and
sandwiches)
119 North Idaho St.
(208) 527-3757
Inexpensive

Pickle's Place
(American)
440 South Front St.
(208) 527-9944
Inexpensive

Index